SMITHSONIAN REPORTS.

NOTICES

OF

PUBLIC LIBRARIES

IN THE

UNITED STATES OF AMERICA.

BY CHARLES C. JEWETT,
LIBRARIAN OF THE SMITHSONIAN INSTITUTION.

PRINTED BY ORDER OF CONGRESS, AS AN APPENDIX TO THE FOURTH ANNUAL REPORT OF THE BOARD OF REGENTS OF THE SMITHSONIAN INSTITUTION.

WASHINGTON, D. C.
1851.

31st Congress, 1st Session. | [SENATE.] | Miscellaneous, No. 120.

APPENDIX

TO

THE REPORT OF THE BOARD OF REGENTS

OF

THE SMITHSONIAN INSTITUTION,

CONTAINING

A REPORT ON THE PUBLIC LIBRARIES

OF

THE UNITED STATES OF AMERICA,

JANUARY 1, 1850.

BY CHARLES C. JEWETT,
Librarian of the Smithsonian Institution.

WASHINGTON:
PRINTED FOR THE SENATE.
1850.

APPENDIX.

SMITHSONIAN INSTITUTION,
Washington, January 1, 1850.

SIR: I have the honor to transmit to you, in compliance with the duty assigned me, the following report upon the public libraries of the United States, prepared in accordance with the plan of rendering the Smithsonian Institution a centre of bibliographical knowledge.

I remain, very respectfully, your obedient servant,

C. C. JEWETT,
Librarian of the Smithsonian Institution.

TO JOSEPH HENRY, LL. D.,
Secretary of the Smithsonian Institution.

PRELIMINARY REMARKS.

Books constitute a large element of the intellectual wealth of a nation. On the shelves of publishers and venders they are an indication of existing demand, and an earnest of usefulness. Nor are they idle even there. The shops of booksellers have, from early times, been the favorite resorts of men of letters. Their contents are, for purposes of reference, more accessible than those of most libraries.

Collections of books for private libraries are also of great public interest. The proprietor of each derives from it his own means of teaching the public. Not only so; private collections are generally made for specific purposes, and are—each in some particular branch of knowledge—as complete as the means of the proprietor will allow. The learning, bibliographical skill, and resources of the collector have been limited to some one object, and that he has pursued to its utmost extent. He has thus formed a complete library in one department. The aggregation of such libraries would constitute a complete universal library. These collections generally become, sooner or later, parts of public collections: such is commonly the wish of the scholars who form them. Therefore, the community may be allowed to watch—so far as they can without intrusiveness—such private accumulations, with interest and satisfaction. In this country, moreover, a narrow and exclusive spirit among book collectors is almost unknown. Gathering for use, and with an appreciating spirit, they are not disposed to debar others from the treasures which they possess. The liberality of proprietors of large collections of books in this country is remarkable, and I believe unparalleled.

But our present object is not to describe private collections. The census board, with an enlightened regard for the interests of letters, have included books, in both public and private libraries exceeding one thousand volumes, among the objects to be enumerated. Mr. John R. Bartlett, before his appointment to the important post which he now holds upon the

Mexican boundary commission, had made considerable progress in procuring from the proprietors of the most valuable private collections such accounts of their literary treasures as would be of public importance, and such as they were willing to have printed. These notes will not be lost, though the publication of them is deferred.

Our immediate concern is with public libraries. It is unnecessary to seek for an exact definition of the word *public* in this connexion. I mean by it libraries which are accessible—either without restriction, or upon conditions with which all can easily comply—to every person who wishes to use them for their appropriate purposes. In this sense I believe it may be said that all libraries in this country, which are not private property, (and indeed many which are private property,) are public libraries.

Of these libraries I have endeavored to collect such historical, statistical, and descriptive notices as would be of general interest; together with such special details as would be beneficial to those who are engaged in the organization and care of similar establishments.

No person who will consider the vast extent of the field to be surveyed, the tedious process by which most of the information is to be collected—namely, by circular letters and private correspondence—the difficulty in this busy land of getting any one to furnish minute information on such subjects, the antiquated statistics, on these matters, which survive all other changes, in gazetteers and geographies, and the fact that there is nowhere in this country a full collection of books and pamphlets relating to the local affairs of the several towns and counties of the different States—no one who will consider these things, and remember that this is but *one* of the topics of inquiry to which I was required to devote my attention, and that, by the other duties of my office, I was prevented from visiting most of the libraries which I wished to describe, will be surprised if he should find that, in some instances, these accounts are not so full nor so accurate as could be desired.

The publication of them, in their present state, is considered a step necessary to their completion and perfection. Copies will be distributed to librarians and others interested in these matters, and all persons who may receive the work are earnestly requested to furnish corrections, additions, and suggestions for a second edition. It is hoped that within a few years materials may be obtained for accurate accounts, embracing all historical facts of importance with reference to every library and every institution possessing a library in this country; and including the history and statistics, with a description of the bibliographical and scientific treasures of each.

The present notices relate almost *exclusively* to libraries. When the library forms but a department (it may be a comparatively small one) of an institution, it has not been the aim to give anything more of the history of such institution than was necessary to illustrate the formation, position or prospects, of the library.

It was at first intended to limit these notices to the answers obtained to the questions of a circular letter.* Many of the circulars have, however,

*The following is a copy of the circular letter:

The following questions have been prepared in order to collect as accurate statistics as possible of the various public libraries in the United States:

1. By what name is the library legally designated? 2. When was it founded? 3. What number

remained to this time unanswered ; others were filled up hastily, and gave but a meagre account of the collections; others, again, simply referred to some sources from which authentic details might be gathered. In order to give anything like completeness or uniformity to the notices, it was found necessary to re-write them, and to seek additional information from all available sources. When the librarian's name is given in connexion with an article, it is an indication that the principal facts were derived from his answers to the queries. When the facts have been gathered from other sources, the authorities have, for the most part, been named.

It is to be regretted that these statistics do not all refer to exactly the same date. They were intended to represent the condition of the libraries at the middle of the year 1849; but when returns were not made, and it was necessary to take the best accounts at hand, these frequently related to a time several years past.

Doubtless many libraries, more important than some which are mentioned in these notices, have been overlooked. The omission is unintentional. It has been utterly impossible to collect, at once, full and reliable accounts of all the libraries, small and large, in the country. This publication will make known our wish to gather all facts worthy of record respecting every one of them; and, in conformity with this plan, we would respectfully and earnestly solicit from the guardians of libraries not mentioned here, or of which the accounts are incorrect or in any way unsatisfactory, to furnish us with the means of improving the work for a second edition. We would direct attention particularly to the following points:

1. The number of volumes of printed books as they stand upon the shelves; the number of pamphlets; the number of manuscripts, in the form of works intended for publication, or of letters, &c.; the number of maps and charts; of loose engravings; of sheets of music unbound, and of bound books of music; the number of coins and medals, pictures, busts, &c., possessed by the institution on the 1st of January, 1851.

2. The expenditure for books, and the number of books purchased, during the year ending December 31, 1850.

3. The number of books lent out, also the number used in the library rooms, during the same period.

4. Important facts not already given with reference to the history of the

---

of volumes does it contain? 4. Has it collections of manuscripts, maps and charts, music, engravings, medals, coins, etc.? If so, please to state the number of articles of each description. 5. Are the numbers, given in reply to the last two questions, ascertained by actually counting the volumes and articles, or are they from a conjectural estimate? 6. What has been the yearly average number of volumes added to the library for the last ten years? 7. What has been the yearly average expenditure for the purchase of books? 8. Is there a permanent fund for the increase of the library? If so, how large is it, and what sum does it yield annually? 9. How many and what officers are employed? What are the names and address of the present officers? 10. Has a building been erected expressly for the library? If so, when, of what material, and at what expense? 11. What are the dimensions, and what is the ground-plan, of the library building or rooms? 12. Are the books arranged on the shelves according to subjects, or on some other system? 13. Is there a printed catalogue of the library? If so, when was it printed, and what is its size, and the number of pages? If more than one, what is the date of each? 14. How often is the library opened, and how long is it kept open each time? 15. Who are entitled to the use of the library, and on what terms? 16. Are books lent out to read? If so, how many are taken out annually? 17. What is the yearly average number of persons consulting the library without taking away books? 18. Have the books been injured at any time by insects? 19. Is there any regulation by which books may be lent by courtesy to persons at a distance? If so, what is it?

library, and the institution with which the library is connected. In this place we would also beg leave, on behalf of the Smithsonian Institution, to solicit for its library the gift of books, pamphlets, or articles, printed or written, relative to the history, condition, or prospects of every literary, scientific, and educational establishment in the country; with catalogues (old as well as new) of all libraries; annual and triennial catalogues of colleges and high schools; and documents relating to common schools, Sunday schools, &c. It is highly important to have upon our shelves the means of tracing the progress of education in this country in the history of schools, colleges, and libraries, from their foundation to the present time. Such a collection would be peculiarly appropriate in a central institution like this. Nothing pertaining to the subject should be thought too insignificant to be sent. Everything will find its place, and, we may safely say, will one day be useful.

5. It would be interesting to have a description, or at least a list, of all remarkably rare and curious books or manuscripts which the library may possess; and we would ask particularly for an account, as minute as may be convenient, of all manuscripts relating to the early history of this country.

To those who have contributed information for this work I beg leave to present my sincere thanks. I have heretofore spoken of the articles contained in the "Serapeum" for 1846, from the pen of Hermann E. Ludewig, esq., of New York, on the libraries of America, as the fullest and most correct account of them that had been published. His was the work of a pioneer. It was faithfully done, and I most cheerfully acknowledge my obligations to him for the assistance which I have derived from his researches.*

MAINE.

AUGUSTA.

State Library—about 9,000 *vols.*—Founded 1836. The average yearly increase is about 500 volumes. From 1840 to 1847, the annual appropriation for the purchase of books was $300; for 1848, $400; for 1849, $400. One of the rooms of the State House (50 feet by 30) is appropriated to the library. It is fitted up with alcoves on two sides—twelve in all. Three catalogues have been printed—the first (60 pages 8vo.) in 1839; the second (105 pages 8vo.) in 1843; the third (120 pages 8vo.) in 1846. Another is in preparation. During the sessions of the legislature the library is open from 8 a. m. to 6 p. m. Books may be taken from the library by the governor, members of the council, senate, house of representatives, heads of departments, judges of the courts, secretary and members of the board of education, and the superintendent of the Insane

*These notices were brought up to January, 1850, at which time they were presented to the Regents of the Smithsonian Institution. As the printing has been delayed for a year, I have added to them such facts as during the interval have come to my knowledge. These additions improve the notices in fullness and accuracy; but they give them a fragmentary character, which could only be avoided by rewriting many of them—a task which was not consistent with my other duties.

C. C. J.

JANUARY, 1851.

Hospital. The privilege to the members of the legislature, board of education and its secretary, is limited to the time they may be in session. No law books, (excepting those of the State of Maine,) nor books presented by the United States, or any other State, or received through Vattemare's exchange, can be taken from the library except for the use of the two houses, and the committees, at the committee-rooms, during their session. Probably 2,500 persons consult the library each year. Ezra B. French, of Damariscotta, Secretary of State and *ex officio* librarian; Abner Oakes, of Sangerville, assistant librarian.

BANGOR.

Theological Seminary Libraries—7,500 *vols.*—The Theological Seminary at Bangor was incorporated in 1814 as the "Maine Charity School." It was at first connected with Hampden Academy. In 1819 it was removed to Bangor. It is under the direction of the Congregationalists. The library was founded in 1832, and contains 7,500 volumes, selected with special reference to the benefit of theological students; with a few maps and charts, and a great variety of curiosities, collected chiefly by missionaries among the heathen; as ornaments, implements of labor, idol gods, &c., &c. The yearly average increase is about 400 volumes. Annual expenditure for books about $500. There is no permanent fund. It is expected that a building will soon be erected for the library. The books are arranged on the shelves according to subjects. No catalogue has been printed. There are two written catalogues—one alphabetical, the other recording the books as they stand on the shelves. Open twice a week for taking out books, and every afternoon for consultation. Students, officers, trustees, clergymen, and other literary gentlemen in the city of Bangor, are entitled to the use of the library, for which no charge is made. The post of librarian is usually filled by a student of the seminary.

The Society of Inquiry on Missions, connected with the seminary, is in possession of a valuable cabinet and library.—[See History of the Bangor Theological Seminary, by Rev. E. Pond, D. D., in the American Quarterly Register for August, 1841, p. 27.]

BRUNSWICK.

Bowdoin College Libraries—24,750 *vols.*—Bowdoin College was established in 1794, but it did not go into operation till eight years later. The college library dates from the organization of the institution, in 1802, and contains at present (1849) 11,600 volumes. For the last ten years the average annual increase has been about 130 volumes, and the average annual expenditure about $200. There is no permanent fund for the purchase of books, but an annual appropriation of $200 is made from the funds of the college. Since 1846 a granite building has been erected, at an expense of about $40,000; a part of which will be the college chapel, and a part contains the library. The room now occupied by the library is 70 feet long, 30 feet wide, and 18 feet high. There are, besides, two wings, to be used when required—each 70 feet long, 18 feet wide, and 18 feet high. The last printed catalogue was published in 1819, containing 120 pages 8vo. It is now out of print, and, were it to be had, would give a very imperfect idea of the present library. It is expected that a new catalogue will soon be prepared and published. The library is open three times a week, one hour each time. During these hours the use of the library is allowed to all persons, without fee. Books are lent out to the students, resident graduates, officers, trustees, and overseers of the college, and to the clergymen of Topsham and Brunswick. The number of charges for volumes lent is about 3,000 annually. Daniel R. Goodwin, Professor of Modern Languages, is librarian.

There are four libraries belonging to societies of under graduates of the college, viz:

The Peucinian Society library - - - -	4,800 vols
Athenæan Society library - - - -	3,800 "
(These two libraries are increased annually, each by about 200 volumes.)	
Theological Society library - - - -	750 "
Peace Society library - - - - - -	500 "
(The books belonging to the Peace Society were presented by the late William Ladd, esq.)	
The medical department of the college, established in 1820, has a remarkably good library of - - -	3,300 "

The Historical Society of Maine was incorporated February 5, 1822. It has a small library of books, pamphlets, manuscripts and papers, relating principally to the history of Maine. The society has received, during the last year, a grant of land from the legislature, which will yield about $6,000, for the express purpose of erecting a fire-proof building. When such a building is completed, a new interest will doubtless be awakened in the community in behalf of the society, and it is expected that large collections of manuscripts and papers of historic value with reference to the State, now kept in reserve waiting for a safe place of deposite, will be received, and will form an important and valuable library. Professor Alpheus S. Packard, of Bowdoin College, Brunswick, librarian.

HOULTON.

Forest Club Library—200 *vols.*—Aroostook county is situated in the northern forests of Maine. Houlton, the shire town, is nearly 100 miles from any settlement of importance in the United States. It is, however, gratifying to record the establishment in this place of a public library, in July, 1849. The number of its volumes is as yet inconsiderable; but we chronicle its formation with the hope that the notice may, in some humble manner, serve its interests by directing towards it the donations of those who have books to bestow. William Butterfield, librarian.

PORTLAND.

Athenæum Library—[illegible]70 *vols.*—This institution was incorporated March 6, 1827. The library contains (1849) 6,170 volumes. The rate of increase cannot be accurately stated; a new system of supervision has lately been adopted, which will hereafter enable the librarian to give such information. The institution has a fund, now amounting to $3,100, and increasing at the rate of $300 to $500 per year, intended for the general purposes of the Athenæum.

An alphabetical catalogue of 88 pages in 12mo. was printed in 1839. Another was printed, December, 1849, entitled "Catalogue of the Library of the Portland Athenæum; with the By-Laws of the Institution, adopted February 19, 1849." 12mo. Portland, 1849: in 150 pages. The books are arranged in 18 chapters. This catalogue is well compiled and handsomely printed.

The library is open twice a week, 3½ hours each time.

The persons entitled to the use of the library are, proprietors of shares, costing $40 each, and others on payment of $10 annually.

8,150 books were lent out during the last year. James Merrill, librarian.

The following historical account of the Athenæum is from a book just published by Mr. Willis, of Portland:

"This institution is the successor to the Library Society, which was established in 1765, by twenty-six gentlemen, who associated together for that purpose. Previous to that time there was nothing in the form of a library existing in town. The library opened in 1766 with 93 volumes, of which 62 volumes were 'Ancient and Modern Universal History,' 'Rapin's History of England,' 7 vols., 'Lardner's Writers of the New Testament,' 3 vols., 'London Magazine,' 9 vols., &c. Not much addition was made till after the Revolution, during which the small collection was scattered, and a number of the books lost. In 1780 a new attempt was made to resuscitate it, and the fragments were reunited. But it was not till the peace of '83 that any successful movement was made to give it vitality. In May, 1784, twenty-six new members were admitted, who were required to pay two dollars each, in money or books. Others were subsequently admitted on the same conditions. On the 3d of April, 1786, the library was valued at £25; the worth was diminished by the number of broken sets of works which it contained. In 1794, the books were again appraised, and valued at £64 3*s.* 8*d.*, and the price of admission was raised to 42*s.* The committee were this year instructed to purchase Sullivan's History of Maine, Hutchinson's History of Massachusetts, Belknap's Biography, Ramsay's American Revolution and Carolina, and the History of the County of Worcester. These are all American publications and on American subjects. In 1798 they procured an act of incorporation. The library went on slowly, and gradually increasing until 1825, when its number of volumes was 1,640, and its proprietors 82; and the whole annual expense $331. At this period the design was formed for enlarging the institution, and giving it a more elevated and diffusive character, better suited to the wants of the age and spirit of the times. The present Athenæum grew out of these suggestions. It was incorporated in March, 1826; purchased the property of the old library, and the former society was dissolved, most of the members becoming proprietors of the new institution. One hundred and thirty-three persons became proprietors in the Athenæum, at $100 a share, of which $60 only were paid, the principal part of which was invested in bank stock, as a fund towards the support of the establishment. The books go into circulation to all the members who pay a tax of $5 a year, and to others who pay $10. The library, which has been continually increasing to the present time, is now conveniently arranged in the large room over the Canal Bank, and contains (1848) 5,750 volumes of the literature of the days through which it has lived, embracing the best periodical publications and standard works. For its size there are few libraries more valuable. A new impulse has been given to it the present year; upwards of 40 new shares have been taken up, at $40 each. The institution is an honor to the city, and should receive a liberal regard from every citizen who is able to contribute to this unexceptionable public improvement. Charles S. Daveis is now president; and Phineas Barnes, secretary and treasurer."—[Journals of the Rev. Thomas Smith and the Rev. Samuel Deane, pastors of the First Church in Portland, with notes and biographical notices and a summary history of Portland. By William Willis: 8vo., Portland, 1849: pp. 441-2, appendix.]

WATERVILLE.

Waterville College Libraries—8,484 *vols.*—The college was founded in 1820. The college library contains 5,200 volumes; other libraries permanently connected with the college, 3,284 volumes; making a total of books to which students have access, of 8,484 volumes. The average increase is about fifty volumes yearly. The sum of $10,000 is pledged as a library fund, but not yet realized. The library is in a building erected for chapel, library and philosophical apparatus; the building is of brick, and cost about $8,000; the room used for the books is about 30 by 40 feet. A catalogue was printed in 1845, containing 47 pages 8vo. The library is opened twice a week, and kept open half an hour each time. The trustees, faculty, and students are entitled to the use of the books without charge; the students pay one dollar a year for the privilege; other persons are allowed to consult the library, at the discretion of the librarian and library committee. Professor M. B. Anderson is librarian.

DISTRICT SCHOOL LIBRARIES—452 VOLUMES.

"The statute of 1844, chapter 106, authorizes school districts to expend a portion of their money in the purchase of books for a district library. The small amount of school money in a majority of the districts, divided and subdivided as they have been, has rendered it inexpedient to divert any portion of it from the ordinary purposes of the school; and for this reason, but little progress has been made in the formation of school libraries."—[First report of Secretary of the Board of Education, presented May 25, 1847.]

The secretary in his second report (1848) states that eleven districts had established libraries. In the last report (1849) the secretary says "there are but seventeen school district libraries in the State, containing in all 452 volumes."

OTHER LIBRARIES.

Besides the libraries already mentioned, there are doubtless others from which no reports have been received. A correspondent, who is intimately acquainted with the different parts of the State, writes: "There are but few town libraries in the State. A large proportion of our religious societies have what are termed Sunday school libraries; these, however, are made up of works designed more particularly for juvenile readers. Some of our academies have libraries, and there may be a few, but a very few, social libraries. * * We have a large number of valuable private libraries, on which dust is not permitted to gather."

NEW HAMPSHIRE.

CONCORD.

The State Library—4,700 *vols.*—commenced prior to the Revolution, and contains at present (November, 1849)—

Judicial reports - - - - - - -	400 vols.
Legislative documents, statutes, &c. - - -	2,486 "
Miscellaneous works - - - - - -	1,625 "
Pamphlets - - - - - - -	1,905 "
Maps - - - - - - -	28
Atlases - - - - - - -	7

For the last two years it has increased about 300 volumes yearly; the eight years previous, about 75 volumes yearly. About $100 per annum have been expended for the purchase of books. There is a standing appropriation of that amount. The library occupies a room in the north wing of the State House, which is 23 feet by 43. A catalogue (57 pages 8vo.) was printed in 1846. The library is open during each day when the legislature is in session. The members and clerks of the Senate and House during the sessions of the legislature, and at all times, the governor and council, judges of the superior court, secretary and treasurer, may take out books, to be returned in one month. Except during a session, any person may take out books by depositing double the value thereof, as security for the return of the book in good order. Few books, however, are lent out in this way—perhaps fifty a year. It is impossible to tell how many consult the library in the room. During the session of the legislature it is generally resorted to by the members. Thomas P. Treadwell, Secretary of State and ex-officio librarian.

The Methodist General Biblical Institute—1,000 *vols.*—This library was commenced in 1846, and contains at present 1,000 volumes and 17 maps. It receives about 250 volumes annually by donation. It is open Tuesdays and Thursdays, during one hour. About 400 books are lent out annually to the students and instructors of the Institute. Professor Osmon C. Baker, librarian.

The New Hampshire Historical Society—1,500 *vols.*—This society owes its origin and much of its early prosperity to the suggestions and active exertions of Mr. John Farmer and Mr. Jacob B. Moore. It was founded March 13, 1823, the two hundredth year after the first settlement of the State, and incorporated the 13th of June following. Its objects are like those of the other Historical Societies in the country. They are thus stated in the first article of the constitution, namely: "To discover, procure, and preserve whatever may relate to the natural, civil, literary and ecclesiastical history of the United States in general, and of this State in particular." The society has published five volumes of valuable collections. The library of the society contained, in 1838, "about 1,500 volumes, a considerable collection of pamphlets and newspapers, a small collection of minerals, some valuable manuscripts, ancient coins and Indian relics." The Hon. William Plumer, its first president, gave to the society several hundred volumes of American state papers, arranged with a copious manuscript index by himself. The Hon. William Bartlett gave his private library, a part of the library of the late Nathaniel Peabody, and a portfolio of autograph MS. letters, amounting to about 200 in all. Deposited in the library "are a considerable number of papers and documents, formerly belonging to the Rev. Dr. Belknap, and used by him in the compilation of the second and third volumes of the History of New Hampshire," transmitted to the society by John Belknap, esq., son of the reverend historian.

An article in the fifth volume of the society's collections, written by Hon. William Bartlett, entitled "*Remarks and Documents relating to the preservation and keeping of the public Archives*," deserves to be particularly mentioned, and commended to the careful perusal of librarians, seretaries of state, and all others to whose care are intrusted the original records of our history.—[See Hist. N. H. Historical Society, in American Quarterly Register, February, 1838, pp. 229-241.]

DUBLIN.

The Union Library, founded in 1793, contains 438 volumes. Proprietors pay $1 50 per share and an annual assessment of 25 cents. 37½ cents per year are paid by those who borrow books. L. W. Leonard, librarian.

Ladies' Library, founded 1799, contains 161 volumes. Mrs. Lucy Marshall, librarian.

Juvenile Library, founded 1822, contains 1,817 volumes on the catalogue; some are *worn out*, some lost; about $16 per year expended for books; the use of the library is free to all persons in town. L. W. Leonard, librarian.

EXETER.

Phillips Academy has a library of about 800 volumes, which has been slowly accumulating since 1783, when the academy was first opened for the admission of pupils. The purchases are made at the discretion of the principal, mostly for the benefit of the instructors.

Connected with the academy is a library belonging to a society of the present members of the institution, containing 1,400 volumes. It is under the immediate care of a librarian chosen each term. It contains valuable books adapted to the wants of the students. Gideon L. Soull, principal.

GILMANTON.

Theological Seminary.—This seminary was established in 1835 by the Congregationalists. The number of volumes in the library is stated in the American Almanac for 1850 to be 4,300.

GREAT FALLS.

Manufacturers' and Village Library—2,200 *vols.*—A catalogue of this library, containing numbers 1 to 1,628, was printed January 1, 1847; 16 pages octavo, with supplements—June 24, 1848, 1 page; March 24, 1849, 4 pages; and March, 1850, 4 pages. Proprietors pay $2 initiation fee and $1 annual assessment. All females in the employ of the Great Falls Manufacturing Company are entitled to the benefit of the library on payment of 25 cents annually.

HANOVER.

Dartmouth College Libraries—20,600 *vols.*—From various sources, principally from the "Bibliotheca Sacra," April, 1850, we gather the following facts: The college was founded in 1769. From that time it has gradually gathered a library which now contains about 6,400 volumes, and 17 portraits in oil. Among these last are: a full-length portrait of the Earl of Dartmouth, a copy of the original by Sir Joshua Reynolds, and a donation of the present Earl; a portrait of Daniel Webster, of Jeremiah Smith, Jeremiah Mason, Francis Hopkinson; a full length portrait of Eleazar Wheelock, the first president of the college; of John Phillips, of Exeter, also full length; of Samuel Appleton, Charles Marsh, &c. The library contains some rare and valuable works, but is deficient in new books.

The libraries of the two societies of students—the Social Friends and the United Fraternity—contain each 6,500 volumes; are well selected, and include many very valuable works, both for reference and miscellaneous reading; some with costly illustrations.

A few years ago a building (costing about $10,000) was erected for the accommodation of the three libraries.

The two society libraries have published catalogues.

The library of the medical department contains about 1,200 volumes.

The Northern Academy of Arts and Sciences—1,300 *vols.*—This society was formed June 24, 1841, and is composed of the professors of Dartmouth College and a few other gentlemen in the vicinity. It has 800 unbound volumes of pamphlets, etc., partially arranged; also 700 unbound volumes of newspapers. This collection also contains some valuable private papers, among which are a meteorological journal kept by Mr. John Farmer, of Concord, New Hampshire, from 1813 to 1830; Governor Bartlett's correspondence from 1774 to 1794; also a MS. journal of the weather, kept by Eleazar Russell, esq., of Portsmouth, New Hampshire. Efforts were early made to procure for the library complete sets of the first newspapers printed in that part of the country. Spooner's Journal, published at Hanover by Judah C. Spooner and Timothy Greene in 1771, and from February, 1781, at Westminster and Windsor, Vermont, is nearly complete. This paper is extremely valuable, as it was published at the time of the American Revolution, and was the first periodical issued in that part of the country, and consequently contains much of its early history. Complete sets of the Vermont Chronicle, the Boston Recorder, and the Dartmouth Gazette, are also contained in the library.—[See American Quarterly Register, November, 1842.]

MERIDEN VILLAGE, PLAINFIELD.

Kimball Union Academy Libraries—2,000 *vols.*—The academy library, founded in 1814, contains 1,000 volumes. About $100 per annum are generally appropriated from the funds of the institution towards purchasing books for the library. The endowment of the academy is rich; (about $40,000 in stocks, and $20,000 in buildings.) The library is open Saturdays from 1 to 2 o'clock. The use is free to all connected with the academy. A catalogue was printed some 15 years ago; another will be put to press very soon. C. S. Richards, A. M., principal, and ex officio librarian.

The Philadelphian Society, composed of students of the academy, possesses a library of 1,000 volumes of choice books. It was founded soon after the academy library, and is increased annually, by the voluntary contributions of the members, about 50 to 70 volumes.

NEW HAMPTON.

Theological Seminary Libraries—2,200 *vols.*—The "New Hampton Academy" was incorporated in 1821. In 1826 its name was changed to the "Academical and Theological Institution at New Hampton." The theological department went into full operation in 1833. It is under the care and patronage of the Baptist denomination. The department has a library of 600 well selected volumes.—[See History of the New Hampton Theological Institution, by W. E. Wording, A. M., in the American Quarterly Register for May, 1842.]

The Literary Adelphi of the Academical and Theological Institution at New Hampton, New Hampshire, was founded A. D. 1827, and incorporated by the legislature of the State in 1829. "There are about 800 volumes in the library, most of which are valuable standard works. Efforts are being made to enlarge the library, and several friends have made valuable donations. The reading room is spacious and convenient, and by the liberality of patrons is furnished with about 20 regular newspapers from different parts of the country. Besides this, the society receives several of the most popular and valuable literary periodicals of the present day."—[See note to the "Catalogue of Members of the L. A.;" 12mo. Concord, 1844.]

In the year 1830 a new society, called the Social Fraternity, was formed. It has a library and reading-room similar to those of the Literary Adelphi.—[See Wording's History.]

NEW IPSWICH.

The academy at New Ipswich was incorporated in 1789. It has a small library, presented by Samuel Appleton, of Boston. The Demosthenean Society, among the students, has also a small library. A valuable town library was destroyed by fire some years since. The present one is small but well selected.—[New Hampshire Historical Collections, vol. 5, p. 161]

NORTHFIELD.

Library of the New Hampshire Conference Seminary—1,000 *volumes.*

PORTSMOUTH.

Athenæum Library—7,284 *vols.*—Incorporated in 1817. The library contains 7,284 volumes, 150 engravings, and 246 coins. The yearly average increase for the last ten years has been 200 volumes. The annual expenditure, $200. The building now occupied by the Athenæum was purchased for $7,500; it is of brick, with slated roof, three stories high; the first story is used as a reading and newspaper room; the second is the library, and the third a museum and cabinet. The books are arranged on the shelves according to subjects. A shelf-catalogue is prepared, containing the titles of the books as they stand upon the shelves; by this the library is annually examined. A "Catalogue of books in the Portsmouth Athenæum, to which are added the by-laws of the institution and a list of its proprietors," 108 pages 8vo., was printed at Portsmouth in May, 1833; at that time the library contained between 4,000 and 5,000 volumes. A "Catalogue of books added to the library of Portsmouth Athenæum, from May, 1833, to January, 1839," was published at Portsmouth in 1839, 31 pages 8vo.; at this time the library contained 5,300 volumes. This catalogue is alphabetical; the titles are recorded under the names of authors, with cross-references from subjects to authors—the subjects and authors being arranged in one alphabet. This is a very convenient way in a small library. Another "Catalogue of books in the Portsmouth Athenæum, to which are added the by-laws of the institution and a list of its proprietors," 192 pages 8vo., was printed January 1, 1849, at Portsmouth. This catalogue is upon the same plan as the preceding. From a note (page 12) we take the following facts respecting the history of the institution: "In 1829, John Fisher, esq., of London, gave his library in this town, amounting to nearly 300 valuable volumes, to the Athenæum. In February, 1830, James Edward Sheafe bequeathed $1,000 to the Athenæum, which sum was invested in the purchase of books for the library. In October, 1843, Horace Appleton Haven bequeathed $2,000 to the Athenæum—one moiety for the purchase of books, and the other for the preservation of the library. These sums have been invested accordingly." The library is open every day from sunrise to ten o'clock in the evening. Persons allowed the use of the library are: proprietors of shares; and subscribers, who, on the payment of six dollars a year, may read in the library room. Proprietors can take out books, two at a time, which they may change as often as they please. George Jaffrey, librarian.

St. John's Church Library—500 *vols.*

Unitarian Church Library—678 *vols.*

SANBORNTON BRIDGE.

Public Library—300 *vols.*

WAKEFIELD.

Wakefield and Brookfield Union Library—500 *vols.*—This library company was incorporated in 1797. It commenced with thirty members; in 1827 there were forty-four members; in 1849 there are only twenty eight members. The library contains 500 volumes, mostly histories and biographies. William Sawyer, jr., librarian.

SCHOOL LIBRARIES—2,500 VOLUMES.

In the State of New Hampshire there are perhaps twenty-five libraries, averaging 100 volumes each, connected with the district schools.

There are doubtless many small social libraries in this State, from which no returns have been received.

VERMONT.

BURLINGTON.

University of Vermont—12,250 *vols.*—This institution was incorporated in 1791. The library was commenced when the college went into operation, in the year 1800. It contains at present (1849) about 7,000 volumes, as near as can be estimated, without including 5 volumes of atlases and 63 unbound maps. The average annual increase for the last ten years has been about 100 by donation, and about the same number by purchase. About fifty dollars a year were appropriated, previous to 1846, for buying books; since then, seventy-five dollars. There is a permanent fund of $1,250 for the increase of the library, yielding 6 per cent. interest. There is a classified "Catalogue of the books belonging to the library of the University of Vermont," 8vo., 93 pp.; printed in 1836, with supplement (alphabetical) 1842, 8vo., 24 pp. The library is opened twice each week, for one hour. The Faculty of the University use the library without charge. Students pay $1 50 per year for the privilege. Others are allowed the use of it by special permission of the president. Books are lent out, to be returned or renewed as often as once in two weeks. Professor Calvin Pease, librarian.

This is one of the few libraries in the United States selected with competent bibliographical knowledge and with good judgment, and purchased with economy. The college had the wisdom to send a learned, zealous, and active agent to Europe to buy the books, instead of trusting their funds to the cupidity of bibliopoles. The selection was made to meet the wants of the officers of the college, and, consequently, of the students. Somewhat less than two-thirds of the books are in the English language. The collections of Greek and Latin authors are nearly complete, and of the best editions.

A large part of the library of the Hon. George P. Marsh, minister of the United States to Turkey, amounting to between 3,000 and 4,000 volumes, is deposited in this library. Nearly all these works are in foreign languages, principally in the Spanish and Scandinavian. There are, however, some very rare books in the English language. [See Bibliotheca Sacra.]

The libraries of the three societies of students contain, respectively, 2,000, 2,000, 1,250 volumes.

MIDDLEBURY.

Middlebury College Libraries—8,417 *vols.*—This institution was founded in 1800. The college library contains about 5,000 volumes, and occupies a room in a building with the cabinet of natural history, lecture-rooms, &c. A catalogue was printed in 1833, containing 16 pp. 8vo., double columns. The library is opened once a week, and kept open for an hour. The students pay four dollars a year for the use of books. Resident graduates, clergymen in the neighborhood, and others, by permission of the librarian and Faculty of the college, are allowed to take out books without charge. The students have three libraries, namely:

The library of the Philomathesian Society (miscellaneous)	2,200	volumes.
" " Philadelphian Society (religious) -	432	"
The Beneficent Library (mostly text books) - -	785	"

Professor R. D. C. Robbins, librarian.

MONTPELIER.

State Library—3,500 *vols.*—This library contains about 3,500 volumes, maps of the several States, a few engravings, and thirty medals. It occupies a room in the State House, 36 feet by 20, with alcoves, and gallery eight feet from floor, with seven and a half feet above it. Open every day during the session of the legislature and council of censors. The books are not lent out, except to members of the legislature and council, on their becoming responsible for their safe return. Cornelius N. Carpenter, Montpelier, librarian.

Historical and Antiquarian Society of Vermont.—This society was incorporated November 22, 1838. Its library and collections are as yet very small. The president, Henry Stevens, esq., of Barnet, possesses a very valuable collection of books, newspapers, manuscripts, &c., illustrative of the history of the State, amounting to about 1,500 volumes.

NORWICH.

Norwich University Library—1,032 *vols.*—This institution was founded in 1834. The library, commenced in 1843, contains 1,032 volumes and a few maps and charts. The average annual increase is 200 volumes; average annual expenditure, twenty-five dollars. The room is adorned by a full-length portrait of the distinguished and lamented Colonel T. B. Ransom, former president of the college. The library has no permanent fund. It is opened at three o'clock on Saturday afternoons, and at such other times as visitors may desire. The faculty, students, members of the corporation, and donors, are entitled to the use of the books. Ira Davis, librarian.

MASSACHUSETTS.

AMHERST.

Amherst College Libraries—13,700 *vols.*—The college library was founded at the opening of the college, in 1821, and contains 5,700 volumes. The average annual increase is about 120 volumes. Three or four years since, David Sears, esq., of Boston, gave to the college, expressly for the library, an estate, in the city of Boston, which yields $120 per annum. He has since given another, yielding a larger income; and has thus established a perpetual fund, called the "Sears Foundation," which is to accumulate slowly, and mainly for the use of the library. The annual amount appropriated for the purchase of books is at present uncertain; probably not over $300. The library occupies a room in the same building with the chapel and other public apartments; it is about 40 feet by 20. A catalogue (38 pages 12mo.) was printed in 1827; but the most valuable part of the library has been purchased since. The library is opened once a week for taking and returning books. The officers take out books *ad libitum;* the students pay four and five cents for each work; some 200 or 300 are usually out at a time, in possession of the teachers; the students take but few on account of the large miscellaneous libraries of the societies. Professor E. S. Snell, librarian.

The libraries of the two literary societies of students contain, together, 8,000 volumes. The Society of Inquiry has a small museum.

An effort is now making, which it is hoped will be fully successful, to enlarge the college library. The library is, at present, "deficient in even the standard works of science. Ten thousand dollars ought to be given to the college for its library, and an equal sum for a library building."—[Independent.]

"The trustees propose to raise, without delay, $30,000 for the increase of the library and the erection of a suitable library building."—[Boston Traveller correspondent, August 10, 1850.]

ANDOVER.

The Theological Seminary Libraries—20,249 *vols.*—This seminary is under the direction of the trustees of Phillips Academy, which was founded April 21, 1778, and belongs to the Orthodox Congregationalists. The library was commenced in 1808, and contains at present 16,300 volumes. During the last ten years there have been added to the library upwards of 4,000 volumes, including a bequest from the Rev. John Codman, D. D., of Dorchester, of 1,250 volumes. During the same period the expenditure for books has been about $700 per annum. There is a permanent fund of about $12,000, the income of which is appropriated to the purchase of books. The library is in a handsome room in the second story of a brick building, erected in 1818, at an expense of about $19,000, for chapel, recitation rooms, and library. The library room is 60 feet by 40, and about 18 feet high, fitted up with alcoves, and adorned with the portraits of the principal benefactors of the institution. The books are arranged but partially according to subjects. In 1819 a catalogue of 160 pages 8vo., by Professor J. W. Gibbs, now of New Haven, was printed. In 1838 an elaborate catalogue, containing 531 pages 8vo., was published. A supplementary catalogue of 67 pages 8vo. was printed in 1849. The library is opened three times a week, from 1 to 3 o'clock p. m. The persons entitled to the use of the books are, besides the officers of the seminary, students and resident licentiates on the payment of $3 per annum, and others by permission of the faculty. Each student is allowed eight books at a time. Probably 4,000 volumes are lent out in the course of the year. Books may be carried out of town by permission from the faculty. Edward Robie, librarian.

Besides the public library, the following collections are connected with the seminary:

Library of the Porter Rhetorical Society - - -	2,600 vols.
(A catalogue of this library was printed in 1839, in octavo form.)	
Library of the Society of Inquiry - - - -	1,349 "

The library of the Andover Theological Seminary is one of the most valuable in the country. The books mostly belong to the departments of theology and philology. It is a selected library, and not a chance accumulation of volumes rejected from the shelves of a multitude of donors. Profound theological learning, thorough bibliographical knowledge and skill, have for the most part presided over the formation and arrangements of the library. The catalogue, by Rev. Oliver A. Taylor, A. M., now a clergyman in Manchester, Massachusetts, has, we believe, no superior among printed catalogues of libraries. It is on the plan of Audifreddi. The books are placed under the authors' names. The names are in alphabetical order. To the name of each author is appended a biographical note. Annotations upon the books are also interspersed through the work. The catalogue is destitute of an index. To supply one, characterized by the same minute accuracy as the catalogue, would be a difficult and expensive undertaking. We cannot help adding, however, that, if accomplished, it would be a most important aid to theological study, and amply repay the cost of the work. The want of such an index is in a great measure supplied to the students of the seminary by the references given by the professors in their lectures.

"The library has ordered a collection of between 2,000 and 3,000 small books and pamphlets, relating to or written by the Puritans and published in England in the time of Charles I, the Commonwealth, and Charles II. The department in the library which is most fully supplied is that relating to the Christian Fathers, and Church History generally. It has also a good collection of works relating to biblical commentary, criticism, and antiquities. It possesses also many of the best early editions of the Greek and Roman classics and works illustrative of them. It is quite deficient in works on the English language and standard English literature; in the productions of the English and American Puritans; in general works of science which would be suitable to a theological library; in the best later editions of the classics, etc."—[Bibliotheca Sacra.]

Phillips Academy Library - - - - 1,000 vols.
English High School Library - - - - 800 "

BOSTON.

The Boston Athenæum Library—50,000 *vols.*—The Athenæum owes its origin to a society of gentlemen who conducted a literary publication, called the "Monthly Anthology." In the year 1806, they issued proposals for establishing a reading-room to contain the most valuable foreign and American journals, with works of reference suitable to such a place of resort, open to subscribers at $10 per annum. The enterprise proved unexpectedly successful. Many valuable books were presented, and the gentlemen who commenced the undertaking, in order more effectually to secure and extend the benefits of their labor and expense, transferred their right in the Anthology Reading Room and Library to trustees, with power to supply vacancies in their number. At the winter session of the legislature in 1807, the proprietors were incorporated under the name of the "Boston Athenæum."*

The price of a share was fixed at $300. Annual subscribers were admitted at $10 per annum. From these sources, occasional voluntary subscriptions and frequent donations, the institution has risen to its present important position.

The principal endowments of the Athenæum before the year 1847 are thus enumerated in an inscription under the corner-stone of the new building:

---

*Snow's History of Boston.

"The sum of $42,000 was raised for the general purposes of the Athenæum, by voluntary subscription for shares created in 1807.

"James Perkins, in 1821, gave his own costly mansion in Pearl street, which from that time has been the seat of the institution.

"In the same year, the sum of $22,000 was raised by voluntary subscriptions for shares.

"Thomas Handasyd Perkins (besides his earlier and later valuable donations,) and James Perkins the younger, seconded, in 1826, the liberality of the brother and the father, each giving $8,000; and the sum of their contributions was increased to $45,000 by other subscriptions, obtained chiefly through the efforts and influence of Nathaniel Bowditch, Francis Calley Gray, George Ticknor, and Thomas Wren Ward.

"Augustus Thorndike, in 1823, gave a choice collection of casts of the most celebrated ancient statues.

"George Watson Brimmer, in 1838, gave a magnificent collection of books on the fine arts.

"John Bromfield, in 1846, gave $25,000 as a fund to be regularly increased by one quarter of the income, of which the other three-quarters are to be annually applied to the purchase of books forever.

"The sum of $75,000, for the erection of the building, was raised by voluntary subscription for shares created in 1844."*

Liberality like this is seldom witnessed, and deserves the most honorable mention.

The institution first occupied rooms in Congress street, whence it was removed to Scollay's buildings, in Court street, and in 1810 to the building on Common (now Tremont) street, north of King's Chapel burial ground. In the year 1822 it was removed to the house in Pearl street presented, as already stated, by James Perkins. In 1823 the King's Chapel Library and the Theological Library, containing together 1,300 volumes of theological works, were deposited in the Athenæum, where they still remain. In 1826 a union was effected with the Boston Medical Library, and its books, valued at $4,500, were added to those of the Athenæum. In the same year, also, an association which had been formed for the purchase of a scientific library became merged in the Athenæum, and its funds, exceeding $3,000, were transferred to the Athenæum to be expended in the purchase of scientific books.—[See sketch of the Boston Athenæum, by Edward Wigglesworth, M. A., in the "American Quarterly Register" for November, 1839.]

In July, 1849, the library was removed to its new home in Beacon street, just above the Tremont House. The location is central, yet free from the dust and noise of crowded thoroughfares. The edifice is elegant, spacious, and convenient. The front is 100 feet long and 60 feet high, in the Palladian style of architecture, and built of freestone. The other walls are of brick. In the basement story are rooms for the packing of books, for a bindery, for the accommodation of the janitor, &c. The main entrance opens into a pillared and panelled rotundo, from which the staircases conduct above. On the first floor are two large reading-rooms, a room for the trustees, and a sculpture gallery, 80 feet by 40. The library occupies the second story, which is divided into three rooms, two in front and

*This sum having been found insufficient for the completion of the building, an additional subscription for two hundred shares has been opened, and is now (April, 1850) nearly filled up.

one large hall (109 feet by 40) in the rear. The western division of this room is filled with Encyclopedias, Transactions of learned societies, Magazines, and other works in long series of volumes. The other and larger portion is divided into 26 alcoves, and contains about 40,000 volumes. This hall is beautifully finished in the Italian style. The shelving is carried to the height of 18 or 20 feet, and the upper shelves are made accessible by means of a light iron gallery, reached by five spiral staircases. The two front rooms will accommodate some 25,000 volumes. The picture gallery occupies the upper story. It is divided into six apartments, each lighted by a skylight. It is admirably adapted to its purposes. The roof affords a magnificent view of the city and the surrounding country. The whole building is constructed in the most substantial and workmanlike manner.

Besides 50,000 bound volumes, including 1,500 or 1,600 volumes of pamphlets, the library possesses 20,000 or more unbound pamphlets, between 400 and 500 volumes of engravings, and the most valuable collection of coins in that part of the country. For an American library it is rich in certain departments, *e. g.* in the reports and transactions of learned societies, in periodical publications in the English language, works in the natural sciences, &c. It has complete sets of the Transactions of the Royal Society of London, the French Institute, the royal societies of Berlin, Copenhagen, Göttingen, Lisbon, Madrid, Stockholm, St. Petersburg, Turin, etc. It has also the Encyclopédie Raisonné, 35 volumes folio; the Encyclopédie Methodique, 258 volumes 4to., including 37 of plates; Buffon's Natural History by Sonnini, 127 volumes 8vo., &c.†

The institution has lately received a valuable collection of books and papers, once forming a part of the library of General Washington. It contains in all about 450 bound volumes, and from 800 to 1,000 pamphlets unbound, nearly all of which belonged to the library of Washington. About 350 contain his autograph, and a few of them notes in his handwriting. One little book has the autograph of Washington in a rude, school-boy hand, at about the age of nine years. There are several autographs of Augustine Washington, the father of the General; of Mary, the mother, and of Martha, the wife. One book contains on the title-page the autograph of John Custis, (first husband of Martha,) and on the next leaf that of George Washington. One volume has the autograph of Thomas Jenifer, a signer of the Declaration of Independence. There are several presentation copies from eminent authors—Sir John Sinclair, Arthur Young, Ebeling, Alfieri, Jefferson, Dr. Morse, and others. Ten volumes contain the name of Richard Henry Lee in his own handwriting. These books came into the possession of the Athenæum in the following manner. General Washington bequeathed his books and papers to his nephew, Bushrod Washington. On the death of Bushrod Washington the library was divided: one portion was left at Mount Vernon, where it still remains; another fell to Colonel Washington. The latter portion included the public papers, afterwards purchased by Congress, and a considerable number of the books, pamphlets, and private papers. The books had been offered for sale. Congress had declined the purchase. Mr. Henry Stevens at last bought the collection, and offered it

---

* Literary World, August 11, 1849. †Bibliotheca Sacra, January, 1850.

for sale to the Athenæum. A few gentlemen of Boston and vicinity subscribed the required amount, and presented these precious memorials of the world's best hero to this institution. An elegant descriptive catalogue, prepared by an accurate and accomplished scholar, will soon be published.

The Athenæum possesses many valuable paintings and statues. Among the latter is the Orpheus of Crawford, in marble.

Several catalogues of the books have been printed; one, without date, in 266 pages 8vo., in which the books are arranged in 16 classes. Another, and the last, was printed in 1827, and contains 356 pages 8vo. It is alphabetical. A supplement (60 pages) was printed in 1829; a second (80 pages) in 1834. These two supplements, with the other additions to the library up to 1840, were in that year printed together in a volume containing 179 pages 8vo. A complete and elaborate catalogue is now in preparation. The printed catalogues have not heretofore contained the titles of the numerous pamphlets belonging to the library. A neat and accurate catalogue of these pamphlets, prepared by Dr. A. A. Gould, and complete to within two or three years, exists in manuscript.

The present librarian is Charles Folsom, esq. It is highly creditable to the wisdom of the trustees that they have chosen for this important post so ripe a scholar, and so accomplished a gentleman. The influence of such an officer is incalculable; not only in forming far-seeing plans for the increase and arrangement of the collection, but in aiding the researches of learned men, in guiding the studies of youth, and in leading the intellectual pursuits of an educated community.

The library is hardly surpassed, either in size or in value, by any other in the country; and its regulations are framed with the design that it shall answer the highest purposes of a public library. Practically it is such; for each proprietor, besides the right for himself and his family to use the library, may grant to two other persons constant access to it, free of all assessments; and tickets for a month to any number of strangers. Any person, indeed, stranger or resident, may be introduced for a special purpose by a note from a proprietor. Thus, the by-laws open the doors of the institution to a large number of persons; so that the proprietor who bestows on others the free use of all the rights he can impart, renders himself thereby a public benefactor.

The following are the principal regulations of the institution:

The proprietors meet annually on the first Monday of January. The officers are chosen annually. They are a president, vice president, treasurer, secretary, and nine trustees. The trustees appoint a librarian, and sub-librarian.

The price of a share is $300; that of a life subscription $100. Annual subscribers pay $10 for the use of the library and reading-room, but are not allowed to take out books.

Every proprietor has, besides his own right, two rights of admission transferable to such persons as he may select. Proprietors and life shareholders, on paying $5 annually, may take books home—not to exceed four volumes at once. Every proprietor and life subscriber may introduce strangers not residing within twenty miles of Boston, and such strangers are entitled to visit the Athenæum for one month from the time of their introduction.

Certain persons by virtue of their offices are entitled to free admission to the Athenæum. These are the governor and council, the lieutenant governor and members of the legislature of Massachusetts for the time being, the judges of the Supreme Court and of the courts of the United States, the officers and resident graduates of Harvard College, of Williams College, of Amherst College, and of the Theological Seminary at Andover, the several presidents of the American Academy, Historical Society, Medical Society, Agricultural Society, Salem Athenæum, and the East India Marine Society of Salem; also clergymen settled in Boston. These last are likewise allowed to take out books on the same terms as proprietors.

The Boston Library—12,150 *vols*.—The first meeting of the members of the Boston Library Society was held the 1st of November, 1792, and the society was incorporated in 1794. At the annual meeting in May, 1849, the number of volumes in the library was 12,150. About 250 volumes, on an average, have been added to the library annually, during the last ten years. The average annual expenditure for books, during the same period, has been, including binding and repairs, $378 69. The library is supported by an annual assessment levied on the proprietors, and by fines incurred. The income from these sources is about $850 per annum.

The apartments occupied by the Boston Library were a donation to the infant society in the winter of 1793–'94 by Messrs. Bulfinch (the architect of the capitol at Washington,) Vaughan & Scollay, "being the hall over the arch of the Tontine Buildings, in Franklin Place." The cost to the society of completing the rooms was $857 57. The society has since purchased, for $1,500 dollars, of the Massachusetts Historical Society, a room of the same area, being the upper story of the building. Each apartment is 37 feet in length by 27 in front, and 33 feet in the rear; from which should be deducted staircase and closets. Catalogues and supplements were printed at various dates, (1795, 1797, 1807, 1815, &c.) A new and accurate catalogue of 335 pages, 8vo., was printed in 1844, and a supplemental catalogue of 48 pages was completed in September, 1849, to which is appended a list of works relating to America, of 20 pages. The library is opened at 3 o'clock on the afternoon of each Tuesday, Thursday and Saturday, for three hours, or till dark, and on the morning of Saturday from 10 o'clock till 1 o'clock.

No one can take books from the library, except the proprietors, without the special permission of the trustees. The price of a share is $25, subject to an assessment of $3 annually. Each proprietor can take out three volumes at one time. The librarian estimates the number of volumes annually charged to proprietors at 15,000. The number of persons that consult the library, without taking away books, is small; but the trustees cheerfully give every reasonable facility to all persons having occasion to consult the library. Occasional applications for books have been made from the neighboring towns, which have always been granted. George S. Bulfinch, librarian.

The principal object of the society has been to form a collection of books for popular use, admitting none of an injurious moral tendency, and preferring those of solid and standard value. History and biography, (particularly American,) travels, the English and French classics, and fiction, are the departments best supplied. Most of the books have been selected and purchased. The donations have been comparatively few.

For some years after the library was founded, the shares were not transferable, and subscribers had only the use of the library for their lives; consequently, by the death of original proprietors, many shares have fallen into the common stock; which has given to the shares of present proprietors a value far beyond their cost. Shares are now, however, transferable, and do not cease at the death of the proprietor.

The Library of the American Academy of Arts and Sciences—8,000 *vols.*—This society was incorporated May 4, 1780. Among the scientific associations of the United States, it is next in age to the American Philosophical Society at Philadelphia, which is the oldest in the country. The average annual increase of the library is about 150 volumes. An annual appropriation of about $600 is made from the general fund of the academy for the purchase of books. The library is opened during the day, every week-day. All members of the academy, and strangers, are allowed the use of the books, which may be taken out by any member, or in his name. A catalogue (57 pp. 8vo.) was printed in 1802. Lists of accessions are, from time to time, printed in the publications of the academy. John Bacon, jr., M. D., is librarian. This library contains a valuable collection of the memoirs and transactions of learned societies, reviews and magazines, and of modern scientific works. It is kept in two rooms leased by the society in Tremont Row, No. 7½.

Library of the General Court—7,400 *vols.*—The State library was established by an act of the legislature, passed March 3, 1826, requiring that "all books and manuscripts belonging to the commonwealth, and now in any of the departments of the State House, shall be collected, deposited, and arranged, in proper cases, in the room in said State House usually called the land office." It contains, at present, 7,400 volumes, 80 maps and charts, 5 atlases, 37 railroad plans, 1 portrait, 3 tableaus, and 6 medals. The yearly increase for the last eleven years is as follows:

	Volumes.
1838	452
1839	396
1840	260
1841	358
1842	348
1843	334
1844	367
1845	583
1846	336
1847	791
1848	455
Total	4,680

Averaging 425 per annum. About $395 per annum has, during this time, been expended in the purchase of books. The regular appropriation for the library has been $300 per annum, with occasional extra allowances "to procure such books, manuscripts and charts, works of science and the arts, as tend to illustrate the resources and means of improvement of this commonwealth or of the United States." "Additions are also made annually of the statutes, legislative journals and documents, and law reports of the United States and of the several States of the Union, received in exchange through the secretary's department. Of *such* works it probably contains a more complete collection than any other library. One thousand and eighty duplicate volumes of laws, public documents, and reports, have been deposited in the law library of Harvard University by a resolve of the legislature.

"The library contains Mr. Audubon's collection of American Birds, in four large folio volumes, at an original cost of about six hundred dollars. An addition was recently made of 440 volumes of French, German and Swedish books of science, arts, history and statistics, some of which are of great value, by international exchanges through M. Vattemare. Among them are the following works, presented by the Chamber of Deputies:—Collection of Etruscan, Greek, and Roman antiquities, from the cabinet of Hon. William Hamilton, Naples, 1766; four large folio volumes, with English and French text, and 520 plates. Presented by the Minister of the Interior:—Monuments of Nineveh, published by order of the government; descriptions by P. E. Botta—designs by E. Flandin: the first ten numbers—*to be continued.* Presented by the Minister of Agriculture and Commerce:—Statistics of France, comprising territory, population, external commerce, etc., from 1837 to 1843; nine large folio volumes. Presented by the National Library of France:—The New Theatre of the World, containing maps, tables, descriptions, etc., of all the regions of the globe; 1639; 3 large folio volumes. This, considering its date, is a magnificent work. The Holy Evangelists, in Arabic and Latin: printed at Rome, in the typographia of Lorenzo de Medici, 1591, large folio; the works of Euclid, in Arabic: printed at Rome, in the 16th century, folio; Acta Historica Ecclesiastica Nostri Temporis: printed at Weimar, 1741 to 1774, *extremely rare*, 43 volumes. Presented by the King of Sweden:—History of the Kingdom of the Moors until their expulsion in 1726, in Arabic and Latin: edited by Professor Tornberg, 2 volumes in one; Ancient Sweden, etc., with 3 volumes of plates of its provinces, cities, buildings, etc., in oblong quarto. The choicest volumes in the State library to a descendant and admirer of the Puritans, and indeed to any true son of New England, are the ancient General Court Records of Massachusetts. They are copies, in manuscript, of original papers in the archives of the Secretary of State, and make 34 large folio volumes. The Records commence with 1629 and extend to October, 1777, and contain the entire legislative and much of the religious history of Massachusetts between those periods. Each volume has a copious index at its close, containing the names of *persons* and *places*, also a list of subjects spoken of, in separate columns, which facilitates reference, and greatly increases the value of these treasures of our colonial history. No books in the library are consulted more frequently or with more interest. Since the first volume was transcribed, several pages have been inserted at the beginning, containing records of a still earlier date."*

The secretary of the board of education is, by a recent law, made *ex-officio* librarian, and is allowed an assistant. Two rooms in the State House are appropriated to the library; one of them is 54 feet by 22, and the other 36 by 25. The books are arranged in cases with glass doors, and generally according to subjects. A catalogue (43 pp. 8vo.) was published in 1831; another in 8vo. was printed in 1839. The last catalogue (125 pp. 8vo.) was printed in 1846. The library is open every week-day from 9 a. m. to about sunset, and, during the session of the

*Bibliotheca Sacra, January, 1850.

legislature, sometimes in the evening. Books are lent to members of the legislature and officers of the State. Rev. Barnes Sears, D. D., secretary of board of education, and librarian; Rev. Charles T. Jackson, assistant.

Mercantile Library—7,059 *vols.*—The Mercantile Library Association was founded March 11, 1820, and incorporated in 1845. The library contains 7,059 volumes. The average annual increase for the last ten years has been 400 volumes; the average annual expenditure $375. There is a fund of $16,100, yielding six per cent. per annum, for the support of the library. The library is in two rooms, each 80 feet by 35. The arrangement on the shelves is according to the date of purchase. A catalogue was printed in 1848, consisting of 135 pages 8vo. The library is open every week-day evening till ten o'clock. Any person engaged in mercantile pursuits may acquire the right to use the library by paying two dollars per annum. Books are lent out, twenty-eight thousand annually. John Stetson, president.

The library is composed of such works in the field of general literature as are suited to the tastes and wants of merchants and merchants' clerks. In the reading-room are 89 newspapers and 21 reviews and magazines.

The number of members of the association is now 1,145. An annual course of lectures is delivered by distinguished gentlemen. The members participate in exercises of debate, declamation and composition. The whole number of tickets for the lectures in 1848–'9 was 1,300.*

Library of the Massachusetts Historical Society—7,000 *vols.*—The foundation of the Massachusetts Historical Society was originally suggested by Rev. Jeremy Belknap and Mr. Thomas Walcutt. It was organized in 1791, and incorporated in 1794. The number of members is limited by the act of incorporation to sixty. The library contains about 7,000 volumes, inclusive of bound newspapers; about 2,000 unbound pamphlets, 300 maps and charts, 450 volumes of manuscripts, a few coins, and 70 portraits. It increases about 100 volumes annually, wholly by donations. The society possesses no funds, not even for the support of a librarian. The entrance fees and annual assessments go for binding and other charges. The library occupies rooms in a stone edifice, erected in 1833. These rooms were purchased by the society for $6,500; $5,000 of which were collected by subscription at that time. These rooms are 84 feet by 40 in their whole length and breadth. The books are placed upon the shelves according to size, without regard to subjects. Two catalogues have been published—the first, 40 pages 8vo., in 1796; the second, compiled by Rev. Timothy Alden, 96 pages 8vo., was printed in 1811. The continuation is in manuscript. The library is open daily from 9 a, m. to 1 o'clock p. m., and from 3 to 6 p. m. It is accessible to members and others pursuing historical investigations. About 200 volumes a year are lent out. About 1,000 persons a year consult the library without taking away books. By permission of the standing committee, books may be lent to persons at a distance. Rev. Joseph B. Felt, librarian.

"Among the most valuable treasures belonging to this society are the manuscripts of the historian Hubbard; of the first Governor Winthrop, 11 volumes; of Governor Hutchinson; of Governor Jonathan Trumbull, of Connecticut, 23 volumes; the manuscript of Washington's Farewell Ad-

*Bibliotheca Sacra, January, 1850.

dress to the officers of the American army. The society has also 98 folio volumes of Commercial Statistics of the United States, embracing the years from 1816 to 1842 inclusive, drawn up with care, and very complete. There is a copy of Eliot's Indian Bible in the library. Thirty volumes of Collections have been printed, in three series, of 10 volumes each. The last volume of each series contains a full index of all the volumes in the series. The portraits of about seventy persons, mostly New England worthies, adorn one of the rooms. Some of these are of special value, *e. g.* the portraits of Rev. Increase Mather and of Rev. John Wilson."*

An interesting "Account of the Massachusetts Historical Society," prepared by William Jenks, D. D., of Boston, was printed in the American Quarterly Register for November, 1837, pages 166-177.

The Mechanics' Apprentices Library—4,000 *vols.*—This institution claims the distinction of being the first of its kind established in the world.† It is due to the wise suggestion and philanthropic energy of Mr. William Wood, now living in Canandaigua, New York. Lord Brougham remarks, that "although the remote origin of these institutions may be traced to Franklin, Mr. Wood has the merit of establishing them on their present plan, and adapting them peculiarly to the instruction of mechanics and apprentices. He founded the first in Boston, in 1820."

Mr. Wood has been actively engaged in the formation of libraries of a similar character in most of our large cities, and has even extended his benevolent efforts to the cities of the Old World. In his own words, "from the establishment of this library, in 1820, until now, as opportunity offered, the circulation of books, in any shape which might do good, has been the hobby of a life now drawing to a close." The name of this gentleman deserves to be held in lasting and grateful remembrance as a public benefactor.

Mr. Wood's efforts to collect a library for apprentices in Boston were warmly seconded by several distinguished citizens, and about 1,500 volumes were soon collected. The library was a gift from the public to the apprentices of Boston. On the 22d of February, 1820, it was formally intrusted to the guardianship of the Massachusetts Charitable Mechanics' Association, a society of long standing and established reputation. They agreed to take upon themselves the management of the institution on condition that they should not be chargeable with its incidental expenses.

The library was accordingly opened and the apprentices gratuitously supplied with books; the expenses being defrayed by public subscriptions. After a few years these subscriptions ceased, and the doors of the library were consequently closed. The apprentices feeling keenly this deprivation, held a meeting and agreed to take upon themselves the cares and responsibilities of the establishment, if the association would appropriate a small amount to aid them in the undertaking. This request met with a favorable answer. The present Association of Apprentices was formed June 19, 1828; and the library committed to their entire control in 1832, by the Mechanics' Association.

---

* Bibliotheca Sacra, January, 1850.

† For a full and interesting history of this institution, see an address delivered before the association on its 24th anniversary, by Frederick W. Lincoln, jr., Boston, 1844, from which this account is substantially taken.

The association consists entirely of apprentices to mechanics and manufacturers—of course embracing only minors. Any young man who is an apprentice to a respectable mechanic, (and learning a mechanical trade,) on producing a certificate that he is worthy of confidence, paying into the treasury the sum of one dollar per year, and signing the constitution, shall be a member. The affairs of the institution have been very ably and successfully conducted by its youthful members.

The association occupies two rooms in Phillips Place, opposite the head of School street; the one for reading and lecture-room, (say 30 feet by 40,) the other (say 30 by 15) for library and conversation room. The library is well selected to promote the intellectual culture of the class for whom it was intended. The reading department contains the principal newspapers and periodicals of the city, and many from different parts of the country, and is in a most flourishing condition. A cabinet of minerals and curiosities has been commenced; an annual course of free lectures is supported by the institution; an elocution class has been formed, the exercises of which consist in the reading of original compositions, declamation, and debate.

The yearly average increase of the library for the last ten years has been 175 volumes. A catalogue was printed in 1847, containing 68 pages 12mo.

The library is open three hours every Tuesday and Saturday evening. About 10,000 volumes are lent out annually. Robert H. Howell, jr., is the present librarian.

Library of the American Board of Commissioners for Foreign Missions—3,500 *vols.*—This library was founded in 1822, and contains, besides 3,500 volumes, a few manuscripts and valuable maps. The average annual increase is about 150 volumes. The library is in the Mission House, Pemberton Square. There is a catalogue, but it has not been printed. The collection is designed mainly for the use of the officers of the board, and is always accessible to them. The books are occasionally lent to persons investigating subjects relating to missions. It is designed to be a library for reference on subjects connected with the work of foreign missions; is in no sense a circulating library, and nothing is paid for the use of the books. Books may be lent to persons at a distance by consent of the prudential committee. Rev. S. L. Pomroy, D. D., Secretary A. B. C. F. M.

Library of the Boston Society of Natural History—3,500 *vols.*—The Boston Society of Natural History was founded in the winter of 1830, and incorporated February 24, 1831. Its great design is to "promote a taste and afford facilities for the pursuit of natural history, by mutual co-operation and the collection of a cabinet and library." The society has been conducted with much energy. It holds regular and frequent meetings, issues a "Journal," and has collected a valuable cabinet and library. "When the society originated, the great difficulty in the way of making advances in the study of natural history was the want of books. When we consider how essential a library is to the study and arrangement of every department of the cabinet, it cannot but be felt that the society have done wisely to contribute largely towards it. It is of vital importance that the naturalist who is engaged in the investigation of any subject, should be able to know *all* that has been written upon his subject. Scientific books are expensive, and no man among us can promise himself such a library as he may need."—[See notices of Boston Society of Natural History, by Dr. A. A. Gould, in the American Quarterly Register, February, 1842, pp. 236, seq.]

The library contained (1849) about 1,600 volumes* and a small number of maps and engravings. The yearly average increase is about 100 volumes. The average annual expenditure for books is about $200. The society has a permanent fund of about $12,000—$10,000 of which were received from a bequest of Ambrose S. Courtis, esq., $300 from a grant by the State, and $500 from the legacy of Simon E. Greene, esq.—one third of the income of which is, by vote, appropriated to the library. This arrangement is liable to alteration. The society owns a brick building with iron shutters. This contains the library and cabinet, and cost $30,000. The library room is 30 by 26 feet. The centre building is 40 by 30 feet, with two wings 26 by 30 feet each. The last catalogue was printed in 1837, and contains 27 pp. 8vo. The library is open daily from 9 till 1 o'clock. Individuals not members of the society are freely allowed to make use of the books on application. About 300 volumes are taken out during the year, and about 150 different persons consult the library yearly without taking away books. Books are lent to persons at a distance who are known to be engaged in scientific pursuits requiring them. The library committee has power to lend them, and so may any member, he being responsible for their safe return. Charles K. Dillaway, librarian.

"It is expected that the choice library of Dr. Amos Binney, formerly president of the society, will be incorporated with that of the society. Both will form a fine collection of the most important works in natural history in the English and French languages."†

The American Oriental Society—400 *vols.*—though yet in its infancy, has commenced the collection of a library. It contains only a few hundred volumes, 68 Muhammedan coins, 17 Arabic MSS., 1 Syriac MS. of a portion of the Old Testament, (600 years old,) and 5 Turkish MSS. These are all donations. The books are lent out only to the members of the society. The collection is at present deposited in the Boston Athonæum. Francis Gardner, librarian.

The Library of the American Statistical Association—2,000 *vols.*—This society was formed November 27, 1839, and incorporated January 7, 1841. Its purposes are to collect, preserve, and diffuse statistical information.—[See a notice of the society in the American Quarterly Register for May, 1841, pp. 451, seq.]

The Library of the New England Genealogical Association—1,500 *vols.*—The New England Historic Genealogical Society was incorporated the 17th March, 1845. Its object is "to collect and preserve the genealogy and history of early New England families." Its library is mostly the fruit of donations, and comprises most of the local histories of New England. The New England Historical and Genealogical Register, published quarterly under the auspices of the society, is a valuable repository of facts relating to the early history of the country.

The Social Law Library—3,000 *vols.*—This library occupies a room in the court-house. A catalogue containing 32 pp. 8vo. was published in 1824.

---

* In the report in 1850, the number is stated at 3,500 volumes.
† Bibliotheca Sacra, January, 1850.

The Bowditch Library—2,500 *vols.*—The late illustrious mathematician, Dr. N. Bowditch, collected a valuable scientific library of about 2,500 volumes. Since his death, his family, with a liberality worthy of their name, have allowed to the public the free use of the books. Although, therefore, this collection is private property, its public usefulness requires that it should find a place in notices of the public libraries of Boston. The proprietors have, we believe, expressed a desire, in case the city should erect a proper building and actively undertake to establish a public library, to bestow their shares upon such an institution. But no provision has yet been made for rendering the library permanently public. The proprietors have established the following "rules for the Bowditch Library, at 8 Otis Place, Boston:

"As this library is peculiarly valuable from the circumstance of its former ownership, it is particularly requested that books taken from it be used with care and returned punctually, subject to the following rules:

"1. No person will be allowed more than four volumes at a time.

"2. If any book be lost, it must be replaced, *although, of course, the loss can never be entirely supplied.*

"3. No book must be kept from the library more than three months, without being renewed upon the record book.

"4. All books must be returned on or before March 1st, of each year, for examination. After the 20th of the same month the library will be again opened.

"5. Omission, for the space of one week, to comply with the requisitions contained either in the third or fourth rule, deprives the party in default of the right thereafter to use the library, unless two at least of the proprietors are satisfied that the neglect is excusable, or are willing to pass over the omission.

"March 16, 1846."

About 250 volumes are taken out annually. None have been lost.

The Prince Library—1,800 *vols.*—"The Old South Church (Congregational) in Boston possesses a valuable collection of books and MSS., bequeathed to the church by Rev. Thomas Prince, one of its pastors, (the learned author of 'the Chronological History of New England,' &c.) Mr. Prince, while in college, in 1703, began a collection of books, and public and private papers, relating to the civil and religious history of New England, to which he continued to make valuable additions for more than fifty years. It is a precious collection, containing many standard works in church history and biblical literature and theology, the works of the early divines of New England, and valuable pamphlets and MSS."—[Bibliotheca Sacra, January, 1850.]

Mr Prince's will was proved in 1758. Since that period, or nearly one hundred years, this has been the public library of that Church, and accessible to any person desirous of using it for literary purposes.

It appears from Mr. Prince's will, that he had made a separate collection (to which he gave the name of the New England Library) of books, papers, &c., either published in New England or pertaining to its history and public affairs. This collection he gave also to the Old South Church, on condition that it should be kept in a different apartment from the other books, and "that no person shall borrow any book or paper therefrom, but that any person whom the pastors and deacons of said Church shall approve, may have access thereto." In 1814, 259 works, as they are numbered on the catalogue, belonging to this library, were deposited in the rooms of the Massachusetts Historical Society. A "catalogue of the library of Rev. Thomas Prince, former pastor of Old South Church, presented by him to the Old South Church and Society," in 112 pages 8vo., was printed at Boston in 1846. It is to be regretted that a catalogue so well printed should be so badly arranged, or rather so entirely destitute of all useful arrangement.

CAMBRIDGE.

Harvard College Libraries—84,200 *vols.*—On the 24th of January, 1764, in a stormy winter's night during the college vacation, Harvard Hall, containing the library of more than 5,000 volumes, the philosophical apparatus, and all the little collections of objects of interest belonging to the college, was destroyed by fire. "Thus perished the valuable books given by John Harvard, Sir Kenelm Digby, Sir John Maynard, Dr. Lightfoot, Dr. Gale, Bishop Berkeley, and other distinguished benefactors; the books and pamphlets connected with the early history of New England, the precious, though scanty, accumulations of a hundred and twenty-six years—a loss which in those days must have seemed appalling, and which the historian, the antiquary, and the bibliographer can never cease to deplore."

The State legislature was in session. Indeed, at the time of the calamity, Harvard Hall was occupied by them in consequence of the alarm excited by the existence of the small pox in Boston. At the instigation of Governor Bernard, they immediately appropriated £2,000 to erect a new building in place of that which had been destroyed while occupied by them. A general subscription was made for the same purpose among the towns and counties of the State, amounting to £878 16*s.* 9*d.** A generous sympathy was shown by many persons in the parent country. The subscription of Thomas Hollis, for the new building, was £200. The friends of the institution manifested not less zeal and liberality in supplying the new hall with books. The General Assembly of New Hampshire gave books to the value of £300 sterling. The Society for propagating the Gospel in New England and adjacent parts gave £200 sterling, and the Society for propagating the Gospel in foreign parts gave £100 for the library. In 1790 the library had increased to 12,000 volumes; in 1830, to 30,000. It is almost entirely the fruit of individual munificence. First among its distinguished benefactors stands the name of Thomas Hollis, whose "deeds of peace" entitle him to our warmest respect and gratitude. The books which, during the first ten years of the present library, he placed upon its shelves, were very numerous,† admirably chosen, and many of them elegantly bound, and containing curious and interesting notes in his own handwriting. At his decease, in 1774, he bequeathed to the college a sum of money which now constitutes a fund of $3,000, the interest of which is laid out in the purchase of books. In a note in Giggeius' Thesaurus Ling-Arab., he states that he has "been particularly industrious in collecting grammars and lexicons of the oriental *root* languages, to send to Harvard College, in hopes of forming by that means,

* See sketch of the history of Harvard College, by Samuel A. Eliot, Boston, 1848.

† The arrivals of 43 "cases" are noted on the records at different intervals during this period.

assisted by the energy of the leaders, always beneficent, a few *prime scholars*, honors to their country and lights to mankind."

Thomas Brand Hollis gave to the library many excellent books, and at his decease, in 1806, one hundred pounds sterling. Hon. John Hancock, in pursuance of the known intention of his uncle, Thomas Hancock, whose estate he inherited, presented to the library in 1767 five hundred and fifty-four pounds sterling. He gave for himself, also, "a large collection of chosen authors." Thomas Palmer, of Boston, in 1772, presented "the Antiquities of Herculanæum, and Piranesi's Views of Rome, in 20 folio vols.;" and at his decease, in 1820, bequeathed his library of nearly 1,200 "choice and costly volumes," valued at $2,500. Samuel Shapleigh, librarian of the university, in 1801, gave a piece of land and the residue of his estate for the increase of the library. The sum obtained from this bequest was $3,000, the interest of which is applied to the purchase of books in modern literature. Israel Thorndike, of Boston, purchased and presented, in the year 1818, the celebrated library of Professor Ebeling, of Hamburgh, containing 3,200 volumes of works mostly relating to America, and a collection of 10,000 maps and charts, "probably unrivalled by any other collection of the kind in the world." The whole cost $6,500. In 1823 Samuel A. Eliot, of Boston, purchased and presented the valuable collection of books relating to America of D. B. Warden, consisting of 1,200 volumes, besides maps, prints, and charts,* costing $5,000. The "Boylston Medical Library," of more than 1,100 volumes, was presented by Ward Nicholas Boylston. The sum of $2,000, given to the university in 1825, by Hon. Peter O. Thacher, "from a fund left him in trust by the late William Breed, esq., of Boston," was applied by the corporation to the purchase of books for the library. The Hon. Christopher Gore, who had previously enriched the law library by frequent and valuable donations, at his death, in 1831, left by will to the college the residue of his estate, of which $38,000 are reserved for annuities bequeathed by him. The whole ultimately receivable by the college amounts to $94,888. From this fund Gore Hall, the present library building, has been erected. In 1842 the sum of $21,008 was subscribed by thirty-four gentlemen in Boston and vicinity, for the purchase of books; not as a permanent fund, but for use when wanted. In 1844 Horace A. Haven bequeathed, for the purchase of mathematical and astronomical works for the library, the sum of $3,000. In 1845 the Hon. William Prescott bequeathed $3,000, which has been expended for books on American history, topography, &c. In 1846 Hon. Thomas Grenville, of London, gave, through President Everett, £100 for the purchase of books for the library.†

The library of the university is at present divided into four departments, viz: public, law, theological, and medical.

The public library contains 56,000 volumes of printed books and bound manuscripts. The volumes in the library were counted July 11, 1849, and found to be 55,605. Including the additions since made, the number may be put down at 56,000; this includes the bound manuscripts. The unbound pamphlets and serial works are estimated, exclusive of duplicates,

---

* Mr. Warden subsequently made a second collection, which was bought by the State library of New York.

† I have been able to notice only the most important donations to the library. For a full list of them, see the appendix to Eliot's History of Harvard College; compare also the preface to the catalogue, by Benjamin Pierce.

to be 25,000; they probably exceed this number. No enumeration of MSS. separate from the foregoing has been made. In 1819, seven Greek MSS. were procured in Constantinople, one a fragment of an Evangelistary, probably of the ninth century; there are some Latin MSS., and several oriental MSS., in Arabic, Persian, Hindostanee, Japanese, etc. Of Roman coins and medals, the library has 671 in copper, 43 in silver, and 1 in gold; of ancient coins other than Roman, 8; there are about 500 modern coins of all sorts, and 35 modern medals. The annual increase of the library since 1832 has been as follows: For the years ending—

		Volumes.	Pamphlets.		Volumes.	Pamphlets.	
July 13, 1832	-	1,299,	255,	including	502 and	190	given.
July 12, 1833	-	602,	212,	do	156	204	do
July 11, 1834	-	815,	737,	do	371	733	do
July 10, 1835	-	227,	184,	do	156	181	do
July 15, 1836	-	1,343,	237,	do	384	153	do
July 14, 1837	-	1,043,	205,	do	310	185	do
July 13, 1838	-	803,	209,	do	317	172	do
July 12, 1839	-	551,	532,	do	238	532	do
July 10, 1840	-	251,	249,	do	161	242	do
July 9, 1841	-	881,	1,402,	do	270	1,119	do
July 11, 1842	-	840,	700,	do	419	700	do
July 11, 1843	-	1,353,	1,597,	do	322	1,421	do
July 9, 1844	-	3,645,	1,333,	do	453	1,318	do
July 15, 1845	-	2,928,	3,806,	do	652	3,122	do
July 14, 1846	-	2,018,	3,477,	do	679	3,319	do
July 13, 1847	-	1,762,	3,321,	do	1,072	3,205	do
July 11, 1848	-	1,523,	2,632,	do	540	2,520	do
July 11, 1849	-	724,	1,645,	do	326	1,580	do.

As the books bought for the last seven years have been procured with the money subscribed in 1842, they are to be considered as donations; so that all the additions since 1842 are strictly gifts. The only permanent fund for the increase of the library yields $450 per annum. In 1842, the sum of $22,000 was raised by subscription, to be applied to the purchase of books, but not as a permanent fund. This sum is now reduced to $5,883, which will probably be entirely expended in the course of two or three years. Among the late additions are works in modern English literature, German literature, with the classical and other departments, scientific works, etc.*

The only permanent fund for the increase of the library is the combined Hollis and Shapleigh fund, which yields about $450 per annum. The principal is $6,000. The public library is kept in Gore Hall, the foundation of which was laid April 25, 1837, and to which the books were removed July, 1841. The outer walls of the building are of rough stone (Quincy granite, or sienite,) laid in regular courses, with hammered stone buttresses, towers, pinnacles, drip-stones, &c. The inner walls, columns, and the main floor (which rests on solid brick arches) are of brick, the floor covered with hard pine boards; the other parts finished with plaster. The partitions are strengthened with iron columns concealed within them, and the roof and galleries rest on iron rafters. The whole cost, including

*Bibliotheca Sacra, January, 1850.

the heating apparatus, was little short of $75,000. It is in the form of a latin cross, the extreme length of which externally is 140 feet, and through the transept 81½ feet. The interior contains a hall 112 feet long and 35 feet high, with a vaulted ceiling, supported by 20 ribbed columns. The spaces between the columns and side walls are divided by partitions into stalls or alcoves for books above and below the gallery, which is 12½ feet from the floor. One transept is used for a reading-room, and the other is divided into three apartments for books. (See Quincy's History of Harvard University, II, page 599.) The books are arranged according to subjects.

A catalogue of the old library in 102 pages 4to. was published in 1723, with the title, "Catalogus Librorum Bibliothecæ Collegii Harvardini quod est Cantabrigiæ in Nova Anglia. Bost. Nov. Angl. typis B. Green."

After the burning of the library a "Selectior Catalogus in usum Academiæ Alumnorum" was published, but no copy of it exists in the library.

Another, "Catalogus Bibliothecæ Harvardianæ. Cantabrigiæ, Nov. Anglorum. Bostoniæ, typis T. and J. Fleet, 1790;" 8vo., 358 pages.

The last printed catalogue is entitled: "A Catalogue of the Library of Harvard University, in Cambridge, Massachusetts; 3 vols. 8vo. Camb., 1830."

This catalogue was prepared by Benjamin Peirce, then librarian. The first two volumes (952 pages) contain an alphabetical catalogue. The 3d volume (223 pages) contains a systematic index, in the five classes: theology, jurisprudence, arts and sciences, belles-lettres, history; with a sixth division, comprising works relating to America. Each class has numerous subdivisions.

As a 4th volume, was published "A catalogue of the maps and charts in the library of Harvard University, 8vo. Camb., 1831;" 322 pages; also prepared by Mr. Peirce.

A "First Supplement" to the catalogue, prepared by the present librarian, was published in 1834, (260 pp. 8vo.) containing the additions to the library up to September 1, 1833.

All officers and students of the University, officers of the State government and members of the legislature, clergymen of all denominations living within ten miles of the library, benefactors to the library to the amount of $40 during their residence in Cambridge, and all persons temporarily residing in Cambridge, for purposes of study, may borrow books from the library, under certain conditions prescribed in the laws. "A ready admittance, and the requisite information and facilities for examining and consulting the works, are afforded to all visitors. The privileges granted to individuals are not exceeded by those enjoyed at any other institution of a similar kind, and are believed to be in all respects as great as a due regard to general accommodation and to the preservation of the books would permit."—[Preface to catalogue.]

A small sum is assessed on the students for the use of the library. All other persons are allowed to take out books without charge. The library is very much used for the purpose of consultation, not only by persons who are entitled to borrow books, but by others. The books have not suffered much by insects. The injury has been confined mostly to old books infested before they came to the library, and to some others which were kept in closed cabinets. The present officers are: librarian, Thaddeus William Harris, M. D.; assistant, Rev. John L. Sibley; temporary assistant, Mr. Ezra Abbot; janitor, Mr. Thomas Kiernan.

The *society libraries* connected with the college contain about 12,000 volumes.

Such deficiencies in contemporary literature as the students have at any time felt in using the public library, they have attempted to supply in their society libraries.

The oldest society of students of Harvard College is *The Institute of 1770*. It was formed in that year, as a debating club, with other literary purposes. Different clubs have since been joined to this society, and the library consists of the collections formed by them for their members from the current literature of the periods when they were purchased. Present library 2,500 volumes; annual increase about one hundred.

The Porcellian Club is a convivial and literary club of many years standing. Considerable annual additions from the periodical and other current literature are made to its library, which is the largest society library connected with the university, and contains a large number of valuable editions. At present it consists of about 5,000 volumes.

The Hasty Pudding Club—a social and literary organization founded in 1795—has a library which was established thirteen years afterwards. It now contains about 3,500 volumes. The annual increase is now about 300 volumes—the additions being made at present solely by the donations of the members. The intention of the library is to give to the members of the club those facilities for reference and relaxation which are ordinarily afforded by a gentleman's private library. It therefore consists of a selection from standard literature, in collecting which an especial design has been to embrace complete sets of the leading reviews, as well as the current literature of the day.

The Cambridge Alpha of the *Phi Beta Kappa* society is the oldest branch of that institution since the parent at Williams College expired. It was founded in 1781. For several years after that time a library of English standard literature was collected, which amounts to about 500 volumes. No additions have been made to it in recent years.

The *Natural History*, *Rumford*, and *Hermæan* societies—associations comparatively recently formed—have small, but increasing libraries. The Harvard Chapter of the *Alpha Delta Phi* society has a small library containing merely the books written by its graduate members, and a collection of periodicals. These may be set down together at 500 volumes.

The *Law Library* was commenced by the purchase of the valuable collection of Judge Story. It is in the building erected for the Law School. It contains about 14,000 volumes—having cost, excluding large donations, more than $35,000. "It includes all the American reports, and the statutes of the United States, as well as those of all the States, a regular series of all the English reports, including the Year Books, and also the English statutes, as well as the principal treatises in American and English law, besides a large collection of Scotch, French, German, Dutch, Spanish, Italian, and other foreign law, and a very ample collection of the best editions of the Roman or civil law, together with the works of the most celebrated commentators upon that law."—[Annual Catalogue, 1849–'50.]

"This library," (say the committee of overseers in their annual report for 1849,) "is one of the largest and most valuable relating to law to be found in the country. As an aid to study it cannot be estimated too highly. Here the student may range at will through all the demesnes of jurisprudence. Here he may acquire a knowledge of the books of his profession; learning their true character and value, which will be of incalculable service to him in his future labors. Whoso knows how to use a library, possesses the very keys of knowledge. Next to knowing the law, is knowing where the law is to be found."

The library is open for the use of students during the term, and those who desire it pursue their studies there, especially in the preparation of their moot-court cases.

Several catalogues of the library have been published; one (not, we believe, the first) was in 80 pages 8vo., 1833; a supplement (16 pages 8vo.) contained the books bequeathed to the library by Hon. Samuel Livermore, of Portsmouth, N. H. A general catalogue of the library was published in 1834, (228 pages 8vo.) This excellent catalogue, prepared by Charles Sumner, esq., is alphabetical, with a systematic index. The preface contains an interesting sketch of the history of the library. The fourth edition, with the additions, was printed in 1846, in 354 pages 8vo.

"The *Theological* library is in Divinity Hall. Persons entitled to its privileges must be connected with the Divinity School. Number of books about 3,000. They consist of valuable select works, principally in modern theology, with some of the early fathers in the original. Means have been recently devised to add to the library valuable modern works in theology and morals, as they are published.

"The *Medical* library is in the Medical College in Boston. It isp laced there for the convenience of students attending the medical lectures. The number of books is about 1,200. It contains all the elementary works which are the most important and the most used by students. Besides these, it has the writings of the early Greek and Latin medical fathers and the works of the later medical classics; and, with the latter, it contains numerous valuable modern works."

CAMBRIDGEPORT.

Parish Library—500 *vols.*—This library was founded in 1849. "One hundred volumes were given by a member of the society; nearly as many more, formerly belonging to the Sunday School Teachers' Library, have been transferred to this; the others have been purchased from the proceeds of the contributions at church." "Every family belonging to the society will be entitled to one volume at a time, which may be kept two weeks." A catalogue containing 8 pages 12mo. was printed in 1849. B. L. Whitney, librarian.

GROTON.

Library of Lawrence Academy—2,650 *vols.*—In 1827, at the recommendation of Mr. Elizur Wright, then the preceptor of the academy, the trustees commenced the formation of a library, by the purchase of eighty-six books. For ten years these, without any additions, were used by the students. They were the only ones ever purchased by the corporation. In 1838, Mr. Amos Lawrence, of Boston, made a donation of 180 volumes, and, up to the commencement of the year 1850, his successive gifts comprise 2,400 volumes—nearly the whole collection. Sixty volumes were presented by the American Tract Society; sixty-three were the relics of the library of a literary society formerly connected with the school; four were a gift from the corporation of Harvard College, through the kindness of President Sparks; a few were received from members of Congress. The library is "well selected, free from all corrupting and trashy literature, and adapted to form a taste for useful and solid reading." The library is open on Wednesday to the male pupils, and on Saturday to the females. A catalogue in 8vo., 206 pages, was printed at Lowell in 1850; it is alphabetical, with a classified index; it is in every respect a well executed work. From the preface, signed by James Means, the present preceptor, we have gathered the facts stated above.

LAWRENCE.

The Franklin Library—850 *vols.*—The Franklin Library Association was incorporated April 24, 1847, and possesses 850 volumes. A catalogue of the books (14 pages 12mo.) was printed in 1848. The library is opened on Tuesdays from 7 to 9 p. m., and on Saturdays from 12 m. to 1 p. m., from 4 to 5 and from 7 to 8 p. m. N. W. Harmon, librarian.

LOWELL.

City School Library—7,492 *vols.*—Founded in 1844. First opened for the delivery of books February 11, 1845. It contains 7,492 volumes. The first purchase consisted of 3,800 volumes. There have since been added from 1,000 to 1,500 volumes annually. The city drew from the State its proportion of a fund that had been accumulating for the purpose of forming school libraries, amounting to $1,215, and appropriated $2,000 to purchase this library. The next year the appropriation was $1,000, and since then it has been $500 yearly for the purchase of books. The library occupies a room 60 feet by 28, on the ground floor of a brick building belonging to the city, and centrally located. The books are arranged according to size, without regard to subjects, and each volume is numbered. The first catalogue (printed 1844) contains 66 pages 16mo. Four annual supplements have been printed, containing each 21 pages. The library is open every day, except Sunday, from 2 to 5 and from 7 to 9 p. m. Every citizen may take books out of the library, by giving satisfactory evidence that they will be carefully used, and by paying fifty cents annually. The number of subscribers is about 800, entitled to two volumes per week each. Josiah Hubbard, librarian.

Library of the Middlesex Mechanics' Association—5,386 *vols.*—Incorporated in 1825. Reading-room established 1834. The library contains 5,386 volumes. During the last ten years, the annual average expenditure for the purchase of books has been $314. In 1833–'34 the association erected a large building of brick, at an expense of $29,486 04, for all the purposes of the association. The library-room is 40 feet by 26, and 11 feet high. The reading-room is of the same size. A catalogue was printed in 1840, containing 136 pages 8vo. 89 pages are devoted to an alphabetical catalogue of the books, and 47 pages to a classified index, the large divisions of which are science, history, literature, government, and politics. Theology is included under science. Each division has several subdivisions. A supplement of 22 pages was printed in 1846. All members of the association, and other persons, citizens of Lowell, by paying an annual subscription of six dollars, are admitted to the privileges of the library and reading-room. The books are lent out. The library is open every day except Sunday from 2 till 5 o'clock p. m., and in the evening from 7 to 9. Strangers may be introduced by members to the use of library and reading-room. Mr. —— Crafts, librarian.

NANTUCKET.

The Athenæum Library—2,552 *vols.*—The Athenæum was founded in 1836. The library was destroyed by fire in July, 1846; refurnished and opened to the public in February, 1847; contained, in January, 1849, 2,532 volumes. It has small conchological and geological cabinets, a few maps, and several hundred coins of small value. 100 volumes were added in 1848. A wooden building was erected for the use of the institution in 1846-'47, containing a lecture-room, library-room, and museum—the cost, about $5,000. The library-room is 49 feet by 24, and 12 feet high. It is arranged in alcoves, and capable of holding 10,000 volumes. Opened daily from 1½ to 5 p. m., and on Saturday evenings from 6 to 9. Shareholders pay two dollars per annum, others three dollars per annum, for the use of the books. During the years 1847 and 1848, 5,230 books were taken out each year. William Mitchell, president.

NEWTON

Library of the Theological Seminary—6,000 *vols.*—Founded in 1825. Contains 6,000 volumes. All persons connected with the institution are entitled to the use of the library. The librarian has discretionary power in regard to lending books to other persons. A catalogue was published in 1833, in 12mo. The Seminary belongs to the Baptist denomination.

PLYMOUTH.

The Old Colony Pilgrim Society was formed 9th of November, 1819, for the purpose of commemorating the landing of the pilgrims upon the rock of Plymouth, of cherishing the memory of their virtues and sufferings, and of preserving such well-authenticated relics as could then be gathered. In 1824 a monumental edifice was erected by the society. It is of unwrought split granite, 70 feet in length by 40 in width, and is two stories in height. It has a handsome Doric portico. The whole expense of the building and appurtenances was about $15,000. In the edifice a room is set apart for a library and a cabinet of curiosities. It has as yet but a small number of volumes. It has also some manuscripts relative to our early history. The cabinet contains a large number of curiosities of great interest. [See History of the Pilgrim Society, by W. Cogswell, in the American Quarterly Register for August, 1838, pp. 82-90.]

ROXBURY.

Athenæum Library—5,000 *vols.*—The Roxbury Athenæum was founded May 1, 1848. The library contains about 5,000 bound volumes, and about 4,000 pamphlets, and, say, 40 maps and charts, and 100 engravings. The first year, $1,500 were expended for the library; the second year, $600. There is a permanent fund of $4,000, yielding about $250 per annum. Many books have been received by donation. The library is open every day from 8 o'clock to 11 a. m., and from 3 to 5 p. m. The price of a share is twenty-five dollars. Annual subscribers pay four dollars. Three books may be taken out at a time by any proprietor or subscriber. Over 4,000 were taken out in 1849. A catalogue, 250 pages 8vo., was printed in 1849. Benjamin Kent, librarian.

SALEM.

The Athenæum Library—11,000 *vols.*—"The Salem Athenæum, incorporated in 1810, was formed by the union of the Social and Philosophical Libraries.

"In the year 1760, a number of gentlemen signed a covenant for the formation of a library in Salem, to be called the 'Social Library.' The number of shares at the commencement was thirty-two, at five guineas per share. This number was afterwards increased by the accession of new members. The library was first deposited in the brick school-house in School street, and there continued till 1786, when it was removed to the new middle school-house, now the centre school-house, in Washington street. The brick school-house was taken down to erect on or near its site the court-house; and this last building was also taken down in 1839 for the accommodation of the Eastern Railroad Company. The library was afterwards removed to the Central Building, Central street, where it continued till the union and the formation of the Athenæum.

"From the year 1775 to 1784, no meetings were held; and the interest which was before manifested in the success of the library was paralyzed by the unsettled state of the country during the Revolution. At the restoration of peace, the attention of the proprietors was again directed to the state of the library. All fines, forfeitures, &c., that had been incurred during the above-mentioned period, were cancelled, and it was determined to begin anew. A fresh impulse; thus imparted, rendered its further progress successful. In 1797 an act of incorporation was obtained. In 1809 a catalogue was printed.

"During the revolutionary war, the vessel on board of which a part of the library of the celebrated Dr. Richard Kirwan* was shipped for transportation across the Irish Channel was captured by an American privateer. These books were brought into Beverly and sold. A company of gentlemen, consisting of the Rev. M. Cutler, LL. D., of Hamilton; Rev. J. Willard, D. D., LL. D., and Joshua Fisher, M. D., of Beverly; Rev. T. Barnard, D. D., Rev J. Prince, LL. D., E. A. Holyoke, M. D., LL. D., and Dr. J. Orne, of Salem, &c., became the purchasers; and thus was laid the foundation of the 'Philosophical Library.' An offer of remuneration was afterwards made to Dr. Kirwan, who generously declined it, expressing his satisfaction that his valuable library had found so useful a destination. Rev. Joseph Willard was the librarian from the commencement till

"* Dr. Kirwan, a chemical philosopher, was born in Ireland about the middle of the last century, and died in 1812. His principal works are, 'An Essay on the Constitution of Acids,' 'Elements of Mineralogy,' in two vols. 8vo., and a work on logic, published in 1809.—*Penny Cyclopædia, art. Kirwan.*"

his removal to Cambridge, in December, 1781, to enter upon the duties of president of Harvard University. The Rev. Dr. Prince was then appointed his successor, and continued in office till the union, in 1810. The late N. Bowditch, LL. D., when a young man, was enabled, through the kindness of the proprietors, to pursue his studies under very favorable auspices, by having free access to this library, which contained many important scientific books. In order to repay the debt of gratitude which he felt he had incurred, he left in his will, made fifty years afterwards, the sum of one thousand dollars for the use of the Salem Athenæum.

"At the formation of the Athenæum, the books were deposited in the rooms occupied by the Social Library. In April, 1815, they were removed to rooms in Essex Place. In 1825 they were again removed to the rooms over the Salem Bank; and finally, in the spring of 1841, to the present spacious hall in Lawrence Place, recently fitted for their reception. The present number of shares is ninety-seven. Number of volumes in the library, 9,000. They have been principally obtained by the sale of shares, and by annual assessments "*

The library increases at an average rate of 250 volumes per annum. About $400 are annually appropriated for the purchase of books. There is a permanent fund for the increase of the library yielding about $150 a year. There have been several catalogues printed.

Catalogue of the Social Library,				1809	8vo.	42 pages.
Do	do	Salem Athenæum,		1811	8vo.	72 "
Do	do	do	do	1818	8vo.	77 "
Do	do	do	do	1826	8vo.	95 "
Do	do	do	do	1842	8vo.	171 "
Supplement to the same				1849	8vo.	13 "

The catalogue of 1842, by Thomas Cole, esq., consists of two parts: the first, of 93 pages, contains the titles of the books, systematically arranged; the second (pp. 95—171) a list of about 1,600 pamphlets, inserted alphabetically under the names of their respective authors. A short account of each author, as far as could be ascertained, is affixed, noticing the year of his birth and death, the college or university at which he was graduated, the principal places of residence, occupation, &c. It is skillfully and accurately prepared.

The library is open every day, except Sundays, from 8 o'clock a. m. till sunset. Proprietors and their families, also settled clergymen of the city and neighboring towns, are entitled to the use of the books. Proprietors have the liberty to introduce strangers as readers. No record is kept of the number thus introduced. Charles J. Whipple, librarian.

The library at present contains about 11,000 volumes. The pamphlets, about 2,000 in number, forming a very valuable collection, are mostly bound in volumes. This is not only an excellent library for popular use, but it contains an unusually large proportion of works of standard value. Early theological and scientific works, and the transactions of learned societies, are more fully represented than in most libraries of this kind. The later additions have been well selected, and mostly in the departments of modern history, biography, voyages and travels, and general English literature.

Library of the Essex Institute—2,522 *vols*.—This society was incor-

*See introductory remarks to the catalogue, 1842.

porated in 1848, and formed by the union of the Essex Historical Society (incorporated in 1821) and the Essex County Natural History Society, (incorporated in 1836.) The library contains 2,522 volumes, 20 MSS., 25 maps, 30 paintings or engravings of the former presidents of the Historical Society, and some of the worthies of New England, a few coins, a good collection of objects of natural history, in the several departments of nature, a few Indian relics, &c. For the last ten years about 250 volumes and 350 pamphlets have been added annually, and principally by donation. For the same period about $100 per annum have been expended in the purchase of books. The room is accessible at all times to members of the society who may take out books. A considerable number of persons visit the library daily for the purpose of consulting the books. Henry M. Brooks, librarian.

Library of the Mechanics' Institute—3,000 *vols.*

NOTE.—For the following additional information respecting public libraries in Salem we are indebted to Dr. Henry Wheatland, of that city:

The East India Marine Society has a library containing 300 volumes, some 20 or 30 of which are manuscript journals of sea voyages, &c. The museum belonging to this society is one of the most valuable and interesting in the country. Charles M. Endicott, president.

This society, whose membership is confined to those who have doubled Cape Horn and the Cape of Good Hope, as masters of vessels, was formed in 1799, and incorporated in 1801. A catalogue of the museum, &c., was printed in 1831, (178 pp. 8vo.)

The Essex Southern District Medical Society, formed in 1805, consists of those members of the Medical Society residing in Salem and the other towns in the southern section of the county. The library contains 1,000 volumes, and is located in the Lyceum Building. Dr. E. B. Peirson, librarian.

The Essex Agricultural Society, formed in 1818 under the auspices of the late Hon. T. Pickering, its first president, has within a few months past purchased the agricultural library of the late Henry Colman, containing 525 volumes. These, with a few volumes previously in its possession, will make the library contain 650 volumes. It is deposited in a room in the City Hall, Salem. John W. Proctor, of Danvers, president.

The Salem Evangelical Library, founded in 1818, contains 1,400 volumes. Rev. B. Emerson, D. D., librarian.

Besides these, three religious societies possess libraries containing together 2,500 volumes; the public school libraries contain 3,600 volumes; the Sabbath school libraries 8,000 volumes—making an aggregate, including the Athenæum, the Mechanics' Library, and the library of the Essex Institute, of 34,192 volumes in the public libraries of the city.

WILLIAMSTOWN.

Williams College Libraries—10,559 *vols.*—The college library was founded contemporaneously with the college in 1793, and contains at present 5,993 volumes, the charts of the United States coast survey, and a very few coins. The yearly average increase for the last ten years has been 188 volumes. Yearly expenditure, $190. A brick building was erected for the accommodation of the library, by Hon. Amos Lawrence, of

Boston, in 1847, at a cost of $7,000. It is called Lawrence Hall. In form it is a regular octagon, each side 19 feet, and is found to be very convenient. A catalogue, 51 pages 8vo., was printed in 1845. The first was printed in 1794, others in 1812 and 1828. The library is opened one hour every Wednesday and Saturday during term time. The students of the two lower classes pay 40 cents each, per term, for the use of books; those of the two upper classes pay 50 cents each. Books are lent out to clergymen and other literary gentlemen, even at a distance from the college, at the discretion of the librarian. About 800 are taken out annually. Prof. John Tatlock, librarian.

Besides the college library, are the libraries of two societies of undergraduates of the college:

The Philologian Society Library - - -	2,416 vols.
Philotechnian Society Library - - - -	2,150 "

As the building erected for the library of this college is one of the few, in the planning of which the *internal conveniences* have been primarily consulted, it may not be amiss to give in this place a somewhat minute description of it.

It was required to erect a building for a library of 6,000 volumes, capable of *accommodating* 30,000, and of being extended so as to hold 50,000, or more, without interfering with the part first built. The edifice was to be of brick, substantial and tasteful, and not to cost more than $7,000. These, it must be confessed, are somewhat difficult conditions to meet.

The building is in form a regular octagon, each side 19 feet, the whole height 40 feet. The elevation presents a principal story of the Ionic order, with arched windows, one on each side, and plain pilasters. There is a rusticated basement 13 feet in height. The entrance is by a single door in one face of the octagon. This door opens upon a vestibule, from which rises a circular staircase conducting to the library story, and intended, when the increase of the library may demand it, to be carried up to the galleries. Leaving, for the present, the basement, we will notice the principal story. This is occupied as the library. It is lighted from the sides and the top; is cheerful, airy, and elegant. In the centre is a circular colonade of 8 Ionic pillars, from which springs a dome, surmounted by a lantern. The cases for the books are to be placed against the walls, and radiating from the columns to the corners of the octagon, thus dividing the room into 8 alcoves and a circular area in the centre. One of these alcoves contains a circular staircase. The shelves at first built are only 7 feet high, and will contain say 10,000 volumes. When more shelves are required, a light iron gallery is to be laid upon the top of the cases, and another set of shelves, also 7 feet in height, is to be placed upon the first. This gallery is reached by a continuation of the circular staircase, one staircase being sufficient for so compact a library. The room will admit three such tiers of shelves. Thus the apartment will hold 30,000 volumes; all of which may be reached without the use of movable ladders. The librarian's desk is in the centre; from it he can see, by simply turning round, every person and every book in the room.

The basement is divided into rooms corresponding in shape to the alcoves of the library. One of these divisions and the central area form together a lobby communicating with the several rooms. Another of the divisions is occupied by the stairs. Two others form a room for the meetings of the trustees and for a reading-room of periodicals. The division of the octagon directly behind the stairs, serves as an entrance to the cellar and as a lumber-room. The first room on the left of the lobby is the "packing-room," into which all boxes of books are to be first brought, to be unpacked and examined. All books to be bound, or to be sent away for any purpose, should be invoiced and packed here. A dumb-waiter communicates with the library above. Next to the packing-room, and opening into it, is the librarian's room; next to that a room for engravings, manuscripts, and other articles which require to be kept apart from the principal collection and guarded with special care.

WORCESTER.

Library of the American Antiquarian Society – 18,000 *vols* —The American Antiquarian Society was incorporated October 24, 1812. The present number of volumes in the library somewhat exceeds 18,000. Its manuscripts, though of much interest to the student of New England history, cannot readily be enumerated. Many maps, charts, engravings, medals, &c., belong to the collection. The average annual increase, for the last ten years, has been 404 books and 1,048 pamphlets. The accessions to the library are chiefly donations. There is no fund solely for the purchase of books, and no regular appropriation. The general funds of the society amount to $30,038 33. About $200 were expended in 1848. A brick building was erected in 1820 at a cost of about $10,000. It consists of a central edifice 50 by 40 feet, and two stories high, with wings each 28 by 20 feet, also two stories high. The only catalogue which has been published was printed in 1837, and contains 582 pages royal 8vo. The regular hours for keeping the library open are from 9 a. m. to 1 p. m., and from 2 to 5 p. m.; Saturday afternoons excepted. The library is free to the public for use on the premises. But books are not lent out, except that, by a special act of the council in each case, permission may be had to take books from the town, a bond being given for their safe return. It is impossible to say how many persons consult the library annually. The number is very large. Samuel F. Haven, librarian.

The preface to the catalogue contains the following sketch of the history of this library, which, from its public interest, we insert in full:

The library of the American Antiquarian Society owes its origin to the sound judgment and sagacious foresight, not less than to the public spirit and zeal for the diffusion of knowledge, which marked the character of Isaiah Thomas, the venerable founder of the institution. The important contributions made by Dr. Thomas, both as an author and a printer, to the cause of good learning, need not here be repeated; they already form a part of our public history. From his press much of the early literature of the country was supplied, and to his pen was it occasionally indebted for suggestions and illustrations, in the form of notes, prefaces and appendices, giving increased value to the publications which issued under his auspices. His "History of Printing," written after his retirement from business, was the fruit of his past industry and research, and is a standard work on the shelves of our principal libraries.

During his active period of life, while engaged in the publication of books, to an extent which kept nearly twenty presses in constant operation, and at the same time in conducting a magazine and newspaper of wide circulation, Mr. Thomas necessarily collected many books, pamphlets, and papers, which already constituted a library of considerable magnitude. To this he subsequently made additions with a view to the preparation of his History. After the publication of that work, he justly considered the library which he had been gradually gathering, as a treasure of too much value to society to be hoarded in private while he lived, and perhaps scattered to the four winds at his decease. He was led by this consideration to propose an association for collecting and preserving the materials of history, to whose charge he might intrust his literary treasures, for the use of the present and future generations, and with the fond expectation that they would be the embryo of a collection hereafter to rival the famous libraries of Europe. His design was submitted to his friends, with whose advice and assistance he matured a plan of organization for the American Antiquarian Society, and procured an act of incorporation October 24, 1812. He was elected the first president, and continued in that office till his decease, April 4, 1831, at the age of 82.

Immediately after the incorporation of the society, Mr. Thomas bestowed upon it his library, then composed of about 3,000 bound volumes, a great number of pamphlets, and a series of newspapers far more complete than any other existing in America. Soon afterwards a donation of 900 volumes was received through the hands of Mrs. Hannah Crocker, a descendant of the Mather family, (in part a gift from herself, and partly a purchase by Mr. Thomas,) being the remains of the library formerly belonging to Increase and Cotton Mather, the most ancient in Massachusetts, if not in the United States. A valuable addition was also made to the library and cabinet by the legacy of Rev. William Bentley, D. D., of Salem. The books bequeathed by Dr. Bentley amounted to several hundred volumes, principally German editions and in the German tongue, besides a collection of oriental manuscripts, including a splendid illuminated copy of the Koran, and several commentaries thereon.

Our munificent founder continued to cherish the child of his old age with truly parental assiduity. Every year he made liberal donations of books and rare curiosities, some of which were procured by him at considerable expense. The whole amount of his donations in books was between 7,000 and 8,000 bound volumes, a large number of unbound tracts, and the greater proportion of all the newspapers now belonging to the society. He was at the charge of printing the first volume of Transactions, published in 1820. In the same year he erected the edifice now occupied by the society, and gave it for their exclusive use. And to crown his benefactions and place the existence and usefulness of the institution beyond the reach of ordinary vicissitude, he endowed it, at his decease, with a fund, which, if not equal to all its wants, is ample compared with many other institutions, and will probably enable it hereafter to do good service in the republic of letters.

There are many other benefactors of the society entitled to their gratitude, among whom it may be permitted to the committee charged with the publication of the catalogue to name the Hon. Thomas L. Winthrop, our present president, whose solicitude for the interests of the institution has been unceasing, and who has enriched the library with many volumes of great price and rarity. Mr. Thomas Wallcut, of Boston, has been the donor of a large collection of old books and pamphlets, especially suited to the objects and taste of the antiquary. The names of all donors, even of a single volume or tract, or any article of curiosity, are entered on our records, and will be transmitted, on the list of our patrons, to those who may come after us.

Soon after the incorporation of the society, the national government made provision for supplying us with copies of the public laws and documents. The legislatures of several of the States have generously made a similar provision. The government of Massachusetts furnishes two sets of all the publications ordered by the legislature, including the statutes and judicial reports. These documents compose a valuable portion of our library; and should the example be imitated by the other States of the Union, a collection of public documents would soon be formed, whose importance to the statesman and the historian cannot be too highly estimated.

The present [1837] number of bound volumes in the library is about 12,000, including upwards of 1,200 volumes of pamphlets, and more than 700 bound volumes of newspapers. There are about 500 pamphlets yet unbound, exclusive of duplicates, and nearly 1,000 volumes of unbound newspapers. Nearly all the American papers printed before the Revolution are in this collection, and of some of them a more complete series is here to be found than is anywhere else in existence.

The manuscripts of the society are of considerable value, especially that portion of them which relates to the early ecclesiastical history of New England. They embrace many of the papers of the Mathers—Richard, Increase, Cotton, and Samuel; those of John Cotton, minister of the first church in Boston, and of John Cotton, the second, minister of Plymouth. There are many other manuscripts which have already been consulted with advantage by authors, and others who have had occasion to investigate the venerable records of the past. The lapse of years will add to their importance; and those time-defaced pages, which are now merely glanced at as objects of curiosity, will hereafter be studied with an intense and eager interest.

The cabinet of the society is not yet of great extent. The articles of most interest are those illustrating the manners of our fathers, and the weapons of war, articles of apparel, and domestic utensils of the aborigines of North America. Specimens of this kind, of American origin, are more to be desired by an American Society of Antiquaries, than any articles, however rare or antique, brought hither from the ransacked domains of the Old World. The cabinet contains a collection of coins, comparatively small, but amounting to nearly 2,000 pieces, of which, however, many are duplicates. Among them is a considerable number of coins of the Roman Empire, and a few said to be of still more remote antiquity. It is believed there are specimens of nearly all the pieces of money ever struck in the present United States.

The library and cabinet of the institution are deposited in a building, in the construction and occupation of which great precaution has been taken for the security of the treasures accumulated within its walls.

The second volume of "Archæologia Americana" has lately issued from the press. The long delay which took place between the appearance of the first and of the second volume is to be imputed, not to the want of materials for the publication, or inclination to spread them before the public, but to the want of sufficient funds, which have but recently come into the possession of the society.

The foregoing sketch of the origin of the society, its objects, history, and present condition, it is hoped by the committee will not be deemed an unsuitable introduction to this volume.

A catalogue of the library has long been a desideratum, not only to the members of the society, but to all who sought access to their archives. Without such an index, a great portion of our volumes were no better than sealed books to every inquirer who had not time or patience to seek, among the undigested mass, for such dates and facts as he desired to ascertain. The catalogue now published is almost wholly the work of the late lamented librarian, Christopher C. Baldwin, whose decease the society deplores as an irreparable loss. It was prepared by him with great care and labor, and is a monument of his untiring industry. It has been completed and brought up to the present date, by the acting librarian, Maturin L. Fisher, esq. Its accuracy, as far at least as regards the bound books, has been since subjected to the test of a careful comparison of its titles with the correspondent volumes on the shelves of the library. It is in the alphabetical form, which has been generally adopted by librarians, as more simple in its arrangement and more convenient for reference, than a systematic index. The plan pursued was to give the name of the author when known, and where the work is anonymous, briefly to state the subject. Each letter of the alphabet has been paged by itself, to facilitate the insertion of future additions under the respective letters, and thus render a new edition of the whole catalogue unnecessary, at least for several years. Our list of books, it will be observed, contains an unusual proportion of tracts, for which reason it is swollen to a size somewhat disproportionate to the solid contents of the library. But we prize this large collection of pamphlets, as a most important part of those materials for history which it is the great object of the society to preserve; and if the list was confined to these alone, we should judge it of sufficient consequence to warrant a publication.

A written catalogue of manuscripts, very minute in its titles and details, is now in a course of preparation, and will be kept in the library for the inspection of all who may have occasion to consult it.

By order of the Council:
JOHN PARK.

The catalogue of this invaluable collection will ere long be reprinted, with the additions since the time of the first printing. Prepared by the present learned and able librarian, it will be a very important contribution to the means of investigating the early history of New England. This society has taken measures to commence the project of stereotyping by titles, so that each library in the country, while it secures a permanent catalogue of its own treasures, will help form the general printed and stereotyped catalogue of all the libraries. This plan, proposed some years ago at the Smithsonian Institution, has received a new impulse through the favor and support which has been accorded it by the Antiquarian Society.

I am indebted to Mr. Haven for the following additional particulars respecting this library:

"A prominent feature in the collection is the *Mather Library*, consisting of about 1,000 volumes, and containing probably the greater portion of the books owned by Increase and Cotton Mather, as well as those of Richard, the father of Increase. The first two were emphatically *the scholars* of their day, in New England; and the works they collected fairly represent the literature and learning of their time, whether historical, theological, or metaphysical, or relating to the natural sciences. This is perhaps the oldest private library in the country that has been transmitted from one generation to another. It was obtained from Mrs. Hannah Mather Crocker, grand-daughter of Cotton Mather, and only remaining representative of the family in Boston—partly by gift and partly by purchase. It is called in the records 'The remains of the ancient library of the Mathers,' and was considered by Isaiah Thomas as 'the oldest library in New England, if not in the United States.' With these books was obtained a large collection of tracts and manuscripts belonging to the Mathers: the latter consisting of sermons, diaries, correspondence, and common-places. Many of the tracts are political, and relate to the period of the Revolution and the Commonwealth in England. Taken together, this Mather collection is unique, and of great historical value.

"The *pamphlets* form another prominent and somewhat peculiar feature. They undoubtedly contain a greater number and variety of fugitive publications, such as illustrate the character and spirit of the time, than can be found elsewhere in the country. Those of ancient date are numerous and curious.

"The *newspapers* begin with the first number of the first paper printed in the United States; and, though the series is not perfect, it is, taking the whole period together, the most perfect that has been preserved. The collection of *almanacs* is, also, the most complete and curious that can probably be found in the country. The *manuscripts* are chiefly such as illustrate New England history. Many are theological; some are treatises and commentaries that have not been printed. There are many letters written by or addressed to the original settlers and their immediate descendants. There are a few diaries, and an untold quantity of manuscript sermons. Besides those of an older period, a mass of military papers relating to the American Revolution belong to the society, which, at the request of the State government, have been deposited in the State House at Boston.

"As to *paintings* and *engravings*, besides the family portraits of the Mathers, five in number, the society possesses an original portrait of Winthrop (received from the late William Winthrop, of Cambridge,) together with the 'stone pot, tipped and covered with a silver lydd,' containing the genealogy of the direct line in which that heir-loom, the pot, had descended. This stone pot is referred to in Savage's edition of Winthrop's journal. We have also portrait of Endicott, Higginson, John Rogers, the martyr; Governors Burnett and Leverett; Hannah Adams; our late presidents, Isaiah Thomas and Thomas L. Winthrop; Mr. Baldwin, late librarian; Charles Paxton, by Copley; Judge Chandler, &c.; and a very considerable collection of engraved heads in frames, bequeathed by the late Dr. Bentley, of Salem.

"There are also many curious and rare old *maps* and *charts*."

Library of the College of the Holy Cross—4,220 *vols.*—Founded in 1843; contains about 4,000 volumes, besides many maps, charts, engravings and pieces of music, and 650 coins and medals. It is opened every day. The professors of the college, and such of the students as have special leave from the president, are entitled to the use of the books. Books are occasionally lent out to persons at a distance from the college. J. O'Callaghan, librarian.

A society of students possesses a library of 220 volumes.

The Library of the Mechanics' Institute contains over 1,000 volumes, nearly all of them choice scientific works recently selected. About $300 per annum are now applied to the increase of the library.

The Lyceum Library contains 1,300 volumes, selected with care. The sum expended for books last year was $100, which is perhaps about the average annual amount.

The Library of the Manual Labor High School, established by the Baptists in 1832, contains about 500 volumes.

PUBLIC SCHOOL LIBRARIES IN MASSACHUSETTS.

From the twelfth report of the secretary of the board of education, presented November, 1848, we learn that the number of volumes in the school libraries was 91,539, and their estimated value $42,707. "It would be difficult," adds the secretary, "to mention any way in which a million of dollars could be more beneficially expended than in supplying the requisite apparatus and libraries for our common schools."

There are sixty-seven incorporated *academies* in the State, many of which possess libraries. Some few of these have already been noticed.

Most of the religious societies possess also *Sunday school libraries.* The number of volumes it is difficult to estimate. It must, however, be very large. These books exert a powerful influence in literature no less than in religion and morals.

Social libraries exist in about two-thirds of the towns in the State. Some of these have been noticed, but only a small part of all that exist. It will be a work of time to gather exact information respecting the whole of them.

By chapter 52, statutes of 1848, the State legislature authorizes the *city of Boston to establish a public library,* and to expend $5,000 a year for its support. Mr. Bigelow, the present mayor of the city, has presented $1,000. Hon. Edward Everett has given a valuable collection of public documents, comprising more than 1,000 volumes. Many books have also been received from Mr. Vattemare. Mr. Winthrop, present Senator from this State, has also presented the documents of the general government for about ten years.

RHODE ISLAND.

NEWPORT.

Redwood Library—4,000 vols.—A catalogue (95 pages 8vo.) of this library was published in 1843.* The preface contains the following historical sketch of this venerable institution, which has been thought to possess sufficient general interest to warrant its publication, with some omissions, in this place:

"The Redwood Library and Athenæum owes its origin to a literary and philosophical society, which was established in Newport in the year 1730. This society was composed of some of the most respectable men of the town of Newport, at that period one of the most remarkable in the

* A catalogue had also been printed in 1764, in octavo.

American colonies, for its wealth, learning, and public spirit. Its origin is connected with a splendid name in literature and philosophy. The celebrated Bishop Berkeley, who resided at this time on Rhode Island, encouraged the formation of this institution, and participated in its discussions. He was the intimate friend of some of its members; and the charm of his conversation, undoubtedly, gave a delightful interest to its meetings. Berkeley resided on Rhode Island from January, 1729, to September, 1731; and from frequent intercourse with these vigorous-minded men, derived that knowledge of American character which prompted his muse to utter the prophetic declaration, 'Westward the star of empire takes its way.'

"At that period, the advantages of the association depended on a system of weekly debates and conversations upon questions of utility or interest. The formation of a library was, subsequently, considered by them as one of the most powerful means of accomplishing their original purpose, 'the promotion of knowledge and virtue.' The system of debates was gradually laid aside, and the energies of the society were solely directed to the collection of valuable books. Had the establishment of a library constituted, originally, an object of the society, the valuable books given by Bishop Berkeley to Yale College and Harvard University, on his departure from Newport, in 1731, would undoubtedly have been presented by him to this institution, to individual members of which he was strongly attached.

"In the accomplishment of this new object, a great impulse was given by Abraham Redwood, esq., who, in 1747, placed at the disposal of the society £500 sterling, for the purchase of standard books in London. To give permanence and usefulness to his donation, Mr. Redwood enjoined on the society the duty of erecting an edifice as a depository for such books as might be purchased. In pursuance of their object, a charter of incorporation was obtained in 1747, and the society, in honor of their most liberal benefactor, asumed the name of the Redwood Library Company. For the erection of a library building, five thousand pounds were almost immediately subscribed by different citizens of the town. Henry Collins,* esq., proved a noble coadjutor of Mr. Redwood, and presented, in June, 1748, to the company, the lot of land then called Bowling Green, on which the present library edifice now stands.

"The library building, which is a beautiful specimen of the Doric order, was commenced in 1748 and completed in 1750. The plan was furnished by Joseph Harrison,† esq., assistant architect of Blenheim House, England. He also superintended the erection of the edifice, with the committee of the company, consisting of Samuel Wickham, Henry Collins, and John Tillinghast. The master-builders were, Wing Spooner, Samuel Green, Thomas Melville and Israel Chapman. The principal front is ornamented with a portico of four Doric columns, seventeen feet in height, and projecting nine feet from the walls of the building.

* "Henry Collins was a merchant of Newport, distinguished for his wealth, liberality and taste. He employed Smibert, who came out with Dean Berkeley, to take the portraits of Callender, Clap, Hitchcock, and Berkeley. Smibert was an excellent artist, and had been previously patronized, while at Florence, by the Grand Duke of Tuscany. The portrait of Henry Collins, taken by Smibert, is supposed to be in the possession of some branch of the Flagg family; but the proprietors of the library have not, as yet, been enabled to obtain it."

† "Harrison was architect of the beautiful little Episcopal church in Cambridge."

The edifice consists of a main building, and two small wings* on each side, ranging in a line parallel with the west end of the building. The wings furnish two rooms, of about twelve feet square. The principal library room, occupying the whole of the main building, is thirty-seven feet long, twenty six feet broad, and nineteen feet in height. The edifice is lighted by seven whole windows and three attic windows in the east and west ends."

* * * * * * * * *

"The library building, on the outside, is worked in imitation of rustic, and is adorned by the ornaments appropriate to the Doric order. The whole building is supported by a substantial foundation, raised several feet from the ground.

"The first meeting of the Redwood Library Company, after their incorporation, was held in the Council Chamber, in Newport, on the last Wednesday of September, 1747."

* * * * * * * * *

"At a meeting of the company in the Council Chamber, on the 4th of July, 1748, the directors presented a catalogue of the books which they proposed to purchase in London. The liberal share given in this catalogue to the ancient classics, evinced a disposition to provide for the scholar the objects of his favorite study. In these times of customary appeal to direct utility, we fear a less liberal expenditure would be allowed for the gratification of classical taste. This catalogue, with Mr. Redwood's bills of exchange, was sent immediately to Mr. John Thomlinson, esq., of London, who appears to have satisfactorily executed the commission of the society. He was elected an honorary member in 1749."

* * * * * * * * *

"In 1750 a tax of twelve hundred pounds was assessed on the members of the company, to defray the expense of completing the building.

"In 1755 the Rev. Ezra Stiles was admitted an honorary member of the society. His distinction as a scholar and theologian, connected with his exertions in behalf of the library, justifies some allusion to his character, in an historical sketch of the institution. The Redwood Library, at the time of his settlement in Newport, contained about 1,500 volumes of standard books. The classical and theological departments were the most valuable, and constituted the principal attraction, which determined Dr. Stiles to fix his residence in Newport. He remained in Newport twenty years, and during the greater portion of the time officiated as librarian of the company. Having constant access to this valuable collection of books, he drew from it, by assiduous study, his great and various learning. He held an extensive correspondence with European scholars, and the principal object of that correspondence was to illustrate and perfect those researches and investigations in philosophy, history, antiquities and physical science, to which his mind had been prompted by the perusal of books which he found on our shelves. His zeal for the diffusion of knowledge led him to solicit for the library valuable works from European authors. Many of these works, obtained through his instrumentality, are still preserved in the library. The copy of Montanus' Hebrew

---

* These wings were not in the original design. They deface rather than adorn the edifice.

Bible and Dictionary, now belonging to the library, enabled him to perfect his knowledge of the Hebrew language; and a folio copy of Homer still bears the marks of his profound study, in the form of Greek annotations, in his own handwriting. He was one of the most eloquent advocates of liberty in the colonies, before the Revolution. The late Dr. Channing says of him: 'To the influence of this distinguished man, in the circle in which I was brought up, I may owe in part the indignation which I feel towards every invasion of human rights. In my earliest years I regarded no human being with equal reverence.' His rare learning, eloquence, and goodness, uniformly supported by tradition, have received, of late, the attestation of great names. The eloquent eulogy pronounced upon this gifted and extraordinary man, by Chancellor Kent, will preserve for many generations the memory of his attainments, genius and virtue.

"In 1770 the proprietors, to evince their grateful sense of Mr. Redwood's exertions for the advancement of the institution, requested him to sit for his picture, the expense of which was to be defrayed from the company's treasury. After repeated solicitations, in 1773 Mr. Redwood gave his consent, agreeably to the wishes of the company. David Cheeseborough, Thomas Vernon, and John Bours, esqs., were appointed a committee to carry the vote of the society into execution. This painting was probably executed, but it is doubtful whether it was ever placed in the library. The beautiful portrait which at the present time adorns the walls of the library room was copied by Charles B. King, esq., from an original portrait of Mr. Redwood, and was generously presented by him to the society, in 1817.

"No meetings of the Library Company were held from 1778 to 1785. During the Revolution, the town of Newport was occupied by various armies. The disastrous state of the town compelled many of the best citizens* to leave their homes, and to seek shelter for themselves and families in the more secure retreats of the country. The tumults of war and revolution interrupted the peaceful pursuits of literature, and exerted a chilling influence on the growth of knowledge, and the prosperity of institutions like that which forms the subject of our sketch. During the war, the library building is said to have been defaced, and many of the books carried off. To the honor of Gen. Prescott, it is said that on being informed of the exposed state of the library, he stationed a military guard to protect it from further injury and depredation.

"At a meeting of the company, held at Mr. Townsend's hotel, on the 14th of October, 1785—it being the first meeting after the conclusion of the war of the Revolution—the following gentlemen were chosen officers of the institution: Hon. Abraham Redwood, Stephen Ayrault, William Vernon, John Malbone, Jonathan Easton, Nicholas P. Tillinghast, Jacob Richardson, and Robert Stevens, *Directors;* William Channing, *Secretary;* Christopher Ellery, *Librarian;* Stephen Ayrault, *Treasurer*. Several important objects engaged the attention of the society: the principal were the remission of the annual tax from 1778 to 1785, the repair of the library edifice, the recovery of missing books, and the formation of a catalogue of the library. William Vernon, Henry Marchant, and William Channing, esqs., were appointed to apply to the honorable General

* "Mr. Redwood resided, during the revolutionary war, on his farm in Mendon, Mass."

Assembly, at their next session, for a renewal of the charter of the company, with alterations and amendments.

"The society experienced a great misfortune in the death of Mr. Redwood, the founder of the library, March 6, 1788. Beneficent objects seemed to have occupied the mind of Mr. Redwood, as will appear from the following obituary notice, taken from the Newport Herald, March 13, 1788: 'Last Saturday morning died the Hon. Abraham Redwood, in the 79th year of his age. He was blessed with an ample fortune and a liberal spirit, which prompted him to encourage useful learning and relieve the distresses of mankind. He founded the library in this town. He subscribed largely to a college to be built in this State, on condition that it should be established in the county of Newport. He subscribed £500 sterling towards a university proposed to be erected in this town; and he offered the same sum to the Society of Friends, of which he was a member, to endow a school in this place for the instruction of Friends' children. His less public acts of generosity will be gratefully remembered by those on whom they were conferred; and the poor will never forget that Abraham Redwood was their constant friend and benefactor.' It is understood that Mr. Redwood removed to Newport from Antigua, where he possessed large and valuable estates.

"After his death, the public interest in the prosperity of the institution seems to have declined. A period of great success in the commerce of the town was allowed to pass away without bringing new resources for the accomplishment of the objects of the institution. In fact, its very existence, at one time, depended on the resolution and efforts of a few individuals. The late Dr. Channing, in a discourse delivered in Newport in 1836, alludes to the neglected condition of the library at this period, during which he pursued his studies in this town. He says: 'I had no professor or teacher to guide me, but I had two noble places of study. One was yonder beautiful edifice, now so frequented and so useful as a public library; then so deserted, that I spent day after day, and sometimes week after week, amidst its dusty volumes, without interruption from a single visitor.'

"The public attention was not directed to the importance of the institution till the year 1810, when the society received an accession of spirit and ability by the admission of a large number of new proprietors. In March, 1810, James Ogilvie, esq., visited the town, and delivered several lectures on the advantages of public libraries, which contributed essentially to awaken the public to the claims of the Redwood Library on their generosity and support. He made the society a liberal donation of select and valuable books. From 1810 to the present time, a very respectable interest has been maintained in the institution, and the funds placed at the disposal of the society have been judiciously managed in accomplishing the plans of its founders."

* * * * * * * * *

"The exertions of the late Robert Johnston, esq., in behalf of the institution, demand honorable mention. By his solicitation, some of the most rare and valuable works in the library were obtained from different individuals in Newport and its neighborhood. In 1834 he made great efforts to enrich the library with the public records of England. He succeeded in obtaining eighty-four volumes (seventy-two large folios and twelve octavos) from the Lords Commissioners and Lord Lyndhurst, in consequence of his application to them, through the medium of his friend and agent, Thomas Bland, esq., of London. These volumes, containing the most valuable materials of English history, were understood to be obtained as a present from the King of Great Britain, on the application of Lord Lyndhurst. As such they will be perpetually preserved in the Redwood Library.

"In 1813 Solomon Southwick, esq., of Albany, gave to the library one hundred and twenty acres of land, in the State of New York, for the purpose of advancing the institution, and thereby perpetuating the memory of Henry Collins, esq., one of its principal founders.

"In 1834 Abraham Redwood, esq., of Dorset Place, Marylebone, England, being desirous of promoting an institution founded by his honored grandfather, gave to the company the homestead estate, situated in Newport, which he inherited from his father, Jonas Redwood, esq.

"In 1837, Baron Hottinguer, a distinguished banker of Paris, who was connected by marriage with the Redwood family, presented to the company one thousand francs, for the restoration of the building.

"In 1840, the Hon. Christopher G. Champlin bequeathed to the company one hundred dollars and some valuable books.

The proprietors are also indebted to the Hon. William C. Gibbs, for his liberality in permitting a free access to a valuable collection of books, at present deposited by him in the library.

"The library room is adorned by several paintings and busts. The beautiful bust of John Marshall was presented in 1839, by Augustus E. Silliman, esq., of New York. The acknowledgments of the company are due to Charles B. King, esq., of Washington, for his numerous and valuable donations; among which are the portrait of Columbus and that of Abraham Redwood, the founder of the library."

The Mechanics' Library—1,100 *vols.*—The Newport Association of Mechanics and Manufacturers was incorporated in 1792. The library was founded in 1828. The average expenditure for books during the last ten years has been about $50 per annum; the average increase of the library from 30 to 60 volumes. As the society has rapidly increased of late, the library will hereafter be an object of special attention. There is a fund of $1,200 belonging to the association, the income of which is applied to various other objects besides the library, which is principally supported by a tax on the members. It is contemplated to erect, so soon as circumstances will allow, a building for public lectures and the library. There is a printed catalogue, but it is very incomplete. Another will be published in the course of the next year. The library is open every Wednesday and Saturday evening from 6 till 9 o'clock. All members of the association, and the apprentices of members who have written orders from their employers, are allowed to take out books. About 1,500 volumes are thus lent each year. W. Nichols, secretary.

PROVIDENCE.

Brown University Libraries—31,600 *vols*—Brown University was incorporated in the year 1764. It was originally established in the town of Warren, where, in the year 1769, the first commencement was celebrated. It was subsequently removed to Providence, where the first college edifice (University Hall) was erected, in the year 1770.

At the period of its removal to Providence, the college appears to have been destitute of a library, or at least of any collection of books worthy of the name. To supply, as far as possible, this deficiency, the Providence Library Company (now merged in the Providence Athenæum) tendered the free use of its books to the officers and students of the college—a privilege which was continued several years.

The books first obtained for the library were probably procured in England, through the agency of the Rev. Morgan Edwards. In the year 1768 Mr. Edwards, then in England, was authorized by the corporation "to purchase such books as he shall think necessary at this time, not exceeding 20 pounds value." This is the only appropriation, small as it is, which is recorded previously to 1784! It is probable, however, that Mr. Edwards and the other agents of the college, while soliciting money, received many presents in books; for, in 1776 the college was in possession of a library, which, at the commencement of hostilities in that year, was removed to the country for safe keeping.

The college was disbanded December 6, 1776, immediately after the British troops took possession of Newport. From December 7, 1776, to June, 1782, the college building (now University Hall) was occupied, first as a barrack for the American militia, and afterwards as a hospital for the French army, commanded by Count Rochambeau. On the return of peace the college edifice was purified and refitted, the library was brought back, and the business of instruction resumed.

In a letter concerning the early history of the library, the Hon. Asher Robbins writes: "At the reorganization of the college, in the autumn of 1782, I was appointed to the office of tutor, and took charge of the library as librarian. It was then kept in the east chamber on the second floor of the central building; the volumes it contained were quite limited in number—these mostly the primary editions of the works in folio and quarto. The precise number I am not able to recollect; my impression is that it did not exceed two or three hundred. Of the previous history of the library I have no certain knowledge; I believe, however, it was acquired by purchase, through the agency of the Rev. Morgan Edwards, and that it was imported, after the removal of the college from Warren and the erection of the college edifice in Providence.

"An addition was made to the library soon after my connexion with it. At a meeting of the corporation, it was proposed by Mr. John Brown to raise a fund, by subscription, for the purchase of books. To encourage a liberal subscription he told the corporation to subscribe what they would, and to procure what they could by subscription elsewhere, and that whatever the amount was, he would subscribe an equal sum. He did so; and, besides, made good the subscriptions of those who failed to pay up theirs. I was employed to make out the invoice of the books to be purchased, under the advisement of President Manning, and also, I think, of the chancellor, Governor Hopkins, who, by-the-by, was a very competent adviser on this subject, being deeply versed in English literature, and an excellent judge of its various merits. The importation was in the course of that year (1783) made by Mr. Nicholas Brown [brother of Mr. John Brown]."

In the year 1784 a valuable donation, containing the works of several of the Fathers of the church, was received from the Bristol Education Society in England.

In the same year (1784) the corporation appropriated the sum of £350 for the purchase of books.

In the succeeding year, Granville Sharp, esq., presented several of his own publications, with a set of the works of his grandfather, Dr. John Sharp, Archbishop of York. He subsequently sent other valuable presents to the library. In 1787, the thanks of the corporation were presented to Mr. John Francis (son-in-law of John Brown and father of J. B. Francis, late Governor of Rhode Island) for a valuable donation of books.

In the year 1792 Nicholas Brown, then a recent graduate of the institution, and a young and enterprising merchant, commenced his benefactions towards the college by the gift of a law library, containing about three hundred and fifty volumes of valuable books, which he had imported from England for that purpose.

The Rev. Isaac Backus, of Middleborough, Mass., author of the Church History of New England, who died in 1806, in the 83d year of his age and the 60th of his ministry, bequeathed to the college a part of his library. The extent or value of this bequest it is now impossible to determine, as no record was made of it at the time. Among the books thus presented, however, there is one which deserves particular mention. It is a copy of Roger Williams's "Bloody Tenent yet more Bloody," being the copy originally presented by Williams to his friend and fellow-laborer, Dr. John Clarke. On a blank leaf it contains the following words in Roger Williams's handwriting: "For his honored and beloved Mr. John Clarke, an eminent Witnes of Christ Jesus, ag'st ye bloodie Doctrine of persecution, etc "

In 1815 Mr. Nicholas Brown gave five hundred dollars for the purchase of books, and Mrs. Hope Ives presented a copy of Dobson's edition of the Encyclopaedia Britannica.

The next, and the most valuable of all the donations to the library which we have to record, is the legacy of the Rev. William Richards, LL. D., of Lynn, England. Mr. Richards was a native of South Wales. He was many years pastor of the Baptist church at Lynn, where he died in the year 1818, in the 69th year of his age.

Mr. Richards seems to have been a man of considerable learning, particularly in English and Welsh history, and in the Welsh language and literature. His writings are historical, political, and controversial. His most important work is the History of Lynn, in 2 vols. 8vo. Dr. Evans says of it: "It is not only well written, the style perspicuous and manly, but it is replete with information as well as entertainment." His Review of Noble's Memoirs of the Protectoral House of Cromwell is characterised by Lowndes as "severe, but at the same time just." "His dictionary of Welsh and English," says Dr. Evans, "a work of minute and wearisome labor, is in high repute." Mr. Richards was of the *General Baptist* denomination, and a strong advocate of religious liberty. It was his love of the liberal character of this institution which induced him to bestow upon it his library, as appears from the following passage in his Memoirs: "Mr. Richards had corresponded with Dr. James Manning, once President of the Baptist College in Rhode Island. From this gentleman he learned the liberal constitution of that respectable seminary, and for some years previous to his death meant to bequeath to it his library. He accordingly made inquiry of Dr. Rogers [of Philadelphia] whether it was still conducted on the same liberal footing, in which case he should cherish the same generous intentions towards it." This inquiry was answered by Dr. Messer, then President of the college, in a letter from which it may be well to extract the following passage: "Though the charter requires that the President shall forever be a Baptist, it allows neither him, in his official character, nor any other officer of instruction, to inculcate any sectarian doctrine; it forbids all religious tests; and it requires that all denominations of Christians, behaving alike, shall be treated alike. This charter is congenial with the whole of the civil government established here by the venerable Roger Williams, who allowed no religious tests, and no pre-eminence of one denomination over another; and none has ever been allowed unto this day. This charter is also congenial with the present spirit of this State and of this town."

Gratified with this letter, Mr. Richards beqeathed his library, consisting of about thirteen hundred volumes, to Brown University. It is a singular fact, that his will was made on the very day on which the honorary degree of Doctor of Laws was conferred upon him by this college. Mr. Richards had received no intimation that the honor was intended for him, nor did he live to hear that it had been bestowed.

The library which he bequeathed to the college is, in many respects, valuable. It contains a considerable number of Welsh books, a large collection of valuable works, illustrating the history and antiquities of England and Wales; besides two or three hundred bound volumes of pamphlets, some of them very ancient, rare, and curious.

For the next valuable accession to the library—designated as "the subscription of 1825"—the college is indebted to the efforts of Mr. Horatio Gates Bowen, who was librarian of the institution from 1824 to 1841. At his request several of the friends of the college subscribed eight hundred and forty dollars, which sum was expended in the purchase of books.

Between 1823—5, fifty-four volumes of valuable scientific works, including Cloquet's Anatomie, Lamarck's and De Candolle's Flore Française, Cuvier's Règne Animal and Wilkins's Vitruvius, were presented by Mr. John Carter Brown and Mr. Robert Hale Ives. Often, since that time, the names of these gentlemen and of Mr. Moses B. Ives appear among the benefactors of the library.

About the year 1823, a splendid donation, consisting of one hundred and three volumes, comprising the best editions, mostly in quarto, of the works of the celebrated French mathematicians, Euler, Lacroix, Lagrange, La Place, etc., besides many valuable theological works, was made by the Rev. Thomas Carlile.

In 1826 Messrs. Brown & Ives presented, through Dr Homer, fifty volumes of rare and expensive theological works. In the same year donations were received from the Hon. William Hunter, LL. D., and from Usher Parsons, M. D.

On the return of Prof. Elton from Europe, in 1827, donations were received, through him, from several distinguished gentlemen in Europe—in all, two hundred and eighty-three volumes; besides eighty five volumes of classical and miscellaneous works purchased by him at the order of Messrs. Brown & Ives.

The libraries of the Philophysian and Franklin Societies, composed of undergraduates, when these societies became extinct, were, by provisions of their constitutions, incorporated with the College Library. They together contained three or four hundred volumes.

The government of Great Britain presented, in 1835, one hundred and ten volumes of the publications of the Record Commission.

In 1838 Mrs. Elizabeth H. Bartol, wife of the Rev. Cyrus A. Bartol of Boston, and Mrs. Hepsy S. Wayland, wife of President Wayland, presented three hundred and fifty six volumes of standard works in French and Italian literature.

The Rev. Jonathan Homer, D. D., of Newton, Massachusetts, at various times, made valuable donations of rare and costly theological books, including some valuable editions of the Bible. Many of these donations contain copious and useful manuscript annotations by the learned donor.

Among the additions to the library, a collection of fifty volumes of Ordination Sermons, presented by the Hon. Theron Metcalf, of Boston, a graduate of the college in the class of 1805, deserves particular notice. These volumes contain more than a thousand discourses preached at ordinations, installations, and inaugurations in the United States, and mostly in New England. This is without doubt the largest collection of the kind which has ever been made, and is of obvious importance as connected with the ecclesiastical history of the country.

The library fund next claims our attention. "At a meeting of the standing committee of the corporation of Brown University, held January 10, 1831, it was unanimously resolved,—

"1. That immediate measures be taken to raise, by subscription, the sum of *twenty-five thousand dollars*, to be appropriated to the purchase of books for the library, and apparatus for the philosophical and chemical departments of Brown University.

"2. *Resolved*, That the chairman and Thomas P. Ives be a committee to carry the foregoing resolution into effect.

"F. WAYLAND,
"*Chairman*."

Soon afterwards, a meeting of the friends of the institution was called for the purpose of seconding this effort. At this meeting the wants of the library and the importance of supplying them were presented and urged. Previously to this, however, the Hon. Nicholas Brown had, with his wonted munificence, subscribed ten thousand dollars towards the fund. The subscription was opened, with the following conditions:

1. "The whole amount shall be invested in a permanent fund, of which the interest shall be, from time to time, appropriated exclusively to the objects stated in the resolution.

2. "The selection of books and apparatus shall be made by joint committee of the corporation and government of the university.

3. "One-third of the amount subscribed shall become due on the 1st day of October, 1832, another third on the 1st day of October, 1833, and the remainder on the 1st day of October, 1834.

4. "A copy of the subscribers' names, and of the sums subscribed by each, shall be deposited in the library, and another among the archives of the university."

The sum thus obtained, amounting to $19,437 50, was placed at interest until it had accumulated to twenty-five thousand dollars, and was then invested in a permanent fund, according to the provisions of the subscription, as above specified. The first dividend became due in July,

1839. Since that time the proceeds have been regularly appropriated according to the design of the donors.

The room appropriated to the library, at the time when the library fund was raised, "was an apartment in University Hall, crowded to excess, unsightly and wholly unsuited for the purpose to which, from necessity, it was devoted." To remedy this defect, the Hon. Nicholas Brown erected, at his own expense, a beautiful edifice for a library and chapel; to which, in testimony of veneration for his former instructor, he gave the name of Manning Hall. This building was dedicated in 1835.

Soon after the removal of the library to the new building it was newly arranged, and in 1843 a full catalogue of its contents printed. This catalogue was favorably noticed in the North American Review, and in other leading periodicals, and drew special attention to this important department of the institution.

Soon afterwards a chair of modern languages was established at the college; and the professor elect was encouraged to visit Europe, partly for the purpose of professional study, and partly to enable the friends of the college to carry out more effectually their wishes for the increase of the library. This agent was authorized by Mr. John Carter Brown to select and purchase, at his expense, such books in the French, German, and Italian languages, to the value of about $2,700, as he might think most useful for the college. The selection was made, both of works and of editions, *without regard to cost;* but the books were purchased with the closest reference to economy. For about $2,600 dollars the number of volumes of bound books purchased was 2,921—viz: 121 folios, 392 quartos, 1,627 octavos, and 781 duodecimos, besides 74 valuable maps and engravings. These books were *all* well bound, most of them newly and elegantly, in half calf, plain gilt. The average price per volume, including binding and all other expenses, was about 89 cents. This collection includes a set of French, German and Italian classics, in the best and fullest library editions; the principal philosophical, scientific, and historical works of late continental scholars; a complete set of the "*Moniteur Universel,*" from its commencement to 1826—a clean, beautiful, well bound copy of the original edition, with the introduction, indexes, &c., in 77 vols. folio; a set of the memoirs of the French Institute since its reorganization,—vols. 4to.; the collection of memoirs relative to the history of France, by Guizot and Petitot, 162 vols. 8vo.; a complete set of the *Allgemeine Literatur-Zeitung*, 134 vols. 4to.; and of the *Allgemeine Deutshe Bibliothek*, 139 vols. 8vo.; *Il Vaticano*, 8 vols. folio, elegantly illustrated; *Il Campidoglio*, 2 vols. folio; the *Museo Borbonico*, 13 vols. 4to., the original Naples edition; the works of Canova and Thorwaldsen—the *Musée Français* and *Musée Royal*, in 6 vols. folio; the *Description de l'Egypte*, Canina's Achitecture, and many more illustrated works of great beauty and value, besides rare and costly maps and prints. These books were mostly purchased at auctions in Paris, Rome, Leipsic, Frankfort on the Maine, and Berlin. Many were purchased at provincial sales. To supply the deficiencies of the library in standard English works, a subscription was opened among the friends of the college, amounting to about $5,000, and the same agent was appointed to select and purchase the books. This collection was received in the library in 1845, and raised the whole number of volumes to nearly 20,000.

The class which graduated in 1821 held a meeting in Providence, a quarter of a century from the time of their graduation, at which a considerable sum of money was subscribed for the benefit of the library, in token of their grateful interest in the institution at which they were educated. The money thus obtained was placed in the hands of Dr. Thomas H. Webb, of Boston, who purchased, with excellent judgment, about five hundred volumes, mostly from the library of the Hon. John Pickering.

The next year, 1847, the Rev. Samuel Osgood, then a clergyman in Providence, and now in New York, proposed to the several religious societies of the city a subscription for the purpose of supplying the deficiencies of the library in the best editions of the Fathers of the church, and the standard theological writers of the Reformation. About $2,000 were raised, and a superb collection was purchased of the Benedictine editions of several of the Fathers; the Bibliotheca Maxima Veterum Patrum, 30 vols. folio; Harduin's Collectio Conciliorum, 12 vols. folio; besides the choicest and most elegant editions of many of the Fathers not edited by the Benedictines, and a large collection of works connected with patristic literature, and the history of the Reformation.

The library committee had before this issued a circular, soliciting the donation of files of newspapers, important pamphlets, &c. In answer to this call a vast mass of pamphlets and papers were sent to the library. From the whole about 5,000 were assorted and arranged, and they form now an invaluable collection. Brown University certainly deserves great credit for the care with which she has garnered and guarded these neglected but precious memorials of our earlier history.

In 1793 the library contained 2,173 volumes; in 1826, 5,818 volumes; in 1843, 10,235; in January, 1849, 21,520, exclusive of pamphlets and of duplicates; in January, 1850, the number of volumes was about 23,000.

It has a large number of maps, charts, engravings, and elegantly illustrated works. Since January, 1843, 11,300 volumes have been added to the library. During the last eight years about $20,000, being the proceeds of the library fund, and donations from individuals, have been expended for the purchase of books. From the income of the fund about $1,200 per annum is appropriated to the purchase of books. The building (called Manning Hall) is built of rubble stone, and is stuccoed. The library occupies the whole of the ground floor. Its dimensions are 64×38 feet, height 13 feet. In the centre is a double row of fluted columns, from which the shelves extend to the walls, forming twelve alcoves. The books are, so far as convenient, arranged on the shelves according to subjects. The first catalogue was printed in 1793; the second in 1826; and the third and last in 1843, [560 pp. 8vo.] This catalogue is alphabetical, according to the authors' names, and has a copious alphabetical and analytical index of subjects. A supplement, nearly as large as the original volume, and on the same plan, is now in preparation. The library is open, during term time, daily from 10 a. m. till 2 p. m.; during vacations, weekly, on Saturdays, from 12 to 1. The members of the corporation; the president, professors, tutors, and register; all resident graduates; all the donors to the library fund; all donors to the fund for building Rhode Island Hall; and all donors to the library to the amount of $40, residing in the city of Providence, are entitled to the use of the library without charge. Undergraduates are entitled to the use of the library, and are charged therefor one dollar per term. During the year 1848, from January 7 to December 5, 4,069 volumes were taken out. The number of books taken out increases every year. The privilege of consulting the library is extended, with such restrictions as the library committee may from time to time prescribe, to all graduates of the University; to all settled clergymen, of every denomination, residing in the city of Providence and its vicinity; and to all other persons on whom, for the purpose of advancing the arts, science or literature, the corporation or library committee may confer it. Books are occasionally lent to persons at a distance, by special permission of the library committee or the corporation.

The present librarian is Reuben A. Guild, A. M.

There are two literary societies of students connected with the University—the Philermenian Society, founded in 1794, and the United Brothers Society, founded in 1806. Each has a library of about 3,600 volumes. They have issued elegant and well prepared catalogues. To the beautiful catalogue of the Philermenian Society, published in January, 1849, is prefixed a history of the society, by Mr. B. F. Thurston.

The Athenæum Library—15,204 *vols.*—The Athenæum was incorporated by act of the General Assembly of Rhode Island, January, 1836. It was formed by the union of the Providence Library (founded in 1753) and of the Athenæum, (founded in 1831.) The library contained, in September, 1849, 15,204 volumes. The yearly average increase for the last ten years has been 800 volumes; the average annual expenditure for books, $1,200. There is a fund of five thousand dollars for the increase of the library, yielding $331 50 per annum. This fund will soon be increased to eleven thousand dollars.

A granite building was erected in 1838 for the use of the Athenæum, at an expense of nearly $15,000. The following description of the edifice is taken from the third report of the directors:

"Principal story.—The floor of the principal story is about fifteen feet from the sidewalk in front of the building; this distance is divided by side steps at each end of the bank in front; steps in the centre of the front of the building, six feet high, approached over a gravel walk on the top of the bank, conduct to the front entry, which is eight feet wide by thirteen feet long. There are two rooms on each side of the entry, communicating with it, thirteen by eighteen feet each—one intended for a reading-room for periodical publications; the other for directors' meetings, committees, &c.

"The library, or principal room, is entered through the front entry, or through either of the rooms just mentioned. It is thirty-two feet long by forty-three feet wide on the floor, and about forty-four long by forty-three wide, from within about seven feet below and up to the ceiling; this difference in length between the upper and lower parts of the room is caused by the space left over the reading and directors' rooms, which is taken off from the library room. Those two rooms are ten feet high; the library room is eighteen feet high. There is also another room eighteen feet high, in the rear of the library room, entered through it, the dimensions of which are twenty by forty-three feet."

A catalogue was printed in 1837, of 116 pages 8vo.; and a supplement of 108 pages 8vo. in 1839. Another is nearly ready for the press.

The library is open every day, Sunday excepted, from the first of April till the 1st of October, from 9 a. m. till sunset; from October to April, from 10 a. m. till 9 p. m.

Persons entitled to the use of the books are owners of shares; the price of a share is $15, subject to an annual tax of $5.

Every shareholder has the right of taking out two books at a time. There are more than 500 shares, nearly all of which are used. It is impossible to say how many consult the library annually. The number, however, is very large. According to article 10th of the library regulations, the board of directors may authorize persons not connected with the institution to make use of the library. Thomas Hale Williams, librarian.

"This is a very well selected library, embracing the most important works in all those departments of English literature which are adapted to the general wants and tastes of an enlightened community." It may perhaps be considered the best English library of its size in the country. The department of periodicals receives particular attention. Fifty-nine reviews, literary and scientific journals, and newspapers, are regularly taken, and are read "with fresh and ever increasing eagerness." With one exception, they are all in the English language. Great care has been exercised to procure all the back numbers, so that the series are generally complete, with all the indexes, &c.

This institution has been justly pronounced "a model for all similar establishments." [Bibliotheca Sacra, January, 1850.] We understand that Mr. Alexander Duncan has recently presented to the institution the sum of ten thousand dollars, in compliance with the wish of his uncle, the late Cyrus Butler, whose estate descended to Mr. Duncan.

Library of the Mechanics' Association—3,300 *vols.*—A catalogue of this library was printed in 1821, in 12mo.

The Rhode Island Historical Society—2,500 *vols.*—This society was founded on the 19th of April, 1822, and incorporated by the General Assembly the June following. The society has published several volumes of "Collections." It has been faithful and active in collecting the materials for the history of the State, and preserving them for future use. "After the decease of the Hon. Theodore Foster, the society purchased of his representatives the collections which he had been engaged in making during a long life devoted to historical research. They have procurod copies to be made of all orders and papers in the office of the secretary of State in Massachusetts, relating to this State. The papers collected by the Rev. Isaac Backus, author of the History of the Baptists, are deposited in the cabinet, as are also the letter-book and correspondence of Ezek Hopkins, the only individual who ever received a commission as admiral in the navy of the United States." The society has taken great pains to complete its files of newspapers printed in the State. Most of them, including the Providence Gazette, are nearly perfect.

Soon after its incorporation the State gave the society $500. The heirs of the late Nathan Waterman presented a lot of land for a building. In 1843 the society had accumulated a fund of $4,000 for an edifice. About $2,000 more were then raised by subscription, and in 1844 a stone building was erected on Waterman street, facing the College square, to which the collections of the society were removed, and in which its meetings have since been held. The library contains about 2,500 volumes, mostly historical. [See account of the Rhode Island Historical Society, by W. R. Staples.—*American Quarterly Register*, *May*, 1839, pp. 362–8.]

Friends' Boarding School Libraries—1,500 *vols.*—The library of this well-endowed institution consists of three parts, of which the principal contains about 1,000 volumes, irregularly arranged in a room in the central building. It embraces a general collection of English, scientific, and literary works, (novels excepted,) mostly the bequests of the late Moses

Brown and his son Obadiah Brown—being their private libraries. No special appropriation has been made for a regular increase of the library; consequently it is falling behind the modern improvements in science. Some small additions of late works are, however, made every year.

Two other collections of books, of rather a juvenile character, are kept in each wing, more particularly for the use of the pupils. These contain about 250 volumes each—making the aggregate of what are termed the library books, about 1,500 volumes. This number does not include the books of reading and study used by the pupils in their daily exercises, for which purpose about 600 volumes are in use. These are the property of the institution; some are furnished gratuitously, and a part are lent to the students for a compensation. There is no printed catalogue of the library. All the pupils are entitled to the use of the books in the juvenile departments, and to those of the central library at the discretion of the librarian. The officers use the central library at their pleasure.

The Franklin Society, Providence, Rhode Island, founded in 1823, has a library of 500 volumes, slowly increasing. Every member of the society has a key to the library room, and may use the books when he pleases.

PUBLIC SCHOOL LIBRARIES—19,637 VOLS.

Within the last four years, under the exertions of Mr. Henry Barnard, the enlightened and energetic commissioner of public schools, public libraries have been established in every town in the State, with the exception of Johnston, Bristol, and East and West Greenwich. These libraries are composed of well-selected books, and are accessible to the whole population. The money for purchasing them was mostly subscribed by public-spirited individuals.

I am indebted to Mr. Barnard for the following list of these libraries, with the number of volumes which they contain.

"Portsmouth—school district No. 1—650 vols.—This was the first library established in the State, as a part of the recent movement to improve the means of popular education. It owes its origin mainly to the liberal donation of $100 by Miss Sarah Gibbs, a resident in the district.

North Providence—four districts—aggregate, 1,200 vols.

Cumberland Hill—500 vols.

Smithfield—Bernon village,		3,475 vols.
"	Lonsdale Athenæum—1,000	
"	Slatersville—800	
"	Hamlet village,	
"	Globe,	

"The library at Lonsdale was purchased by the commissioner, at an expense of about $550, which was paid by the Lonsdale Company. The books are lent out to the inhabitants, old and young, of the village, at a small charge of one cent per volume. More than seventy dollars were realized the first year from the circulation of the books.

"The library at Slatersville was purchased out of an appropriation of $500 made by Messrs. Slater, Lockwood and Carter.

"Burrillville—Pascoag Manton Library—900 vols.—This library and the libraries in Glocester, Foster, Cranston, Hopkinton, Richmond, Charleston, Exeter, Little Compton, New Shoreham, Jamestown, and Barrington, owe their existence mainly to the liberality of Amasa Manton, esq., of

Providence. By an aggregate expenditure of about $1,000, he has been instrumental in raising in these towns double that amount, and has thus secured the establishment of ten libraries, with at least five thousand good books. Who can estimate the blessings, individual and social, which will flow directly and indirectly from the dissemination of these books, and which will continue to flow yet more abundantly when the liberal donor has himself passed from the earth, and another generation has risen up to have access to these libraries?

Glocester—Manton Library - - - - - -	800	vols.
Foster—Manton Library - - - - -	1,000	"
Scituate—Aborn North School Library - - -	500	"
Cranston—School Library - - - - - -	400	"
Middletown—School Library - - - - -	300	"
Little Compton—Manton Library - - - -	600	"
" Social Library - - - - -	500	"
New Shoreham - - - - - - -	400	"
Jamestown Library - - - - - -	700	"
" Manton Library - - - - - -	400	"
Coventry—Washington village - - - - -	400	"
Bowen's Hill Library - - - - - -	400	"

"The library first named was given to the district by subscribers residents thereof. The Bowen's Hill library owes it origin to a liberal contribution from Mr. Tully Bowen, of Providence.

Warwick—Ladies' Library - - - - - -	500	vols.
" Old Warwick Library - - - - -	250	"
Westerly—Pawcatuck Library - - - - -	2,000	"
Hopkinton and Richmond—Manton Union Library -	800	"
Exeter—Manton Library - - - - - -	662	"
Charlestown—Manton Library - - - - -	500	"

"South Kingston.—Besides a small library (200 vols.) at Kingston, there is an itinerating library consisting of about 400 volumes, which are divided into four cases, each case containing about 100 books, and these cases pass in succession through the several villages in the town.

Warren Lyceum - - - - - - -	500	vols
Barrington—District No. 2 - - - - - -	500	"
Tiverton—Globe district - - - - - -	150	"

"Most of the libraries recently established are open to all persons resident in the town, who will pay one cent a week for the use of a volume, and comply with the regulations which may have been adopted for the preservation of the books."

Mr. Barnard (in the "Report and Documents relating to the Public Schools of Rhode Island for 1848," pages 425 seq.) has given a historical and statistical account of the several libraries in the State, with a sketch of the organization and the history and by-laws of the Pawcatuck Library Association, as a favorable specimen of a public school library. He has also published the catalogue of this collection, in 94 closely printed 8vo. pages. This library was selected by Mr. Barnard, and the catalogue, with some very judicious explanatory remarks and select hints on reading, was prepared by him. We extract the following paragraphs descriptive of the catalogue, remarking, that admirable judgment has been shown in the choice of books and in the means adopted for rendering them useful:

"The first of the following catalogues is a *catalogue of subjects.* Its design is not simply to give *the titles of the books* of the library, but to furnish an *index to the subjects considered in the books.* To effect this, the various books in the library have been analyzed with considerable care, and the several subjects exhibited by them have been arranged under their proper heads. The analysis has been confined to distinct treatises and separate articles on subjects. The design of the analysis, it is thought, has been accomplished—viz: to make the catalogue so full that no one shall be obliged to remove a book from the shelves in order to learn its contents or subjects, and that those who use the library may make their selection of books directly from the catalogue. Thus the convenience of persons in their selection will be greatly promoted, and the injurious handling of the books be prevented.

"In addition to the catalogue of subjects, a *catalogue of authors* is also given, in which *the names of all the authors in the library are placed alphabetically,* and under each name all such works of that author as belong to the library.

"By the aid of these two catalogues any person, even those the least familiar with books, may very readily refer to any work or any subject which they may wish to examine.

"In both catalogues the number of each book, as it stands on the library shelves, is carried out on the margin of the page against its title."

CONNECTICUT.

EAST WINDSOR.

Library of the Theological Institute—3,500 *vols.*—The books in this library (founded in 1833) are mostly theological. They are primarily for the use of the faculty and students of the institute.. The library is open twice a week. The institute was founded in 1833 by the Congregationalists. It was incorporated in 1834.

HARTFORD.

The Library of the Young Men's Institute—10,000 *vols.*—This library contains about 10,000 volumes, increasing at the rate of about 500 volumes per annum.

An excellent catalogue, prepared on the same plan as that of the library of Brown University, was printed in 1844, containing 359 pages 8vo. A supplementary catalogue (in 32 pages 8vo.) was printed in 1847.

The preface to the catalogue contains the following historical sketch of the institute:

"The Hartford Young Men's Institute owes its origin mainly to the interest awakened on the subject of lyceums and associations for mutual improvement by the lectures and discussions before the American Lyceum, at its annual meeting held at Hartford, May, 1838. The importance of establishing an institution in which all the young men of the city might associate for purposes of moral and mental improvement, was discussed among individuals, and notice for a public meeting at Union Hall, on Friday evening, May 19, 1838, was given in the newspapers of the city.

"A public meeting was accordingly held, of which the Hon. Thomas S. Williams was made chairman, and William James Hamersley secretary. On motion of Erastus Smith, and after remarks by Rev. T. H. Gallaudet, General Johnson, Rev. Mr. Sprague, and Erastus Smith, it was resolved, *that the young men of Hartford associate together for the purpose of mutual improvement.* The plan of an association was then discussed, and its further consideration postponed to an adjourned meeting to be held on Monday evening, June 4. On that evening the meeting was organized by appointing Henry Barnard, 2d, chairman, and Erastus Collins secretary. The articles of association, under the name of the 'Hartford Young Men's Institute,' were then discussed and adopted."

On the 5th of June the association was organized by the appointment of officers.

"The officers of the institute immediately issued a circular, [setting forth the importance of such an institution, and appealing to the public for support,] and on the evening of the 4th of July the president delivered a public address, setting forth the claims of this and similar institutions upon the liberal support of the community, and especially upon the young men.

"These appeals were promptly responded to by a large accession of members, and liberal subscriptions in books and money, so as to enable the executive committee to put the main departments of the institute into successful operation. A reading-room was opened, a library of twenty-six hundred volumes was established, a course of twenty lectures secured, two debating classes formed, and eighty-three life members and three hundred and forty-four annual members subscribed to the constitution of the institute.

"Before the close of the first year an arrangement was effected with the share-holders of the Hartford Library Company, by which their valuable collection of books, amounting to about three thousand volumes, was transferred to the institute.

"At the first quarterly meeting of the institute, the executive committee were directed to take the necessary steps to procure an act of incorporation. Application was accordingly made to the General Assembly, at its next session, in May, 1838, and a special act of incorporation was obtained under the name of the 'Hartford Young Men's Institute.'

"At the first annual meeting of the institute this act of incorporation was accepted, and the former constitution, with some modification, adopted as the by-laws for its future government. During the year 1839-'40, the number of annual members was four hundred and five. At the close of the year 1842, there were five hundred and forty members; of which number, seventy one were life-members, twenty-six were members in virtue of being share-holders in the Hartford Library Company, and twelve were members having the privilege of the library only.

"During the year 1843-'44, the library was enriched by a larger and more valuable purchase of books than in any former year—eight hundred and eighty-two volumes having been purchased by the library committee, besides one hundred and sixteen volumes which were presented by friends of the institute. The interior of the rooms in *Wadsworth Athenæum,* appropriated to the institute, have been fitted up under the direction of the executive committee, mostly from subscriptions obtained for that purpose.

"During the brief period of its existence, the success of the institute has more than realized the anticipations and promises of its earliest friends. More than one thousand young men, from every walk and employment of life, have been enrolled among its members; and through them, more than two-thirds of all the families of the city have felt the influence of the institution in some one or all of its departments of usefulness. Two classes for debate have afforded opportunities for acquiring mental discipline, and the correct, ready, and elegant use of the English language, in discussions of questions of civil, social, and literary importance, at the weekly or monthly meetings which have been held during the whole time. The reading-room, embracing the most valuable publications in the periodical literature of this country and of England, has been visited at all hours during the day and evening, by members, and strangers introduced by them, who have had any leisure to spend in this form of relaxation and instruction. The library (which, within six months after the first meeting for organization, comprised over five thousand valuable works) has every year, since, received large accessions of whatever of good, or great, or beautiful, the English or American mind has produced, till the range of selections embraces about nine thousand volumes. It has scattered the pleasures and advantages of knowledge broadly through society—more than one hundred thousand books having been drawn from its shelves. The lecture-room, for upwards of one hundred evenings in all, in the autumn and winter of each year, has attracted crowded audiences of the members and their friends, to listen to addresses by some of the most eminent professional and literary men of our land, who have thus brought philosophy, science, and literature from the office, the study, and cells of scholars, to the workshop, the daily business, and the firesides of men. And, in entering on the seventh year of its existence, the institute is in the permanent occupancy of one-third of Wadsworth Athenæum—a spacious, safe and massive edifice; chaste, beautiful and attractive in its architecture; central in its location; affording ample accommodations for the library and reading-room, the classes for debate and mutual instruction, the weekly meetings of the executive committee, and the regular quarterly and annual meetings of all the members, under the same roof with the other literary and scientific institutions of the city—a structure consecrated to the pursuits of literature, science, and the arts; a monument at once of the munificence of the individual whose name it bears, and of the public-spirit of the citizens by whose liberality it was erected.*

"Every member of the institute who shall have paid all sums due from him to the institute, and made good all damage and loss which he may have occasioned, and any person by paying $3 a year in advance to the librarian, shall be entitled to all the privileges of the library and reading room.

"The library shall be open for the delivery and receipt of books every day (Sundays excepted) from 10 a. m. until 9 p. m."

In the eighth annual report, presented June 6, 1846, we find the fol-

*The Wadsworth Athenæum was erected for the joint accommodation of the Young Men's Institute and the Connecticut Historical Society. It also contains a gallery of art. Daniel Wadsworth gave the land, valued at $15,000, and the citizens subscribed about $32,000 for the building.

lowing table, exhibiting the number of volumes in the library at the close of each year; the number of volumes presented; the number of volumes purchased; and the amount of money annually expended upon this department:

	No. of vols.	Donations.	Purchases.	Money expended.
First year.........	5,620	Vols. 800	Vols. 1,500	$1,261 91
Second year........	6,335	" 159	" 597	831 80
Third year........	6,924	" 126	" 463	678 57
Fourth year........	7,453	" 175	" 478	443 39
Fifth year.........	7,819	" 75	" 280	393 43
Sixth year.........	8,701	" 116	" 882	1,078 80
Seventh year.......	8,871	" 121	" 49	596 13
Eighth year........	8,989	" 21	" 97	46 21
	Whole amount of money expended			5,330 24
	Average amount per annum -			666 28

Owing to the time and labor required in making the necessary estimates, few of the reports announce the number of volumes annually circulated by the institute.

The following are the estimates that have been made:

Circulation, first year - - - - 2,000 volumes.
Circulation, fourth year - - - 25,178 "
Circulation, fifth year - - - - 23,250 "
Circulation, eighth year - - - 25,115 "

The State Library of Connecticut, at Hartford.—Under the care of the Secretary of State are some 3,000 volumes of public documents and miscellaneous books, forming a nucleus for a State library. No distinct department of the kind has as yet been organized.

The Library of the Historical Society of Connecticut—7,000 *vols.*—This society was incorporated in 1825. Owing, however, to the removal of several of the more prominent members from the State, its operations were suspended for several years. Its charter was revived in 1839. Soon after which time, chiefly through the intervention of Mr. Henry Barnard, (now the commissioner of schools in Rhode Island,) the present library was obtained.

This remarkable collection was made by Rev. Thomas Robbins, D. D., a clergyman of Rochester, Massachusetts, formerly of East Windsor, Connecticut, one of the founders of the society. In early life he determined to buy about $200 worth of books every year. This he continued *nearly half a century*, till he had accumulated about 5,000 volumes. It is a curious and valuable collection. In the year —— it was transferred to the Historical Society, by an arrangement, which constitutes the venerable collector librarian for life, and gives the library to the society.

Trinity College Libraries 9,000 *vols.*—Trinity College, formerly called Washington College, was incorporated by act of the legislature in 1823.

"There are 3,000 volumes belonging to the college, arranged in alcoves, and occupying a room in Seabury Hall, in which are also the portraits of several officers and benefactors of the college. There are also two *libraries* belonging to societies of under graduates, containing an aggregate of 6,000 volumes."—[*College Calendar.*]

MIDDLETOWN.

Wesleyan University Libraries—11,123 *vols.*—The Wesleyan University was incorporated in 1831; the library was commenced the same year. It contained August 1, 1848, 5,623 volumes, a few MSS., maps, and coins. About 100 volumes are yearly added, and about $100 expended annually for the purchase of books. An income of about $225 per annum is derived from a tax upon the under graduates. A catalogue was printed in 1837, containing 50 pages 8vo. The library is opened every Monday and Thursday in term time, at 12 m., for half an hour. The persons entitled to the use of the books are: the faculty, president, graduates, and under-graduates. The last pay $2 per annum. Professor John W. Lindsay, librarian.

Besides the college library, the Peithologian and Philorhetorian Societies of students, connected with the university, possess 5,500 volumes. The following remarks, prefixed to the catalogue of the college library, give some account of that publication and of the history of the collection:

"The following catalogue has been prepared for the convenience of the librarian and students of the university. As the time which could be devoted to its preparation would not admit of a detailed account of the subjects, edition, and other particulars of each work, which are necessary to a full and complete catalogue, nothing further has been attempted than an enumeration of the titles, briefly stated as might be, and alphabetically arranged, generally with reference to the subjects.

"The library has been enriched by many valuable donations, only a few of which can be here noticed. The most valuable was made by Thomas Chapman, esq., of Camden, New Jersey, and is called, as a token of respect to the donor, the Chapman Library of the Wesleyan University. This portion of the library, in number about 2,000 volumes, consists of all the books in cases D, E, and F, except such as are marked with a †. There are among them 177 folios and 121 quartos. Of these, 1,655 volumes were fixed at a low price: one half of the amount was presented by Mr. Chapman, and the other half paid by the trustees. The remainder of the 2,000 volumes was given with no reserve but the privilege of adding to the number. Among the latter is a splendid copy of the Antwerp Polyglot, in 8 folio volumes. That part of the catalogue distinguished by a §, numbering 375 volumes, was the library of the late John Summerfield, and presented to the university by his brother-in-law, James Blackstock, esq., of New York. Those distinguished by a *, are books presented by the British conference, valued at £100. Other valuable presents have been made by authors and other individuals, of which more specific notice cannot be taken in this place."

The Friendly Association of Upper Middletown—434 *vols.*—The following notice is from a historical sketch furnished by Mr. Horace G. Williams. It would be difficult to point in this country to a better model for a village literary society, or to one which has been for a longer time uninterruptedly prosperous and useful, than the Friendly Association of Upper Middletown:

"A little more than a year preceding the establishment of the Friendly Association in this village, several gentlemen met together and formed a social club for mental improvement, under the name of the 'Debating Society.' It appears to have commenced with a very respectable number of members, and was conducted with considerable spirit for a time. The number of members became, after a while, greatly reduced; and it was resolved by the few remaining to make some changes in its management, preserving whatever of the constitution and by-laws was thought excellent. The new plan being favorably received by several individuals who were not connected with the 'Debating Society,' its reorganization under a better system seemed to promise success.

"On February 20, 1810, the first meeting was held, commencing with thirteen members; and, their object being the mutual improvement of each other, the name of the 'Friendly Association' was very appropriately chosen. After the adoption of the constitution for the society, the proceedings were regularly organized by the appointment of officers.

"Of the early members who were particularly active in establishing and sustaining the associations, the names of Messrs. William C. Redfield, Silas Sage, Joseph Williams, and Martin Ranney, may be mentioned with some degree of pride; the former of whom has, by his contributions to natural science since his residence abroad, secured a very distinguished reputation throughout the world. Many valuable features in the management of the society were suggested by him; he is still warmly attached to it, and has repeatedly manifested his interest in its prosperity. The foundation of a permanent library was a favorite measure with several of the original members of the association, and one of the first resolutions adopted was to appoint a committee for soliciting aid from its friends in the village. As the result of this effort, the sum of $11 25 in cash and 53 books, chiefly on biography, travels, and religious subjects, were received, the most liberal donations being from individuals not connected with the society. About two years later, an additional fund was raised by subscription among the members, amounting to $32 25; all of which was invested in the purchase of books for the library.

"The expenses of the association have been managed with considerable economy, its principal resources being the fee of one dollar paid by each person upon signing the constitution. Whenever an applicant for admission is elected, he receives a suitable address from the president, explaining his duties and privileges. As the society is always very cautious respecting the character of such, it has in no instance been forced to expel a member for a breach of its regulations. Quite a number of young ladies have joined the association, and the effect of their frequent presence at the meetings has been to stimulate the zeal of the gentlemen, and to render their performance more interesting. Neither sex is exempt from contributing a share of their time and labor for the mutual benefit; but, if any are too diffident to exhibit their own productions or prefer to communicate anonymously, a 'reader' is appointed for the purpose. The miscellaneous exercises usually embrace a variety of subjects; they consist principally, however, of original compositions, recitations of dialogues and selected pieces, reading of choice extracts, translations from the classics and modern languages, and reviews of literary publications. The meetings occasionally assume a conversational character: interesting anecdotes are related, natural curiosities and relics of 'old times' are shown, and chemical experiments are performed; and the members are always free to ask for information or to make critical remarks.

"The practice of inviting strangers to deliver occasional addresses and lectures before the society originated about twelve years since, and has been continued to the present time, with marked benefit to the members.

"The return of every anniversary of the association is always an event of some importance throughout our village, it being celebrated with a variety of performances appropriate to the time. Considerable preparation is made for these exhibitions, which usually include orations, essays, dialogues, and dramas, mostly original, together with songs and glees, or instrumental music. Of late years a small fee has been charged for admittance, and with the funds thus realized additions are regularly made to the library.

"Until 1834 the meetings of the association were held in an old schoolhouse which afforded very inadequate accommodations, the library being crowded into the space of a few feet, called the 'lobby,' in one corner of the room. By private subscription among the members, and a generous arrangement with the proprietors of the 'academy' building, the free use of a spacious and convenient hall was secured so long as the society might choose to occupy it. The room is neatly furnished, and, as the library can now be displayed to advantage, it presents quite an imposing appearance. The number of books has increased to 434, exclusive of several printed essays and documents; and of these about 75 volumes have been received from different members within a few years past. For a short time a regulation was in force allowing a person to join the society for one year on payment of fifty cents, but it has since been repealed. The actual number of life members is now 270. Since its organization 802 weekly and monthly meetings have been held, their interest being very uniformly sustained, and only twice have they been suspended for a longer period than usual. The young men of the village, either clerks, apprentices, students, or teachers, are generally its active members, the oldest and most capable of them being intrusted with the management of its affairs. Possessing a respectable library and a surplus in the treasury, the future success of the association alone depends upon the persevering efforts of its friends.

"HORACE G. WILLIAMS.

"UPPER MIDDLETOWN, *Conn., July* 11, 1850."

NEW HAVEN.

Yale College Libraries—50,481 *vols.*—In the year 1700, ten of the principal ministers met at New Haven and formed themselves into a society, and agreed to form a college in the colony. At their next meeting, which was at Branford, the same year, each of them brought a number of books, and, presenting them to the society, said: "*I give these books for the founding of a college in this colony.*"

Bishop Berkeley, about 1733, sent to the library from Europe "the finest collection of books that ever came together at one time into America." Sir Isaac Newton, Sir Richard Steele, Drs. Burnet, Woodward, Halley, Bently, Kennet, Calamy, Edwards, the Reverend Mr. Henry, and Mr. Whiston, presented their own works to the library.

The growth of the library till 1845 was very gradual. In that year a very large and valuable accession, selected and purchased in Europe by Professor Kingsley, gave to the library a new and vigorous impulse, and placed it among the best collections of books in this country.

It contained January 1, 1849, 20,515 volumes, including duplicates, of which there may be 200 to 300 volumes. The number of pamphlets is probably 3,000. The library contains also a few MSS., charts and engravings—not easy to specify in numbers. The MSS. bequeathed by President Stiles are in about 40 volumes. For the last ten years about 900 to 1,000 volumes have been added annually. During the same period the average annual expenditure for the purchase of books has been $1,620. There is a permanent fund of $27,000 for the increase of the library, yielding annually $1,620. In 1845-'6 a building was erected for the use of the College Library and the three society libraries. The material is red sandstone from Portland, Connecticut. The total cost, when stone steps and pinnacles are added, will be near $40,000. The books are arranged on the shelves according to subjects, as far as may be conveniently practicable. The books are not numbered. Catalogues were printed in 1743, 1755, 1791, 1808; the last (102 pp. 8vo.) in 1823. The library is opened every day in the year (except Sundays and three or four public days) in term time from 10 a. m. to 1 p. m., and from 3 to 5 p. m., and in summer commonly an hour or two more: in vacation, every day from 3 to 5 hours. The persons entitled to the use of the books are, the professors, members of the professional schools of the college, and members of the senior and junior classes. Seniors and juniors pay a small charge—others pay nothing. The privileges of the library are granted to many literary and scientific persons in town. Books are lent out, but consultation in the library is encouraged in preference. The number drawn out yearly, not known. The number actually out on one day when an examination was made, April 2, 1849, was 541. The term of loan is one month, except to the officers of the college, who frequently retain books until the general return in August. The number of visitors from curiosity and study is, in fair weather, large. The number of consulters may vary from five to fifteen daily. In answer to the question, Have the books been injured at any time by insects? Mr. Herrick remarks: "The *Lepisma saccharina* is common; brought in, probably, by old books. I cannot discover that it eats much. In my own library, at home, two books have been injured by some boring beetle or its larva, (probably a species of anobium,) so that I cannot doubt that books in our public libraries need examination once a year, at least, with reference to this matter." Books are lent to persons at a distance on application to the library committee, and without charge. For two or three years past books have been constantly out of town under this regulation. Edward C. Herrick, librarian.

See also American Quarterly Register, vol. 8, p. 14: Boston, 1836: 8vo.

Medical Library—900 vols.

Law Library—1,900 vols.

In the same building with the College Library, but in separate apartments, are the libraries of the three literary societies of the college, viz: the Linonian, Brothers in Unity, and Calliopean.

Statistics January 1, 1849:

	No. of vols. by actual count.	Average No. of vols. added per year for ten years past.	No. of volumes drawn out per annum.
Linonian Society - -	10,646	440	11,530
Brothers in Unity Society -	10,500	430	about the same.
Calliopean Society - -	6,020	170	about 5,000

The society libraries are opened statedly every day (or nearly) in term time for about 35 minutes, ending at 2 p. m. Each society librarian has usually three or four assistants. The librarian is selected from the senior class; the assistants are from the lower classes.

The last catalogue of the library of the Linonian Society, printed November, 1846, contains 274 pages 8vo. It has the following preface:

"The Linonian Society was founded in September, A. D. 1753. To the members of the society of the class of 1769, and of the classes immediately following, we are indebted for the foundation of the library. In the records of the society at that time is found a vote of thanks to Timothy Dwight, Nathan Hale, and James Hillhouse, for the first contribution of books.

"From the records and catalogues we are enabled to show the number of volumes at different periods. In 1770 there are stated to be nearly 100 vols.; 1780, 152 vols.; 1790, 330 vols.; 1800, 475 vols.; 1811, 724 vols.; 1822, 1,187 vols.; 1831, 3,505 vols.; 1837, 5,581 vols.; 1841, 7,500 vols. The present catalogue numbers 10,103 volumes.

"It has been attempted to adapt the present catalogue to general convenience. To this end it has been made as accurate and systematic as possible; each book is inserted under the name of the author, as far as could be ascertained, and again under the most prominent word of the title. The classified index will afford a view of the resources of the library in the respective departments therein designated."

The last catalogue of the library of the Brothers in Unity, containing 224 pages 8vo., was published in April, 1846. The following is the preface:

"The library of the society of Brothers in Unity is located in the north wing of the new College Library-building, and numbers at the present time 9,140 volumes.

"The oldest catalogue which we have seen, (probably the oldest in existence,) is a manuscript originally prepared by Judge Baldwin of this city, and by him lately presented to the library. Judge Baldwin was librarian of the class of 1781, thirteen years subsequent to the formation of the society. This valuable relic contains a list of only 163 volumes—but those carefully selected standard works. The library was at that time kept in a private room, and jealously closed against all except *members*. A collection of the printed catalogues, nearly if not quite complete, is to be found in the library of the college. It appears from these, that from 1808 to 1825 the various societies issued joint catalogues. The number of volumes in the Brothers library, at various periods since 1808, is as follows: 1808, 723 vols.; 1811, 756 vols.; 1814, 860 vols.; January, 1818, 937 vols.; September, 1822, 1,187 vols.; November, 1825, 1,730 vols.;

April, 1829, 2,550 vols.; September, 1832, 3,562 vols.; January, 1835, 4,565 vols.; June, 1838, 6,078 vols. It will be seen from this table that it has increased with much greater rapidity within the last few years than at any former period.

"The present catalogue differs in several respects from those which have preceded it. The list of authors has been very much increased—completed, so far as time would allow—and inserted in the body of the work. The whole has been rewritten, and in very many cases the titles of books given with greater distinctness. The index has also been rendered more perfect by the addition of three or four new divisions. Books can, therefore, be found almost invariably under the *name of the author*, usually also under the most prominent word of *their own title*, and finally under their appropriate subject in the index."

The Calliopean Society published a catalogue (94 pages 8vo.) on the same general plan as the others in February, 1846.

All these catalogues are well prepared, and elegantly printed. The libraries themselves are of great value. The societies are conducted with remarkable spirit. To the Brothers Society we are indebted for the publication of a very useful work, prepared by William Frederick Poole, entitled "An Alphabetical Index to subjects treated in the Reviews, and other Periodicals, to which no indices have been published; prepared for the library of the Brothers in Unity, Yale College. New York, Putnam, 1848: 154 pages 8vo."

Library of the Young Men's Institute—3,800 *vols.*

NEW YORK.

ALBANY.

State Library—23,274 *vols.*—Founded in 1818 It is in two departments, *the Law Library* and *the Miscellaneous Library*, containing—

Law Library—Law	5,825 vols.	
Statute law	1,253	
State papers	2,792	
		9,870 vols.
Miscellaneous library		13,353 vols.
Maps, atlases, &c., bound in volumes		51
Maps		97
Engravings		299
Painting and busts		4
Medals		25
Total		23,699

There is also a large collection of manuscripts connected with the history of the State, most of which have lately been received from the office of the Secretary of State, from which they were transferred to the State Library in pursuance of a joint resolution of the senate and assembly. A separate catalogue of these, forming 55 pp. 8vo., was printed in 1849, being No. 148 of the Assembly documents. Some of these manuscripts are of great interest and value. Among them are the original charter, or grant, of Charles II to his brother, the Duke of York, of this State, amongst others, in 1664; several royal commissions, of which the oldest is that of William and Mary, in 1689, constituting Henry Sloughter captain general of the province of New York; oaths of allegiance and office, extending from 1698 to 1810; certificates of entry for land and land patents; rolls of laws passed by the legislature of the province, &c.

The following appropriations have been made for the State Library since its foundation, in 1818, for the purchase of books, maps, charts, &c.:

1818 ($3,000 for books and fitting up rooms, &c.)	$1,500 00
1819 (annual appropriation)	500 00
1820 (annual appropriation)	500 00
1821	500 00
1822	500 00
1823	675 00
1824	500 00
1825	1,500 00
1826	1,300 00
1827	1,000 00
1828	1,000 00
1829	1,300 00
1830	801 44
1831	562 78
1832	1,645 44
1833	1,399 51
1834	1,236 38
" Globes	60 00
" 1st vol. Audubon	220 00
1835	1,240 93
" 2d vol. Audubon	220 00
1836	1,972 25
1837	1,219 39
" 3d vol Audubon	200 00
1838	611 51
1839	1,309 32
1840	1,006 43
"	163 49
" 4th vol. Audubon	200 00
1841	3,148 60
"	680 13
"	13 00
1842	2,560 91
"	155 83
1843	1,500 00
1844	3,972 53
1845	3,560 37
" Warden library	4,000 00
1846	3,328 64
1847	3,584 91
1848	4,347 18
1849	4,800 00
	62,995 97

The value of the donations to the library has been estimated by Dr. T. Romeyn Beck, secretary of the trustees, as follows:

Previous to 1844	$1,000
During 1844	253
1845	1,215
1846	1,915
1847	2,068
1848	800
1849	2,250
	9,501

"If to these we add the hundreds of volumes of laws, journals, documents, and law reports; the copies of the Natural History of New York, of the Journals of the Provincial Congress, &c., &c., presented by the State itself to the library, the total amount will considerably exceed ten thousand dollars."

Respecting the general character of the collection the select committee of the assembly on the library say, in their report dated February 3, 1849: "We feel constrained to say that we have been surprised and gratified to find such completeness in some of the departments, and the whole to be of such great value. An examination will convince all that it has become a worthy object of State pride. Already the law department is considered the most perfect of any similar collection in the States. It is believed, also, that nowhere can be found so many useful works on America and American affairs. The most unwearied pains have been taken; Europe and this country have been ransacked to procure everything valuable in this department. The value of these books cannot be estimated in money, for money could not replace very many of them. There are, also, valuable scientific, statistical, documentary, and miscellaneous works, otherwise inaccessible to Americans generally."

This library has, at different times, received large and valuable accessions through the agency of M. Vattemare. Nearly one thousand volumes, mostly in folio and quarto, besides maps, charts, &c., have been thus added to the library.

It is required by law that a catalogue of the State Library be published every five years. The trustees present an annual report to the legislature containing the lists of books added to the library since the previous report. The catalogue published January, 1844, contains two hundred and forty-five pages 8vo. The regents of the university, having been constituted trustees of the State Library by act of the legislature, (passed 4th May, 1844,) requested, in their report, (January 10, 1845,) permission to prepare and print, immediately, a new and improved catalogue. The legislature acceded to their wishes, suspending the enactment requiring quinquennial catalogues.

The catalogue published in 1846 is in two parts, paged separately. Part 1, is the catalogue of the law library, (252 pages 8vo.,) prepared by John L. Tillinghast: Part 2, catalogue of the miscellaneous library, (294 pages 8vo.,) prepared by George Wood. Pages 214-252 contain a minute and carefully prepared descriptive catalogue of the publications of the Record Commission of Great Britain. A new edition, dated January 1, 1850, has been printed. It contains 1,058 pages large 8vo., in parts. The first part, (245 pages) is an alphabetical catalogue of the law books, registered with the necessary fulness, under the names of the authors. The second part, in 35 pages, double columns, is a catalogue or index of the same books, arranged according to subjects. The titles of subjects are arranged alphabetically. The third part (pages 283-365) contains statute laws and State papers. This includes a list of Congressional documents since the formation of the government, in a tabular form, exhibiting the number and titles of the volumes published at each session of Congress, with the time of the commencement and termination of each session. The fourth part (pages 367-376) is a classification of statute laws and State papers, under nineteen heads, as commerce and navigation, debates, digests, diplomatic correspondence, &c. The fifth and largest part is a catalogue of the miscellaneous works, (pages 377-815) Part sixth is a classification of the miscellaneous works into five leading classes, namely: (1) theology, (2) government and political economy, (3) sciences and the arts, (4) history, (5) belles-lettres, with several subdivisions under each class. Part seventh contains a catalogue of works of art, globes, atlases, maps, plans, painting, engravings, busts, and medals, (pages 909-950.) Appended to these are lists of books received while the catalogue was in press, a list of donations to the State Library from its foundation to January, 1850, and a descriptive list of manuscripts received from the Secretary of State.

"The works in the miscellaneous department of the library, when not anonymous, are *lettered* with the author's name, and a brief title of the work. Each work is arranged on the shelves alphabetically, under the initial letter of the surname of its author. Anonymous works are *lettered* agreeably to their subjects, and placed in like manner under their initial letters. The octavos and smaller sized volumes are disposed on one set of shelves—the quartos and folios separately, on other sets of shelves. There are, however, some few exceptions to this order. Periodical works, such as magazines, registers, and reviews, scientific journals and publications of learned societies, together with the dictionaries, encyclopædias, and gazetteers, and other similar works of repeated reference, are withdrawn from the general arrangement and placed by themselves for more convenient consultation. The Warden collection it was thought advisable to keep, likewise, by itself. The works of this collection had been numbered by Mr. Warden, in his published catalogue, as they followed in his classification. These numbers have been cancelled, the works new numbered in their order in this catalogue, and indicated by the capital letters W. C., with the number. The maps, charts, and atlases have been treated in a somewhat similar manner, and arranged in the catalogue among the other maps and charts. The words *vide* and *see* are used in the catalogue for two distinct purposes: *vide*, when the reference is from one part of the catalogue to another; *see*, when the reference is to the book itself, on the shelves."

The library is open, during the session of the legislature and the courts, from 9 a. m. to 4 p. m., Sundays excepted. On Christmas, New Years, and other holidays, it is open one hour, from 9 to 10 a. m.

It is accessible for reading and consultation to every citizen. The following statutes and regulations of the trustees relate to the use of the library:

Revised Statutes, volume 1, part 1, chapter IX, title 8, *section* 6.—"It shall be the duty of the trustees to provide, in their regulations, that any member of the senate or assembly, during the session of the legislature, or during the sitting of the court for the correction of errors, or of the senate only, shall be permitted, under proper restrictions, forfeitures and penalties, to take to his boarding house, or private room, any book belonging to the library, except such books as the trustees shall determine are necessary always to be kept in the library as books of reference; but no member of the legislature shall be permitted to take or detain from the library more than two volumes at any one time.

Ibid., sec. 7.—"Before the president of the senate, or the speaker of the assembly, shall grant to any member a certificate of the time of his attendance, he shall be satisfied that such member has returned all books taken out of the library by him, and has settled all accounts for fines for injuring such books, or otherwise.

"The trustees hereby declare, agreeably to the provisions of the revised statutes, that the law library, in its most extensive sense, comprehends such books of reference as should always be kept in it; but during the session of the legislature, of the senate, of the court for the correction of errors, and of any court held in the capitol, law books may be taken from the library to any room in the capitol, to be returned on the same day. The librarian shall previously charge each person so taking with the book or books, and a fine of fifty cents shall be imposed for each day's detention beyond the above time. The regulations above ordained, as to loss, injury, or damage of books, shall apply in the present case.

"No books belonging to the law library are to be taken to the miscellaneous library to be read; nor are books, maps, charts, or prints, be longing to the miscellaneous library, to be taken to the law library to be read or examined."

The number of persons consulting the library is said to be very large, but it cannot be accurately stated.

The library is at present in the capitol. It is very inconveniently lodged. The rooms, too, are completely filled. The trustees and the governor of the State recommend the erection of a new building. From the spirit, good judgment and taste manifested in the general arrangements of the trustees, we are led to hope that they will not add yet another to the long and melancholy list of opportunities neglected for giving to the world the plan of a building *suitable* for a public library. The present librarian is Alfred B. Street.

The Assembly Library contains 6,000 to 8,000 volumes. "It is impossible for the librarian, or any one else, to tell the exact number, so long as they are kept in the present manner. All that can be crowded, two rows deep, upon the shelves in the clerk's room, are there. The rest are in the garret of the capitol. This library is increasing very rapidly." The select committee of the assembly on the library (from whose report the above extract is taken) recommend the providing of better accommodations for this collection. It should be remarked that this collection contains several copies of most of the public documents of the State. The number of different works is consequently much smaller than the aggregate number of volumes would seem to indicate.

The Library of the Young Men's Association—4,500 *vols.*—The Young Men's Association for Mutual Improvement, in the city of Albany, was founded on the 13th of December, A. D. 1833. "The plan originally contemplated, and which has been hitherto carried into successful operation, was to furnish, at the cheap rate of two dollars per annum, admission to a news and periodical room, in which all the leading journals and periodicals of the State and nation, and such foreign ones as were deemed proper, should be taken; the privilege of taking books from a library, to which additions are constantly being made of new and valuable publications; attendance upon popular lectures on literary and scientific subjects at least once a week during the winter months, and opportunities for debate during the same period. Such extended means of information, of so varied and practical a character, it is confidently asserted, were never before offered at so cheap a rate." [See introductory remarks to a pamphlet containing the charter, with the rules, &c., of the Young Men's Association in Albany, 1847.]

The association was incorporated by act of legislature, passed March 12, 1835.

The library contained (January, 1848) 4,015 volumes, valued at $3,726 26. There were added during the previous year, by purchase 370 volumes, by donation 24 volumes.

The following summary statement of the affairs of the association, taken from the annual reports of its presidents, from the time of its organization to 1847, is annexed to the pamphlet, before mentioned, containing the charter, &c.:

Year.	No. newspapers taken.	Other periodicals.	Volumes in the library.	Annual increase.	Number of members.
February, 1834	92	23	811	811	614
Do 1835	87	20	917	106	378
Do 1836	84	16	1,169	252	642
Do 1837	80	30	1,369	200	608
Do 1838	80	25	1,711	342	726
Do 1839	91	29	2,205	494	901
Do 1840	85	30	2,244	39	1,036
Do 1841	81	25	2,618	374	1,053
Do 1842	88	31	3,067	449	1,084
Do 1843	78	20	3,208	141	906
Do 1845	68	18	3,323	....	844
Do 1846	76	19	3,616	293	933
Do 1847	76	20	4,015	399	1,204

A catalogue of the library, classified with an alphabetical index, was published in January, 1848. It contains 103 pages 8vo. An earlier catalogue was printed in 1843 The librarian is A. F. Lansing.

Library of the State Normal School—6,858 *vols.*—In the report for 1846 of the executive committee of the State Normal School of New York, established at Albany in 1844, it is stated that "a donation for an educational library has been made to the Normal School, by the executors of the Hon. James Wadsworth, out of certain funds left by that distinguished friend of education, to be disbursed in such manner as would best promote the interests of the schools of the people." This valuable donation has been received, and composes the principal part of the "Miscellaneous Library."

"There are at present 745 volumes in the Miscellaneous Library. The Text Book Library numbers 6,113 volumes."—[Report January 12, 1849.]

With reference to the general character of the books, in the "First Quinquennial Register and Circular of the State Normal School, September, 1849," it is stated: "Besides an abundant supply of text books upon all the branches of the course of study, a well selected miscellaneous library has been procured, to which all the pupils may have access free of charge. In the selection of this library particular care has been exercised to procure most of the recent works upon education, as well as several valuable standard works upon the natural sciences, history, mathematics, &c. The State Library is also freely accessible to all. The library is under the charge of Mr. Webb, one of the teachers of the school, who deserves especial commendation for the care taken by him, in arranging and preserving the books. The Miscellaneous Library now numbers 783 volumes, showing an increase of 38 volumes since the last report. In the Text Book Library there are 4,338 volumes fit for use."—[Annual report for 1850.]

Library of the New York State Agricultural Society—600 *vols.*—This society was organized in February, 1832, and was incorporated the same year. It has gradually been collecting a library, composed mostly of agricultural works, pamphlets and periodicals. During the last year (1848) about 100 volumes were added by purchase, and upwards of 100 by donation. The library is now much used, and the Executive Committee, in their report for 1848, urge that it should be so increased as to contain all the valuable works on agriculture, horticulture, &c., published in this and other countries, both for the benefit of the officers of the society, who are frequently called upon for information, and for the farmer and others interested in agriculture.

Library of the Albany Medical College—2,212 *vols.*—The books are most of them new and in good preservation. Their value is estimated at $5,900.—[Regents' report, 1850.]

Library of the Albany Institute—3,323 *vols.*—The Albany Institute was established in 1828. In 1832, the library consisted of 1,592 volumes, and the museum of 10,444 specimens in natural history. The library at present (1849) contains 3,323 volumes.

AUBURN.

Theological Seminary Library—6,000 *vols.*—This seminary was founded by the Presbyterians, and commenced operations in 1821.

BROOKLYN.

The Library of the United States Naval Lyceum—2,971 *vols.*—The lyceum was founded in 1833, and possesses a library of 2,971 volumes, 478 maps and charts, 531 coins, 49 medals, and 75 engravings. It is open daily from 8 o'clock a. m. to 3 p. m. Members of the lyceum may take books out of the library. Few, however, are taken out. The officers of the station resort to the library for reading. The library is at present under the charge of Dr. Thomas L. Smith, surgeon of the United States navy.

City Library—3,000 *vols.*—Founded and incorporated in 1839. The books (400) of the Hamilton Association have lately been purchased. The whole now occupy a part of the Free Library room of the Brooklyn Institute, but are not merged in the library of the institute. It is hoped that the City Library will be the nucleus of a large and valuable collection. A right in the library costs $25; annual assessment, $3. Persons not owning "rights" may enjoy the privileges of the library on paying $5 per annum. An alphabetical catalogue (80 pp. 8vo.) was published in 1841. The act of incorporation and by-laws are prefixed to the catalogue. The library is under the care of the institute, and no separate librarian is employed.

Youths' Free Library of the Brooklyn Institute—3,028 *vols.*—The institute was founded August, 1823; chartered September, 1824, by the name of the Apprentices' Library Association of Brooklyn; charter renewed April 13, 1843, and name changed to the Brooklyn Institute. The Free Library dates from 1828. The present rate of increase is from 200 to 500 volumes a year. The expenditure for books varies from $50 to $250 a year. Many books are annually worn out by constant use. There is at present no permanent fund for the increase of the library. A part of the rent of the institute rooms is devoted to that purpose. The sum of $5,000 is about to be invested as a permanent fund for the library. A building of granite and brick was erected for a lyceum, at an expense of $30,000. It was sold under mortgage, bought by an individual, and presented to the trustees expressly for a library. It is eighty feet long, fifty feet wide, and three stories high. Four catalogues have been printed since 1829; the last in 1849 (114 pp. 12mo.) The library is open three times a week, for three hours each time, for taking out books, and every evening for consultation. About 30,000 books are taken out each year. The librarians are volunteers, and frequently change.

"Minors of twelve years of age and upwards may have free access to the Youths' Free Library, Brooklyn Institute, subject to the following rules and regulations, viz:

1. "A guarantee will be required for the safe return of all books loaned.

2. "Each reader will be required to purchase a catalogue, at twenty-five cents. The numbers of the books wanted must be legibly marked on the card supplied for that purpose previous to coming to the library.

3. "Books may be returned every week, or kept out two weeks; if kept longer, they must be renewed, or the reader will be fined as follows: each quarto volume 12½ cents, octavo volume 6 cents, duodecimo volume 3 cents per week.

4. "Books lost, defaced, or injured in any way, by being torn, soiled, written in, or leaves turned down, such damage to be paid for by the reader as the librarian may deem proper. If a volume of a set be lost or injured, the whole set to be paid for.

5. "No conversation allowed among the readers in the room during the time of giving out books, and all disorderly conduct in or near the library will forfeit them the use of the books, and also the admission to the lectures. Readers are required to leave the room as soon as they have received their books.

6. "Books marked with an asterisk (*) shall not be taken from the library except by special permission.

7. "No reader can receive a book from the library until he shall have

paid all fines, and made good all damages he may have occasioned, and no book belonging to the library can be lent by the reader to any person out of the dwelling of the reader.

8. "The library will be open for girls every Thursday from 3 to 4 o'clock p. m; for boys every Monday and Saturday evenings—from May to November, from 7 to 9 o'clock; November to May, from 6 to 8 o'clock.

9. "Members of the institute may have the use of the library, subject to the above regulations."

BUFFALO.

Library of the Young Men's Association—6,500 *vols.*—This society was incorporated 3d March, 1837. It has (January, 1849) a library of 6,500 volumes, which is well selected and arranged, and contains many rare and valuable works. The collection in English and American history and literature is very full and valuable. Many of the editions are rare and costly. The library is increasing rapidly—say 400 volumes per annum. It is open daily from 8 a. m. to 9 p. m. There is a separate reading-room for newspapers and periodicals. Most of the leading reviews of the day are subscribed for. A lot of ground has been purchased in the city for the purpose of erecting thereon a suitable building for its purposes, and the executive committee are now engaged in raising the means to erect the same; the estimated cost of the lot and building being about $14,000.

The number of volumes drawn from the library during the past year (1848) is 14,200; being an increase of 3,600 volumes over the preceding year. Of the volumes thus read, 38 per cent. were works of fiction; 36 per cent. history, biography, travels, &c.; 17 per cent. standard literature; and 9 per cent. science.

The number of volumes drawn in each year since the foundation of the association is as follows: 1836, 5,500; 1837, 7,500; 1838, 6,300; 1839, 6,600; 1840, 6,400; 1841, 10,400; 1842, 11,100; 1843, 9,000; 1844, 8,000; 1845, 8,200; 1846, 9,250; 1847, 10,600; and in 1848, 14,200, as before stated.

In 1847 a handsome and convenient catalogue was printed, containing 146 pages 8vo., in two parts. "Part one comprises a complete descriptive catalogue of all books in the library at this date, (except novels and works in foreign languages,) with the names of the authors arranged alphabetically, the arrangement including the first and second letter of each name. All works published anonymously will be found under the head of '*anonymous.*' Part two is a catalogue of the titles of the works comprised in part one, classified according to subjects, and arranged alphabetically. Appended to the catalogue is a list of all works in the library published in foreign languages."

Of the last mentioned class there are but few books, and those mostly medical works in Latin.

Besides the library, the association possesses a cabinet of natural history, containing about 250 mineralogical and geological specimens, a catalogue of which is appended to the thirteenth annual report (1849.) The association also provides an annual course of lectures, free to members; others are charged 12½ cents each lecture. The annual reports are generally printed. The librarian is Phineas Sargent.

The Medical Department of the University of Buffalo possesses a library of 519 volumes, the estimated value of which is $800.—[Regents' report, 1850.]

CLINTON.

Hamilton College Libraries—10,300 *vols.*—The College Library was founded with the college, in 1812, and contains about 3,500 vols. The average annual expenditure for books the last ten years has not exceeded $60. There is no permanent fund, except an income of $50 attached to the department of classical literature. The library room is about 75 feet by 20 feet, in the same building with the chapel. A catalogue was published soon after the college was organized, but it is now out of print. The library is opened on Wednesday and Saturday of each week, between the hours of 12 and 1 o'clock. All persons connected with the college—trustees, officers, and students—are allowed the use of the books gratuitously. Anson J. Upton, librarian.

The Union Society, formed in 1834, has a library of 3,400 vols. The triennial catalogue, printed at Utica in 1847, 55 pages 8vo., contains names of members, catalogue of the library and of the cabinet. The cabinet contains about 4,300 specimens, including minerals, shells, plants, birds, and objects of curiosity; about 250 rare and beautiful Chinese birds were collected for the purpose, and presented by Rev. Dr. Parker of China.

The Phœnix Society, formed ——, has a library of 3,400 vols. The triennial catalogue, published in November, 1847, 61 pages 8vo., contains the names of members, catalogue of books, and of articles in the cabinet.

EAST HAMPTON.

Library Company—563 *vols.*—This library was founded by Dr. Lyman Beecher, in the year 1803, and has been a useful institution. It increases slowly from the proceeds of assessments. Sylvanus Jones, librarian.

FLUSHING.

St. Paul's College Library.—2,800 vols.

FORDHAM.

St. John's College Library, and St. Joseph's Seminary Library—9,500 *vols.*—These two libraries (founded in 1840,) though distinct, are under the same management. St. John's College Library contains 5,500 vols., St. Joseph's Seminary Library 4,000. The latter possesses an illuminated manuscript of the bible, probably of the fourteenth century; the first four pages missing. About 4,000 volumes of the St. John's College Library have been received within the last three years, by donations and the transfer of the library of another institution. This library occupies two rooms—one circular, (18 feet in diameter,) the other oblong, 18 by 30 feet; the books are arranged according to subjects. St. Joseph's Library occupies a room 15 by 30 feet. It contains only works in divinity and kindred sciences. The catalogue is well kept in a folio manuscript, but has not been printed. The libraries are opened daily from morning till night. The faculty and students are allowed the use of the books gratuitously;

books are lent to others on application, when there is prospect of their safe return. Rev. I. Legouais, librarian.

GENEVA.

Geneva College Libraries—6,429 *vols.*—The library commenced with the college, in 1825, and contains about 2,000 vols. and 1,600 pamphlets; and increases at the rate of 70 or 80 vols. yearly, most of which are gifts. A very imperfect catalogue, now out of print, was published some years ago. There is no regular time of opening the library. There is also a library, founded in 1835, connected with the medical department; it contains about 600 volumes, valued at $1,500. A society of under graduates of the college (the Hermæan Society) possesses a library of 3,669 volumes, to which additions are annually made from the proceeds of a tax upon the members. From this library the students are mostly supplied with books, though they are allowed to use the College Library without charge. The Hermæan Library is opened daily for an hour. Joseph M. Clark, A. B , tutor and librarian of the College Library.

HAMILTON.

Madison University Libraries—7,000 *vols.*—This institution was established in May, 1820, by the Baptist Education Society of the State of New York. It was called, till within two or three years, the Hamilton Literary and Theological Institution. "One principal object aimed at by the early conductors of the institution, was to lay the foundation of a good library. Many of the first donations were received in books, and at the end of the seventh annual report we find a 'list of books, &c.' from which we learn that the library contained 450 volumes." [See History of the Hamilton Institution, by Professor J. H. Raymond, in the American Quarterly Register for February, 1843.] Most of the library is owned by the Baptist Education Society of the State of New York. A small portion is owned by the University board. It was begun in 1822, though, for many years, scarcely any additions were made, except by occasional donations, and those small. It contains, at present, 4,900 vols. The books are arranged according to subjects, particular portions of the room being assigned to a particular class, as classical literature, sacred philology, church history, modern languages, &c. Within each section the books are arranged according to their size. There is no printed catalogue. The library is opened for consultation every day at 1½ o'clock, and is kept open until 4 o'clock, except Saturday. Books are drawn three times a week. The students are entitled to the use of the library by the payment of 25 cents per term; the board of trustees, faculty, and clergymen of the place, gratuitously. Books are always lent by the librarian to gentlemen of responsible character who desire them. Books are thus occasionally lent to persons at a considerable distance. Professor A. C. Kendrick, librarian.

Students' libraries, 2,100 volumes.

HARTWICK.

Theological Seminary Library—1,000 *vols.*—This is a Lutheran institution, and was incorporated in 1815.

HUDSON.

The Franklin Library—1,058 *vols.*—The Franklin Library Association was incorporated in April, 1838. Its library contains 1,058 volumes. It has also a philosophical apparatus. The library is open every Saturday evening from 7 to 9 o'clock. The members pay two dollars a year for the use of the library, and for all the privileges of the institution. The executive committee have power to extend the use of the library to others. During the summer, about 35 books per week are lent out; during winter, about 70 per week. J. C. Newkirk, corresponding secretary. A catalogue, with the by-laws, was printed in 1849, containing 21 pp. 12mo.

NEWBURG.

Library of the Theological Seminary of the Associate Reformed Church—3,230 *vols.*—This seminary was incorporated in 1835. The library of the Associate Reformed Church was founded in 1802, and contains 3,230 volumes, and some manuscripts. The only considerable accession during the last ten years was the donation of the Rev. R. Forrest, containing 855 volumes. A catalogue, 16 pages 8vo., was printed in 1848. The library is open for one hour on Thursday of every week in term time, and the use of it is free to all persons connected with the institution. H. Connelly, librarian.

NEW YORK CITY.

Mercantile Library Association—31,674 *vols.*—Founded in 1820. The library contained January 1, 1850, 31,674 volumes; a respectable cabinet of specimens in geology and mineralogy; also a small collection of curiosities, belonging to the association. The yearly average number of volumes added to the library, for the last ten years, is 1,561. The yearly average expenditure for books, during the same period, is $2,126 58. A brick building was erected for the association in 1830, at a cost of $53,000. It is 50 feet by 90 feet. The rooms appropriated to the use of the association are upon the 2d and 3d stories. The library, lecture room, and directors' room, are on the 2d floor; the reading-rooms and conversation room on the 3d floor. There is no systematic arrangement of the books according to subjects. The books are placed in alphabetical order, separating languages and fiction, and dividing according to size. The alphabetical arrangement has been adopted solely on account of its practical convenience. Catalogues were printed as follows: 1st, in 1825, in 12mo.; 2d, in 1828, in 12mo.; 3d, in 1830, in 8vo.; 4th, in 1834, in 8vo.; 5th in 1837, prepared by Edward Johnston, esq., in 8vo., and supplement in 1840; 6th, alphabetical, with a classified index, in 1844, 300 pp. 8vo.; another is in preparation. The library is open every day from 10 o'clock a. m. to 10 o'clock p. m., except Sundays and holidays. Merchants' clerks are entitled to the use of the library, on subscribing the constitution and paying an initiation fee of $1, and $1 for the first six months. Merchants and others are admitted on the payment of an annual subscription of $5, but are not eligible to office. More than 75,000 volumes are lent out annually! About 6,000 persons annually consult the library without taking away books. S. Hastings Grant, librarian.

From reports of the directors we gather the following additional facts:

"The first public meeting of merchants' clerks, for the purpose of considering the expediency of establishing a library and reading-room, was held on the 9th of November, 1820. A subsequent meeting was held on the 27th of the same month, at which a constitution was adopted, and the first officers elected. An appeal was made to the public for money and books; and clerks were invited to become subscribers. The library was opened February 12, 1821, in a room at No. 49 Fulton street, and contained, at that time, 700 volumes. The number was increased before the year expired to 1,000 volumes. The number of subscribers was 175.

"The institution, during the early years of its existence, encountered a good deal of hostility from a class of short-sighted and narrow-minded merchants, who fancied their clerks could not devote their whole souls to their business if they were allowed the recreation which the library furnished. In 1825 special efforts were made to sustain and increase the usefulness of the institution; within six months, more than 200 additional members were obtained, and subscriptions of money were raised to the amount of $795, besides many valuable books. During this year the first catalogue was issued. The next year, 1826, the library was removed to more spacious apartments in Cliff street, and a reading-room was established.

"In 1827 lectures were established, which have since become one of the most popular and useful parts of the plan of the establishment. In February, 1828, at a meeting of prominent merchants, interested in the success of the institution, it was agreed to raise, by subscription, a sum sufficient for the erection of a building for the permanent accommodation of the library. The contributors formed themselves into a company called the Clinton Hall Association. The sum of $33,500 was raised during the year in sums varying from $1,000 to $100. A building was erected on the corner of Beekman and Nassau streets, and, under the name of Clinton Hall, was dedicated on the 2d of November, 1830, with appropriate ceremonies, to literature, science, and the arts. The entire cost of the land and building was about $55,000. This left an indebtedness of $21,500, secured by a mortgage which has been gradually reduced to $4,000, which the net income of two years, arising from rents of rooms not occupied by the association, will more than cancel. The Clinton Hall Association stands in the relation of guardian to the Mercantile Library Association; the latter being assured of a full and perpetual ownership in the building as effectually as if the title were in its own coporate name. On the removal of the library to the new building, it numbered 6,000 volumes.

"In 1830 the trustees of Columbia College conferred upon the institution two scholarships, and in 1848 the University of the city of New York placed two foundations at the disposal of the directors of the association.

"The class department originated with the board of 1838, and has been in active operation every succeeding year. Up to January, 1850, 1,281 members have received instructions in the following branches: French language, 629; Spanish, 173; German, 93; Italian, 11; book-keeping, 125; penmanship, 89; chemistry, 48; music, 48; elocution, 43; drawing, 11; mathematics, 11."

The twenty-ninth annual report, presented January, 1850, contains the following table, exhibiting—

Annual additions of members and books, expenditures for books, total receipts, &c., from the 9th of November, 1820, to 1st January, 1850.

Years.	Members admitted.	Volumes added.	Expended for books.	Expended for binding.
1820 } 1821 }	204	1,000	$600 00	......
1822	76	250	150 00	......
1823	81	100	273 00	......
1824	77	175	208 00	......
1825	257	675	619 00	$73 00
1826	471	1,000	756 72	190 28
1827	360	1,200	695 12	31 38
1828	295	1,000	330 27	146 25
1829	414	600	562 30	154 28
1830	486	600	567 91	99 25
1831	507	750	1,177 19	68 44
1832	383	864	1,107 36	197 55
1833	382	1,397	1,303 98	224 20
1834	393	1,090	1,278 20	223 29
1835	680	1,522	2,126 32	238 51
1836	867	1,845	2,286 74	250 70
1837	936	2,547	2,806 47	186 04
1838	1,003	2,471	3,115 72	423 91
1839	1,097	3,583	4,278 23	729 60
1840	501	390	1,995 19	615 42
1841	627	1,136	1,495 12	591 75
1842	308	1,252	2,179 79	670 77
1843	252	465	797 90	536 85
1844	387	745	708 35	271 25
1845	582	1,428	1,628 60	402 65
1846	609	1,883	2.072 59	500 34
1847	687	2,258	3,311 95	549 19
1848	681	2,276	3,392 71	445 52
1849	1,013	2,517	3,531 83	600 35
	14,616	37,019	45,356 56	8,420 77

The directors add: "This account does not show the full value of our literary property. The donations of books, in a period of 29 years, are worth several thousands of dollars. There has been, it is true, a loss by wear and decay of some 6,000 volumes, but these are mainly of trifling value, consisting chiefly of novels, not deemed worthy the expense of rebinding, even in the cheap style necessary to their preservation. Most of the standard books originally purchased or presented, are still preserved in good order."

The institution has lately received a legacy of $3,000 from Miss Elizabeth Demilt, said to have been the first bequest ever made to this library.

The New York Society Library—35,000 *vols.*—(346 and 348 Broadway.) The trustees of the New York Society Library were incorporated the 2d of April, 1754. The establishment was engrafted upon the "Public Library of New York," founded in 1700. (See Grahame's United States' Minutes of the Common Council of New York, &c.) Grahame says, "a library was founded under the government of Lord Bellamont, in 1700."

A copy of Clarendon's History of the Rebellion, marked "Public Library of New York, 1811," is now in the Society Library.

In 1729 the Rev. Dr. Millington, rector of Newington, England, bequeathed his library to the society for the Propagation of the Gospel in Foreign Parts. By this society the library of Dr. Millington was presented to the corporation of the city, for the use of the clergy and gentlemen of New York, and the neighboring provinces. The New York Society Library was founded in the year 1754, having for its object, as expressed in the original articles of association, "the use and ornament of the city, and the advantage of an intended college."

Smith's History of New York thus adverts to the subject: "In 1754 a set of gentlemen undertook to carry about a subscription towards raising a public library, and in a few days collected near 600 pounds, which were laid out in purchasing about 700 volumes of new, well chosen books," &c.

The library of the corporation above alluded to, appearing to have been mismanaged, and at length entirely disused, the trustees of the New York Society Library offered to take charge of it, and to deposite their own collection with it in the City Hall. This proposal having been acceded to by the corporation, the institution thenceforward received the appellation of "The City Library"—a name by which it was commonly known for a long time.

On this foundation the library increased and prospered. In 1772 a charter was granted to it by the colonial government, and the official style of "The New York Society Library" was adopted. The war of the Revolution, however, which soon after occurred, interfered with these pleasing prospects. The city fell into the possession of the enemy. The effect on all our public institutions was more or less disastrous, and to the library nearly fatal. An interval of no less than fourteen years here occurs in the history of the society. At length it appears from the minutes, that "the accidents of the late war having nearly destroyed the former library, no meeting of the proprietors for the choice of trustees was held from the last Tuesday of April, 1774, until Saturday, 21st December, 1788, when a meeting was summoned, and the operations of the society were resumed. In 1789 the original charter was revived, and the society commenced almost a new collection of books. In 1793 a building was begun for the library in Nassau street. In this year the first catalogue of the books, with the charter, names of members of the society, &c., was printed, in 99 pp. 8vo. The library is said to have contained, at this time, 5,000 volumes. In 1813 the second catalogue was published. The library then comprised about 13,000 volumes. In 1825 a supplement was published. The library then contained about 16,000 volumes. In 1836 the trustees sold the property in Nassau street, and purchased a lot in Broadway, on which they have erected the present edifice.

In 1838, when the last catalogue was printed, the library contained 25,000 volumes.

In the year 1849 the society received a bequest of $5,000 from Miss Demilt.

The library at present (1850) contains 35,000 volumes, a few manuscripts of modern date, maps and charts of great value, a few sheets of ancient church music on vellum, numerous collections of engravings, a small but beautiful collection of bronze medals, one set of casts of the Elgin marbles, forty eight in number, and one set of Waterloo medals, fifty in number. About one thousand volumes are annually added to the library. About two thousand dollars per annum are expended for the purchase of books. There is no permanent fund. The rents of the building, the annual payments and some minor sources, afford about nine thousand dollars annually. The debt, however, is large, and leaves but a limited sum for increase. The persons employed in the service of the library are a librarian, assistant, room keeper, janitor, and a boy. A building was first erected for the library in 1794, previous to which the library was kept in the old City Hall. The present edifice was erected expressly for the library in 1838–'39, at an expense of forty seven thousand dollars for the land and seventy thousand dollars for the building and furniture. The material is brick, with façade and basement, &c., of brown freestone. It fronts on Broadway 60 feet, and extends back 100 feet of uniform width. The principal floor is divided into two large and two small rooms. There is a lecture-room below and a picture-gallery above. The arrangement of the books upon the shelves is according to subjects, "but with as many analogous subjects united as possible, in order to avoid the necessity of a complicated distribution in restoring continually the volumes returned, to their places."

Catalogues of the library are known to have existed before the Revolution, but the dates of their publication are not ascertained. Besides the catalogues of 1793, (99 pages 8vo.) 1813, and supplement 1825, (135 pages 8vo.,) a catalogue was printed in 1838, containing 328 pages 8vo., a supplement in 1841 of 72 pages, and another in 1843 of 24 pages. A new catalogue with the following title has just been published: "Alphabetical and analytical Catalogue of the New York Society Library, with the charter, by-laws, &c., of the institution, 8vo.: New York, 1850." Prefixed to the catalogue are a history of the library; the articles of subscription, 1754; the charter, 1772; acts of legislature, by-laws, names of trustees since 1754, and librarians since 1793; alphabetical catalogue, 491 pages; catalogue of the Winthrop library. (This ancient and curious collection of books was presented by the late Francis B. Winthrop, esq. They were the property of his distinguished ancestor John Winthrop, the founder of Connecticut. It contains about 275 volumes.) An analytical index of 112 pages follows the catalogue. This laborious and valuable work was prepared by Mr. P. J. Forbes, the present librarian. It is very handsomely printed.

The library is open daily, Sundays excepted, from 8 a. m. till sunset; but the reading rooms are open till 10 p. m.

Persons entitled to the use of the library are, members who pay $25 for a right, and then $6 annually, and temporary subscribers at $10 per annum. Strangers may be introduced, for the use of the books, &c., in the rooms, for one month. The number of members in 1793 was nine hundred. The present number is eleven hundred.

Books are lent out, with the exception of very expensive works—those of reference, as encyclopædias, dictionaries, bound newspapers, &c. About 2,000 volumes (nearly 8,000 works) were charged in eight months. About 1,500 persons a year consult the library without taking away books. The trustees have full power to extend the use of the library to persons at a distance. Philip J. Forbes, librarian.

Astor Library—20,000 *vols.*—One of the noblest gifts to learning, of which any city can boast, is that for which not only New York, but this whole country, owes a debt of lasting gratitude to the memory of John Jacob Astor. The munificence of the endowment is only equalled by the judicious, enlightened, and liberal provisions made for its usefulness and perpetuity. Mr. Astor died in 1848.

The Astor Library was endowed by the third codicil to his will, which was dated August 22, 1839, and is in these words:

"I, John Jacob Astor, do make this additional codicil to my last will, bearing date the 4th day of July, in the year of our Lord 1836.

"Desiring to render a public benefit to the city of New York, and to contribute to the advancement of useful knowledge and the general good of society, I do, by this codicil, appropriate *four hundred thousand dollars* out of my residuary estate to the establishment of a public library in the city of New York.

"For this purpose, *I give to my executors four hundred thousand dollars*, to be taken from my personal estate, or raised by the sale of parts of my real estates, to be made by my executors, with the assent of my son, William B. Astor, upon condition and to the intent that the said amount be settled, applied, and disposed of as follows, namely:

"1. In the erecting of a suitable building for a public library.

"2. In furnishing and supplying the same from time to time with books, maps, charts, models, drawings, paintings, engravings, casts, statues, furniture, and other things appertaining to a library for general use, upon the most ample scale and liberal character.

"3. In maintaining and upholding the buildings and other property, and in defraying the necessary expenses of taking care of the property, and of the accommodation of persons cousulting the library.

"The said sum shall be payable one third in the year after my decease; one third in the year following; and the residue in equal sums, in the fourth and fifth years after my decease.

"The said library is to be accessible, at all reasonable hours and times, for general use, free of expense to persons resorting thereto, subject only to such control and regulations as the trustees may from time to time exercise and establish for general convenience.

"The affairs of the institution shall be conducted and directed by eleven trustees, to be from time to time selected from the different liberal professions and employments in life, and the classes of educated men. The mayor of the city of New York, during his continuance in office, and the chancellor of the State of New York, during his continuance in office, shall always be trustees. The vacancies in the number of trustees occurring by death, resignation, incapacity, or removal from the State, shall be filled by persons appointed by the remaining trustees. The acts of a majority of the trustees, at a meeting reasonably notified, shall be valid.

"All the property and effects of the institution shall be vested in the said trustees. They shall have power to direct the expenditure of the funds, the investment, safe-keeping, and management thereof, and of the property and effects of the institution; also, to make such ordinances and regulations, from time to time, as they may think proper, for the good order and convenience of those who may resort to the library, or use the same; also, to appoint, direct, control, and remove the superintendent of the library and all librarians, and others employed about the institution; and, also, they shall have and use all powers and authority for promoting the expressed objects of this institution, not contrary to what is herein expressed.

They shall not receive any compensation for their services, except that if any one of their number shall at any time be appointed superintendent, he may receive compensation as such.

"The trustees shall be subject to the visitation of the proper courts of justice, for the purpose of preventing and redressing all mismanagement, waste, or breach of trust.

[By a subsequent codicil the testator authorized the trustees to select a site on the east side of Lafayette Place, to contain 65 feet front and rear, and 120 feet deep.]

"I further direct, that a sum not exceeding seventy-five thousand dollars may be expended in the erection of a building for the library; one hundred and twenty thousand dollars may be expended in the purchase of books and other objects for the establishing of the library; and the residue shall be invested as a fund for the maintaining and gradually increasing of the library.

"All investment of the funds of the institution shall be made in the public debt of the United States of America, or of the States of the Union, or of the city of New York, as long as such subjects of investment may be had, giving a preference according to the order in which they are named. And in case the income of the fund shall at any time exceed the amounts which the trustees may find useful to expend for the purposes above named and particularized, they may expend such surplus in procuring public lectures to be delivered in connexion with the library, upon useful subjects of literature, philosophy, science, history, and the fine arts, or in promoting in any other mode the objects of the institution, as above expressed. I direct my executors to cause and procure the necessary legal assurances to be made for establishing and securing the application of the funds and property hereby appropriated for the purposes of these presents, and in the mode herein pointed out. And it is my request that the trustees would apply to the legislature of this State for such acts as may fully secure, establish, and perpetuate this institution, and render its management easy, convenient, and safe, both to themselves and the public. And as this property is devoted wholly to public purposes, I trust that the legislature will so far favor the institution as to exempt its property from taxation. And, as a mark of my respect to the following gentlemen, I name them to be the first trustees: that is to say, the mayor of the city of New York and the chancellor of the State for the time being, in respect to their offices; Washington Irving, W. B. Astor, Daniel Lord, junior, James G. King, Joseph G. Cogswell, Fitz Green Halleck, Henry Brevoort, junior, Samuel B. Ruggles, and Samuel Ward, junior.

[By a further codicil the testator appointed Mr. Charles A. Bristed one of the trustees; and also authorized the funds of the library to be invested in bonds, secured by mortgaged improved real estates.]

"In witness whereof, I have set my hand and seal to this codicil, and publish the same as a codicil to my will, this twenty second day of August, in the year of our Lord one thousand eight hundred and thirty-nine.

"JOHN JACOB ASTOR. [L. S.]"

The Trustees of the Astor Library were incorporated by the legislature of the State, 18th January, 1849. The act of incorporation corresponds in all respects with the provisions of Mr. Astor's will, with the following additional provisions:

"The property, real and personal, of the said corporation, shall be exempt from taxation in the same manner as that of the other incorporated public libraries of this State; and it shall be the duty of the said trustees to effect such insurances as can be obtained upon said buildings and library, and other property, against loss by fire or otherwise, and pay the expenses thereof out of the fund described in the fourth subdivision of section second of this act.

"The said trustees shall, in the month of January in every year, make a report to the legislature for the year ending on the 31st day of December preceding, of the condition of the said library, of the funds and other property of the corporation, and of its receipts and expenditures during such year.

"If any debts of the said corporation, lawfully contracted, shall not be paid out of its funds, when due, the trustees shall be individually liable for such funds, to the creditors in such cases, and to such extent as they would be if not incorporated."

From the "Literary World" (September 22, 1849) we take the following description of the building now in progress for the Astor Library. This account was originally published in the New York "Journal of Commerce":

"It will be built in the Byzantine style, or rather in the style of the royal palaces of Florence, and consequently will present a strongly imposing appearance, both in its external and internal structure. Its dimensions will be 120 feet in length by 65 wide, and from the level of the side-walk to the upper line of the parapet its height will be 67 feet; built of brown cut stone, and brick; very little wood will enter into its composition. We are informed that no building in the United States, of this character, will be formed to such a large extent of iron. According to the estimates, the iron-work will form one of the heaviest expenditures. Its uses, too, will be altogether novel, at least in this country, and ingenious. For instance, the truss beams, supporting the principal weight of the roof, will be constructed of cast-iron pipes, in a parabolic form, on the same plan with the iron bridges in France and other parts of Europe, with a view to secure lightness and strength.

"The library hall, which will occupy the second floor of the edifice, will be a truly elegant apartment, 100 feet in length by 60 wide in the clear. The ascent from the front will be by a single line of thirty-eight Italian marble steps, decorated on either side at the entrance by a stone sphinx. Upon nearing the summit of these steps the visitor finds himself near the centre of this immense alcove, surrounded by 14 brick piers, plastered and finished in imitation of Italian marble, and supporting iron galleries midway between the floor and the ceiling. The side walls from 'pit to dome' form one continuous shelving of a capacity sufficient for 100,000 volumes. This is reached by means of the main gallery, in connexion with which are four iron spiral stairways, (one from each corner of the building,), and an intervening gallery of a lighter and smaller description, also connected by its staircases, eight in number, with the main gallery. The whole are very ingeniously arranged, and appropriately ornamented in a style corresponding with the general architecture of the building. At an elevation of 51 feet above the spectator is the principal sky-light—54 feet long by 14 broad, and formed of thick glass set in iron. Besides this are circular side sky-lights of much smaller dimensions. All needful light is thus furnished, in connexion with the windows in the front and rear walls. Free ventilation is also had by means of iron fret-work inserted in suitable portions of the ceiling. In the extreme rear are the two librarians' rooms, to which access is had by means of the main galleries.

"The first floor will contain the lecture and reading-rooms, with accommodations for 500 persons. The latter are located on each side of the building, and separated from the library hall stairway at the front entrance by two corridors leading to the rear vestibule, and from thence to the lecture room, still further in the rear. The basement contains the keeper's rooms, cellars, coal vaults, hot-air furnaces, &c. The floors are composed of richly wrought mosaic work, resting on iron beams.

"The library building in its exterior, especially as seen from the street, will present an appearance at once grand and imposing. The basement story will be faced with high rustic ashler, projecting six inches, thus imparting an extremely bold relief. The window frames are placed near the inside line of the wall, forming deep recesses, in order to secure the same effect. These consist primarily of six, occupying the central portion and admitting light to the library hall, placed three above and three below a given point—the upper connected with the lower by columns supported by figures representing the genii of literature. Between these sets of windows is inscribed 'Astor Library, 1849.' The remaining windows are two in number, one on either side of the entrance, and connected with the lecture room.

"The amount authorized to be expended in the erection of the building is $75,000, and the contract is made within this sum—of course, exclusive of furniture and shelving. The latter will cost probably $8,000. Two years it is expected will be required to complete it. The architect is Mr. Alexander Saeltzer, from Berlin, a pupil of the celebrated Schinkel. The entire appropriation for the library and building is $400,000, of which about one-half is to be funded for the benefit of the library, thus insuring to it a perpetuity such as similar institutions but seldom possess. Through the efforts of Mr. J. G. Cogswell, in England and on the continent, about 20,000 volumes have been collected, and are now in his keeping at No. 32 Bond street, where they are accessible to visitors, though the public are not generally aware of the fact."

The excellent management of this admirable institution is, we presume, mainly due to the learning, energy, and practical good judgment of the librarian, Joseph Green Cogswell, LL. D. At his suggestion an early appropriation was made for the purchase of books, at a time when the revolutions of Europe offered the best opportunity that has ever occurred to buy books cheap. The result is seen in the opening of the library with a superb collection of 20,000 volumes, purchased at probably one-half, or perhaps one-quarter of the price that they would have commanded at other times.

Library of the New York Historical Society—17,000 *vols.*—This society was founded in 1804: incorporated in 1809. Its library (January 4, 1849) contained:

Printed books and pamphlets - - -	15,000
Bound volumes of newspapers - -	1,395
MSS., original letters, papers, &c. - -	15,000
Maps and charts - - - - -	2,100
Engravings, several hundred—say - -	400

Medals, about - - - - - - 200
Coins, about - - - - - - 1,400

Also an extensive collection of Indian relics, curiosities, &c.; also, a collection of portraits, busts, &c.

As nearly all the additions are from donations, it is difficult to ascertain, from the records, the yearly average increase. The number added during the year 1848, (printed books and pamphlets,) was 1,290. From one to two hundred dollars are annually expended for the purchase of books. The society has no funds; the library is supported by annual subscriptions of its members. The society occupies leased rooms in the University of the city of New York. A catalogue, prepared by Rev. Timothy Alden, and the only one printed, was published in 1813, 139 pp. 8vo. A complete catalogue has recently been prepared, and is soon to be put to press. The library is open daily from 10 until 2 in the morning, and from 4 to 6 in the evening, in summer, and from 7 to 9 in winter. Members of the society, and persons introduced by members, are entitled to the use of the books. Books are only to be consulted in the library. The yearly average number of persons consulting the library is estimated at five hundred. Jacob B. Moore, librarian.

Since the above account was written, Mr. J. B. Moore has been appointed postmaster in San Francisco, and has left his charge in New York. His son, George H. Moore, has succeeded him as librarian. The sum of thirty-five thousand dollars has already been obtained for the erection of a suitable building for the meetings of the society, and the preservation of its valuable collections. Of this sum, five thousand dollars were from a bequest of Miss Elizabeth Demilt, of New York, received in 1849. Mr. James Lenox subscribed five thousand dollars.

Library of the Union Theological Seminary—17,000 *vols.*—The library of this institution was founded in 1838. It is sometimes called, by courtesy, "The Van Ess Library," as having been purchased of the Rev. Leander Van Ess, of Germany. It contains about 17,000 volumes, mostly theological. About 700 volumes were added in 1847 by gift, and others occasionally in like manner. The average annual increase cannot be stated. The library occupies a hall in the seminary building, No. 9 University Place. The room is a parallelogram, about 65 feet in length, much broken by windows and badly contrived. The books are arranged on the shelves according to size. There is only a MS. catalogue. The library is opened each week day, except Saturday, from 10 o'clock a. m. to 3 or 4 p. m.; closed from the 3d Wednesday in June to the 3d Wednesday in September. Persons entitled to the use of the library are: all connected with the seminary, and those who may have permission from a professor. The books are lent out. Of the number no estimate can well be made. Rev. Edward Robinson, D. D., librarian.

Columbia College Library—12,740 *vols.*—Columbia College received its charter in 1754. The library was founded about the year 1757. About this time Mr. Joseph Murray "bequeathed to the college property worth about £8,000, including his library." Rev. Dr. Bristowe, of London, also bequeathed his library of about 1,500 volumes. From these sources, from purchases, from presents by the Earl of Bute and others, and from the University of Oxford, the college was in possession of a considerable library; when, on the 6th of April, 1776, the treasurer of the college was ordered to prepare it in six days for the reception of troops. "The students were in consequence dispersed, the library and apparatus were deposited in the City Hall or elsewhere, and the college edifice was converted into a military hospital. Almost all the apparatus, and a large proportion of the books belonging to the college, were wholly lost to it in consequence of this removal; and of the books recovered, 600 or 700 were so only after about thirty years, when they were found, with as many belonging to the New York Society library, and some belonging to Trinity Church, in a room in St. Paul's chapel, where, it seemed, no one but the sexton had been aware of their existence, and neither he nor anybody else could tell how they had arrived there." [See Moore's Historical Sketch of Columbia College, page 62.] In 1792 "a large addition to the College Library was made by a grant of money obtained from the legislature. In 1813 the college purchased the library of Professor Kemp. In 1838 it purchased the library of Professor Moore, who was 'employed for about a year in making a new arrangement and a catalogue of the whole library.'" The library contains (1849) 12,740 volumes, exclusive of pamphlets, which, if bound, would form about 500 volumes more. A single Egyptian papyrus, several volumes of engravings, a series of 48 bronze medals illustrative of the Elgin marbles, and two marbles bearing Greek inscriptions, though of little interest, belong to the library. About 120 volumes have been added annually for the last ten years, and about $200 expended annually for the purchase of books. The library room is 44 feet by 26; and has, both on its lower floor and gallery, five alcoves on each side, lighted by as many windows. There is no printed catalogue. The library is opened twice a week while the college is in session, and from one to three o'clock p. m. each time. The officers of the college and the students of the three higher classes use the library, and without charge. Books are lent out, about six hundred annually. The yearly average number of persons consulting the library without taking out books is about one hundred and ten. Lefroy Ravenhill, librarian.

The Apprentices' Library—14,000 *vols.*—The General Society of Mechanics and Tradesmen (Nos. 32 and 34 Crosby street) was founded A. D. 1785. The Apprentices' Library, established in 1820 by this society, contains about 14,000 volumes, kept for the gratuitous use of the apprentices of the city. [New York State Register, 1845, page 319.]

Library of the Theological Institute of the Episcopal Church—10,000 *vols.*—The American Almanac, for 1850, gives the date of the foundation of this institution as 1817, and states the number of volumes in its libraries to be 10,000.

Library of the New York Hospital—6,000 *vols.*—The Society of the New York Hospital, New York city, was founded in 1770, and incorporated June 13, 1771. The following account of its library is taken from a pamphlet, published in 1846, containing the charter, laws, &c., of the society, and of the Bloomingdale Asylum, page 68:

"Upon the recommendation of the medical faculty of Columbia College, the governors of the hospital, in August, 1796, appropriated the sum of $500 towards the purchase of a *medical library*, to which the members of that faculty contributed books from their private libraries, and part of their fees of public instruction. A hospital library was thus instituted, which was further augmented by the purchase of the medical library of the late

Dr. Romayne, in 1800, and by the accession, in 1805, of the library of a private association of physicians, then called 'The Medical Society of New York,' who gave their books on condition that they, and such of their sons as should become practitioners of medicinè in the city of New York, should have free use of the hospital library. In 1805 the governors appropriated the annual sum of $250 for the purchase of books; and other larger additions were afterwards made to it, by special purchases and donations from time to time, amongst which was the valuable botanical library of Dr. Hosack, bought by the hospital.

"For some years past there have been appropriated for the support and increase of this library all the proceeds arising from the sale of tickets to students of medicine, which permit them to see the practice of the house, to attend the clinical instruction, and to take books from the library. The moneys thus accruing are appropriated to the purchase of medical and scientific publications, selected by the library committee, (composed of three governors, one physician, and one surgeon,) to the payment of the librarian's salary, binding, and other contingencies.

"The annual average expenditures and receipts on account of the purchase of books, are now from $500 to $800.

"The library now consists of more than 5,000 volumes, confined entirely to medicine and surgery, and those collateral branches of science (as chemistry, botany, &c.) specially connected with the healing art. It is believed to be as useful and complete in this department as a library can be made in that number of volumes, and contains many of the most splendid and costly works on anatomy and natural history. During the last year the governors have fitted up, in the large hospital building, two spacious apartments, one above the other, communicating by a central spiral staircase, and deposited the library in them, the lower room being used as a reading and consultation chamber."

Books may be lent free of charge to the present or former governors, physicians, surgeons, apothecaries, and other officers of the hospital; to all donors of books (approved by the library committee,) or money to the amount of $25; and to other persons on the payment of $5 a year.

A catalogue of the books (194 pages 8vo.) was published in 1845. It is very well prepared. It is alphabetical, with an alphabetical and analytical index. The present librarian is John L. Vandervoort.

Library of the American Institute—6,000 *vols.*—"The American Institute of the city of New York was organized January, 1828; incorporated May 2, 1829; for the purpose of encouraging and promoting domestic industry. The library contains about 6,000 volumes, mostly works of reference for the mechanic, the manufacturer, the farmer, and the statesman. It is open, free of expense to all strangers and is conducted on more liberal principles than any other library in our country." [New York State Register, 1845, page 320.]

Library of the New York Law Institute—4,424 *vols.*—The New York Law Institute was incorporated February 22, 1830. Its library, composed almost exclusively of law books, contains (1850) 4,424 volumes. Its average increase is about 225 volumes a year. From the commencement of the institution to 1850, the sum of $21,894 had been expended for books, making a yearly average of $1,094 70. The annual income, varying from $1,200 to $1,500, is derived from charges for membership, ($80 for each member.)

The corporation of the city at present furnishes two rooms in the City Hall for the accommodation of the institute. The one used for the library is 50 feet by 56. The conversation room is 18 by 33.

A catalogue was published in 1842, containing 120 pages 8vo. This catalogue, prepared by Lewis H. Sanford, contains also "a chronological list of contemporary English reporters." The library is open daily from 8½ o'clock a m. to 6 p. m. Only those members of the New York bar who belong to the institute are entitled to the use of the books; but those who do not practise law in the city, Kings county, or Jersey City, and strangers generally, are permitted to use the library free of charge. No book is allowed to be taken out of the library except to be used in the different courts in the City Hall. The present librarian is H. S. Dodge, 54 Wall street.

Libraries of the University of the city of New York—4,000 *vols.*—This institution was founded in 1831.

In the American Almanac for 1850 the number of volumes is stated as above. In the report of the regents of the New York University, for 1850, the value of the library of the university is stated to be $7,000.

The Library of the Mechanics' Institute—3,000 *vols.*—The Mechanics' Institute of New York, 105 Bowery, New York city, was founded in the winter of 1830–'31, and incorporated April 24, 1833. The library contains at present about 3,000 volumes. The funds of the institute are derived from assessments of members, school-fairs, exhibitions, lectures, &c. A catalogue of the library was printed in 1835, containing 26 pages 12mo.; and another in 1844, of 64 pages 8vo. The library is open daily, Sundays excepted. Members only are entitled to the use of it; others may be admitted by courtesy. The books are lent out, with the exception of large and valuable works. Edward Henry, actuary and librarian.

"This institution was founded for the purpose of promoting the general diffusion of useful knowledge among the mechanical classes by means of *lectures* on natural and mechanical philosophy and other scientific subjects; by founding a *library* and *museum;* by forming *classes* for mutual improvement; holding *conversational meetings, debates,* and *discussions* for the benefit of its members; by having from time to time *public exhibitions* for the promotion of excellence in the mechanical arts; and by establishing *schools* for educating on the most approved principles, as well as on the most reasonable terms, the apprentices and children of its members. During the brief space of time this institution has existed, all and even more has been accomplished than its deserving founders could reasonably have expected.

"Connected with the library is a reading-room, amply supplied with the most popular and scientific American and foreign periodicals.

"The terms on which persons may become members, and with their families enjoy all the privileges of the library, reading-room, lectures, meetings, debates, classes, exhibitions, school, &c., are: initiation fee, $1, and a yearly payment of $2. Life membership $25."

Printers' Reading-Room and Library—2,500 *vols.*—The New York Typographical Society was instituted in 1809, for the purpose of affording relief to indigent and distressed members and their families, and to other proper objects of charity. In 1818 the society was incorporated; re-chartered in 1832 for fifteen years; and in 1847 incorporated under the general law of the State, enacted in 1848. The members commenced making donations of books to establish a library in 1823; contributions have been made from time to time, and at present the library numbers about 2,500 volumes, comprising many valuable works in nearly every department of literature. The increased interest manifested in the society during the past year has extended to the library. Many valuable donations of books have been received from publishers and others, and the society has been encouraged to procure a suitable room for the library and reading-room, as well as for social intercourse. The success of this commendable project seems now to be fully assured. [See address of Peter C. Baker, printed in "Proceedings at the Printers' Banquet, January 17, 1850:" 8vo: New York. The rooms obtained for library and reading room are at 300 Broadway. Address C. C. Savage, 13 Chambers street.]

Library of the Lyceum of Natural History—1,653 *vols.*—The Lyceum of Natural History, in the city of New York, was founded in 1818. The library contains 1,653 volumes, consisting chiefly of works on natural history, voyages, travels, &c., containing natural history, and the transactions of kindred societies. The lyceum has, also, extensive collections in mineralogy, geology, fossils, conchology, ichthyology, entomology, amphibia, reptiles, radiata, corals, botany, and small collections of birds and quadrupeds. Very few books have been purchased. Nearly all are donations from individuals, or have been received from societies in exchange for the publications of the lyceum. The rooms occupied by the society consist of three large apartments on the 2d floor of the large fire-proof building, No. 659 Broadway, and known as the medical department of the University of the city of New York. The premises are leased, by the lyceum, of the Medical Faculty for the term of ten years. A catalogue of the books was printed in 1825, 8vo.; another in 1836, 72 pp. 8vo.* A new one has been prepared, and will shortly be printed. The library is open every Monday evening, during the meeting of the society. Members have access at any time, on application to the librarian. Books are lent out to members Persons of standing in science, residing at a distance, have, by special vote of the society, been allowed to take out any work from the library. This is seldom done. Any person not a member, wishing to consult the books, can do so on application to the librarian. Robert H. Brownne, 39 Crosby street, librarian.

The American and Foreign Bible Society possesses a library, which, according to the Baptist Almanac for 1850, contains 1,576 volumes.

The College of Physicians and Surgeons in the city of New York possesses a library of 1,200 volumes, valued at $1,500. [Regents' report, 1850.]

The American Ethnological Society, New York city.—The object of the society, thus far, has been the preparation and publication of original memoirs on ethnology. A few hundred pamphlets and books have been presented, a list of which is prefixed to the 2d volume of its transactions. It is intended to form a cabinet at an early day. John Russell Bartlett, secretary.

Free Academy of New York City.—This establishment has but recently commenced operations. Preparations for a library are making, which, it is hoped, may be realized at no distant day. Horace Webster, president.

POUGHKEEPSIE.

Library of the Lyceum of Literature, Science, and Mechanic Arts.—Founded April 6, 1838. Contains about 650 volumes, of which 295 are periodicals and pamphlets; a small collection of manuscripts, maps, charts, engravings; large collections of minerals and natural curiosities. Increases at the rate of about 100 volumes annually. A catalogue in 12mo. was printed in 1845. Open daily from 1 to 8 p. m., Sundays excepted.

The Library of the Lyceum is free to members and their families, to whom books are lent out. The lyceum furnishes the public, gratuitously, with a course of weekly lectures, from distinguished men, during the winter. This has been kept up for several years. J. J. Underhill, R. C. Southwick, C Swan, committee.

The *Public Library* occupies the rooms of the lyceum, and contains over 3,000 volumes.

ROCHESTER.

Athenæum Library—5,050 *vols.*—Founded in 1832. The library contains 5,050 volumes, 18 maps, and a small collection of minerals. A public building has been erected, one half of which is occupied by the athenæum, and the other by the "Library of the Court of Appeals." Above is a splendid hall for lectures, 82 feet by 70, and 27 feet high, called "Corinthian Hall." The library rooms are 80 feet long, 34 feet wide, and 15 feet high.

A catalogue was printed in 1847, (40 pages 8vo.;) another is in press. The library is open every day (Sundays excepted) from 8 o'clock a. m. to 9½ p. m. Any person, by paying one dollar per annum, can become a member of the association. Two books can be taken out on one name, and they are usually kept out from two to four days. About 2,000 per week are thus lent. L. R. P. Stockton, librarian.

Library of the Court of Appeals—Contains 3,400 volumes, of law and miscellaneous books, a part of the old Chancellor's Library of the State of New York.

This is the proper place to notice a publication of great value to the bar of this city, and which deserves to be imitated in other places. It is "A catalogue of law books in the different libraries in Rochester on the 31st August, 1847, with references to the several owners of each, by William F. Liddle. 8vo., 55 pages: Rochester, 1847." This catalogue contains the law-books in 63 private libraries, besides those in the public library. The catalogue is alphabetical, and under each title all the attorneys owning the books are referred to by means of numbers. An index of subjects is appended to the catalogue.

SCHENECTADY.

Union College Libraries—14,526 *vols.*—The college library was founded (with the college) in 1795, and contains 7,776 volumes. The yearly average number of volumes added to the library for the last ten years is 468. The annual expediture for books during the same period is $400 39. An imperfect catalogue, intended merely for present use while the librarian is preparing one more perfect, was printed in 1846, (80 pages 12mo.) The new catalogue is nearly completed. The library is opened twice a week, one hour each time. Officers, students, and resident graduates are entitled to the use of the library. About 2,110 volumes are lent out annually. Jonathan Pearson, librarian.

The societies of under graduates possess 6,750 volumes.

Library of the Young Men's Association—3,200 *vols.*

SOMERS

Public Library—210 *vols.*

TROY.

Library of the Young Men's Association—4,000 *vols.*—This association was founded in 1835. The library contains 4,000 volumes, 18 maps, and 40 engravings. The yearly average increase is about 180 volumes; the average expenditure about $100 per annum. There is a small fund of $1,800, raised by the sale of life-membership tickets, the interest of which goes into the contingent fund for general expenses. The library room is 36 feet by 18, newspaper room 40 by 30, and one room 36 by 18, containing 200 volumes of newspapers bound. A catalogue (32 pages 8vo.) was printed in 1845. The library is open for the delivery of books from 11 to 1 o'clock, and from 7 to 9 in the evening, of every week-day. All members of the association are entitled to free access to the library, at all hours of the day, by an annual payment of $2. Clergymen of all denominations are honorary members, and entitled to all the benefits of the association. Books are lent out to members of the association—about 14,000 annually. About 3,000 persons consult the library annually without taking away books.

The Lyceum of Natural History possesses a library, besides a valuable cabinet.

UTICA.

Library of the Young Men's Association—2,200 *vols.*

WEST POINT.

Library of the United States Military Academy—15,000 *vols.*—This library was founded in 1812, and contains (January 1, 1849) about 15,000 volumes, exclusive of pamphlets.

It has, of manuscripts, 4 volumes.
maps and charts, 100.
music, 4 volumes.
engravings, 55 volumes.
busts, 4.
paintings, (portraits) 10.

Additions to the library since 1838:

In 1838, 250 volumes.	In 1843, 171 volumes.	
1839, 602 "	1844, 50 "	
1840, 159 "	1845, 130 "	
1841, 377 "	1846, 25 "	
1842, 108 "	1847, 50 "	

Average, 192 volumes per annum. Average expenditure, for the last ten years, $838 43. There is no permanent fund for the increase of the library. There is usually an appropriation made by Congress of $1,000 annually for the library, but for the years 1846, 1847, and 1848, no such appropriation was made. The sum of $1,500, however, was given for the fiscal year ending June 30, 1849.

The library occupies one wing of a gneiss building, of the Elizabethan style of Gothic architecture, erected in 1840 and 1841. The remaining portion of the building contains four public offices and rooms for philosophical apparatus; the east tower bearing a transit instrument, the middle one an equatorial telescope, and the west one a mural circle. The cost of the entire building was $50,216 86. The library-room is 46 feet square, with a gallery and two tiers of cases. Height of room 31 feet.

The books are arranged upon the shelves according to subjects—alphabetically under subjects. There are two printed catalogues—the first, August, 1822, 22 pp. 8vo.; the second, 1830, 132 pp. 8vo.; and one in manuscript, nearly complete, will probably be printed soon. The library is open daily, Sundays excepted, between 8 and 12 a. m., and between 1 p. m. and sunset. Only members of the institution and officers residing at the post are entitled to the use of the books. Cadets may draw books on Saturday, to be returned on the ensuing Monday—at other times by special permission of the superintendent in writing. Officers can draw four volumes—professors, eight volumes—for a period not exceeding two months. The annual number drawn is on an average 1,070. The yearly average number of persons consulting the library without taking out books is between 6,000 and 7,000, exclusive of strangers, of whom there are a good many who visit the library during the summer.

The officers are a librarian, a member of the academic staff; and an assistant librarian, a private soldier. The office of librarian is at present (January, 1849) vacant. André Freis is the assistant librarian.

ACADEMY LIBRARIES, (157 IN NUMBER)—66,442 VOLS.

The annual reports of the Regents of the University of the State of New York enable us to give (what we would gladly be able to furnish with respect to the other States of the Union) an exact list of the academy libraries, with the number of volumes contained in each.

The volumes in the libraries for the last three years number as follows:

No. of academies.	No. of volumes.	Average number.
In 1848, 153 academies reported	63,365	414
In 1849, 154....do......do............	65,524	424
In 1850, 157....do......do............	66,442	423

The following list of academies, with the number of volumes in the academic library, and the value of the library, is taken from the 63d annual report of the regents, made to the legislature March 1, 1850:

Names of academies.	No. of volumes in the academic library.	Value of library.
Academy at Little Falls	384	$329 00
Addison Academy	166	158 00
Albany Academy	797	1,645 00
Albany Female Academy	1,066	958 00
Albany Female Seminary	707	900 00
Albion Academy	358	397 00
Alfred Academy	451	398 00
Amenia Seminary	1,837	1,698 00
Ames Academy	270	280 00
Amsterdam Female Seminary	397	390 00
Argyle Academy	126	194 00
Auburn Academy	181	164 00
Auburn Female Seminary	112	153 00
Augusta Academy	153	301 00
Aurora Academy	615	566 00
Ball Seminary	130	159 00
Binghamton Academy	587	650 00
Brockport Collegiate Institute	185	198 00
Brookfield Academy	141	156 00
Brooklyn Female Academy	1,660	1,220 00
Cambridge Washington Academy	306	498 00
Canandaigua Academy	528	400 00
Canajoharie Academy	189	277 00
Canton Academy	125	180 00
Cary Collegiate Seminary	307	374 00
Cayuga Academy	322	396 00
Champlain Academy	237	272 00
Cherry Valley Academy	129	211 00
Chester Academy	170	217 00
Claverack Academy	346	221 00
Clinton Academy	345	232 00
Clinton Grammar School	340	250 00
Clinton Liberal Institute	1,177	1,000 00
Clover Street Seminary	325	225 00
Cortland Academy	1,086	1,100 00
Cortlandville Academy	474	461 00
Coxsackie Academy	313	150 00
Delaware Academy	771	1,026 00
Delaware Literary Institute	685	520 00
De Ruyter Institute	242	345 00
Dutchess County Academy	276	190 00
East Bloomfield Academy	361	360 00

LIST OF ACADEMIES—Continued.

Names of academies.	No. of volumes in the academic library.	Value of library.
Elmira Academy	348	$288 00
Erasmus Hall Academy	2,065	496 00
Fairfield Academy	401	840 00
Falley Seminary	202	190 00
Farmer's Hall Academy	379	182 00
Fayetteville Academy	225	235 00
Fort Covington Academy	100	161 00
Franklin Academy, (Malone)	173	213 00
Franklin Academy, (Prattsburgh)	1,182	419 00
Fredonia Academy	1,471	620 00
Friendship Academy	117	168 00
Galway Academy	90	317 00
Genesee Wesleyan Seminary	1,677	1,460 00
Genesee and Wyoming Seminary	412	425 00
Geneseo Academy	777	300 00
Genoa Academy	133	202 00
Gilbertsville Academy and Collegiate Institute	320	401 00
Glens Falls Academy	258	263 00
Gouverneur Wesleyan Seminary	376	400 00
Grammar School of Columbia College	862	362 00
Grammar School Univ. City of New York	none.	....
Granville Academy	217	188 00
Greenbush and Schodack Academy	82	150 00
Greenville Academy	165	180 00
Groton Academy	298	334 00
Hamilton Academy	805	800 00
Hartwick Seminary	854	1,155 00
Hobart Hall Institute	588	469 00
Hubbardsville Academy	97	153 00
Hudson Academy	151	189 00
Ithaca Academy	444	434 00
Jamestown Academy	256	203 00
Jefferson Academy	197	166 00
Jefferson County Institute	972	623 00
Johnstown Academy	187	189 00
Jordan Academy	203	300 00
Keeseville Academy	218	281 00
Kinderhook Academy	540	600 00
Kingsboro' Academy	154	211 00
Kingston Academy	534	500 00
Lansingburgh Academy	441	570 00
Le Roy Female Seminary	581	573 00
Liberty Normal Institute	129	161 00
Lowville Academy	328	167 00

LIST OF ACADEMIES—Continued.

Names of academies.	No. of volumes in the academic library.	Value of library.
Macedon Academy	129	$153 00
Manlius Academy	364	273 00
Mayville Academy	171	152 00
Mexico Academy	480	640 00
Middlebury Academy	736	722 00
Millville Academy	193	180 00
Monroe Academy	144	159 00
Montgomery Academy	398	150 00
Moravia Institute	425	409 00
Mount Pleasant Academy	1,320	1,020 00
Munro Academy	314	308 00
New Berlin Academy	201	176 00
Newburgh Academy	414	370 00
New Paltz Academy	237	282 00
New York Free Academy	not stated.	369 00
North Salem Academy	253	524 00
Norwich Academy	558	455 00
Nunda Literary Institute	191	192 00
Ogdensburgh Academy	312	393 00
Oneida Conference Seminary	1,381	1,328 00
Onondaga Academy	504	456 00
Ontario Female Seminary	559	478 00
Ovid Academy	428	330 00
Owego Academy	219	231 00
Oxford Academy	1,219	922 00
Peekskill Academy	283	207 00
Phipps Union Seminary	383	416 00
Plattsburgh Academy	146	215 00
Pompey Academy	351	374 00
Poughkeepsie Female Academy	213	186 00
Prattsville Academy	201	150 00
Red Creek Union Academy	188	206 00
Rensselaer Institute	407	1,035 00
Rensselaerville Academy	197	169 00
Rhinebeck Academy	386	292 00
Riga Academy	141	224 00
Rochester Collegiate Institute	284	328 00
Rochester Female Academy	170	176 00
Rome Academy	133	177 00
Rutgers Female Institute	2,303	2,141 00
Sag Harbor Institute	95	125 00
St. Lawrence Academy	649	428 00
Sand Lake Academy	242	181 00
Sauquoit Academy	83	171 00

LIST OF ACADEMIES—*Continued.*

Names of academies.	No. of volumes in the academic library.	Value of library.
Schenectady Lyceum and Academy........	325	$590 00
Schoharie Academy	219	272 00
Schuylerville Academy	160	173 00
Seneca Falls Academy...................	245	438 00
Seward Female Seminary................	358	401 00
Sherburne Union Academy...............	514	521 00
Spencertown Academy...................	203	159 00
Springville Academy	127	180 00
S. S. Seward Institute..................	82	150 00
Starkey Seminary.......................	860	539 00
Stillwater Seminary......................	304	361 00
Troy Academy...........................	338	300 00
Troy Female Seminary..................	909	1,379 00
Union Hall Academy....................	464	634 00
Union Literary Society	132	121 00
Union Village Academy..................	432	337 00
Utica Academy	185	235 00
Utica Female Academy..................	76	154 00
Vernon Academy	374	320 00
Wallkill Academy........................	318	330 00
Walworth Academy	114	164 00
Washington Academy....................	359	350 00
Westfield Academy.......................	424	478 00
Whitehall Academy......................	180	164 00
Whitesboro' Academy...................	153	100 00
Whitestown Seminary....................	821	880 00
Wilson Collegiate Institute	671	627 00
Windsor Academy	181	189 00
Yates Academy..........................	329	324 00
Totals........................	66,442	69,881

SCHOOL DISTRICT LIBRARIES, (8,070 IN NUMBER)—1,338,848 VOLUMES.

"The number of volumes in the school district libraries was, in 1844, 1,145,250; in 1845, 1,203,139; in 1846, 1,310,986; and in 1847, 1,338,848.

"Selections for the district libraries are made from the whole range of literature and science, with the exception of controversial books, political or religious. History, biography, poetry; philosophy, mental, moral and natural; fiction—indeed every department of human knowledge contributes its share to the district school library. The object of this great charity was not merely to furnish books for children, but to establish in all the school districts a miscellaneous library suited to the tastes and characters of every age."

"By means of this diffusive benevolence, the light of knowledge penetrates every portion of the State, and the sons of our farmers, merchants, mechanics, and laborers have daily access to many well-selected books, of which, but for this sagacious policy of our State, a majority of them would have never heard. If knowledge is power, who can calculate the energy imparted to the people of this State by the district school and district library?" [See Annual Report of the Superintendent of Common Schools, January 2, 1849.]

"In 1835 the districts were, by act of legislature, authorized to tax themselves $20 each the first year, and $10 each year afterwards, for the establishment of a library. But few districts availed themselves of this privilege. In 1838 it was made imperative upon each district, the State paying half of the sum." These libraries are "not so much for the benefit of children attending school as for those who have completed their common-school education. Its main design was to throw into school districts, and to place within the reach of all their inhabitants, a collection of good works on subjects calculated to enlarge their understandings, and store their minds with useful knowledge." [Report, 1836.]

NEW JERSEY.

BURLINGTON.

College Library—1,000 *vols.*—Founded A. D. 1846; contains about 1,000 volumes, 3 MSS., 25 maps and charts, a good collection of sacred music, and several hundred coins. No catalogue has been printed. The library is open daily from 3 to 4 p. m. Books are freely lent, mostly to students, to be returned in a week. The college is yet in its infancy, and of course no annual average of expenditure or use can be stated. Rev. A. Frost, librarian.

NEWARK.

Library of the New Jersey Historical Society—825 *vols.*—The society was instituted in 1845. The library was definitely located in Newark in the year 1846. It contains 825 volumes, 410 pamphlets, 760 manuscripts, 20 maps, 2 portraits, and several engravings. The larger portion of the collection has been presented. About $150 per annum have been appropriated to the purchase of books and MSS. The society occupies a room in a building erected by the Newark Library Association. The room is 48 feet by 18, and 12½ high. No catalogue of its collections has been printed. There is no specified time for the opening of the library. Members have access on application to the librarian. The books are not lent out. Samuel H. Pennington, librarian.

The Library Institution—3,000 *vols.*—This institution was chartered by the State in 184–. The library contained in 1849 3,000 volumes, open to the public on the most liberal terms. A handsome building has been erected expressly for the institution. W. A. Whitehead, secretary.

NEW BRUNSWICK.

Rutgers College Library—8,000 *vols.*—Rutgers College was founded in 1770. The library was commenced about the year 1807, and contains (January, 1849) not far from 8,000 volumes. It increases at the rate of about 150 volumes per annum.

Persons entitled to use the library are: officers of the institution, gratuitously; students of the college, and of the theological school, by paying one dollar per annum. None except professors and students are allowed to take books from the library. The number that consult the library without taking books is very limited. Professor C. K. Van Remondt, librarian.

ORANGE.

Lyceum Library—1,000 *vols.*

PRINCETON.

Libraries of the College of New Jersey—16,000 *vols.*—The College of New Jersey was founded in 1746. The college library was commenced as early as 1755, but was entirely consumed in 1801 by the fire which destroyed the college building. The present library (August, 1849) contains 9,000 volumes, and upwards. It has a collection of maps, and also a small one of medals and coins, and has lately received more than 8,000 sulphurets—fac-similes of ancient Roman and other coins. For some years past about $400 per annum have been expended for the purchase of books. The library is kept in a room 66 feet by 33, and is arranged according to subjects. There is no printed catalogue, except one printed in 1760, in 12mo. The library is open twice a week—one hour each time. Persons entitled to the use of the library are, the instructors and students of the college and theological seminary, and resident graduates. Books are lent out, and occasionally to persons at a distance. Professor G. M. Giger, librarian.

There are connected with the college two literary societies possessing libraries—namely: the American Whig Society has 3,500 volumes; the Cliosophic Society 3,500 volumes. Each of these societies has a handsome building, erected exclusively for its purposes by its members. Both are conducted with much spirit.

Library of the Theological Seminary—9,000 *vols.*—This institution went into operation in the year 1812, with a small number of books. The present number of volumes may be from 8,000 to 10,000, mostly theological, including all the Polyglots and most of the Fathers, besides a very valuable collection of about 1,000 volumes of bound pamphlets, collected mostly by one individual. It is a very choice and valuable library. Most of the books have been presented; there is, therefore, no uniformity in the number of books added yearly. No certain sum is devoted annually to the purchase of books. The average annual expenditure would not exceed $200. On one occasion a private library was purchased for about one thousand dollars.

A beautiful Gothic building, 80 feet by 50, of brown stone, has been erected by the liberality of a single individual. The floors are of marble.

The roof is slated. The whole, except the vestibule, is in one room, with a gallery. There are alcoves on the two sides of the room.

The arrangement of the books is partly by subjects, but not uniformly. The library is open twice a week for taking out books; and every day, Sunday excepted, for consultation. The professors and students of the seminary and of New Jersey College are entitled to the use of the library. The institution is connected with the Presbyterian denomination. Rev. A. Alexander, S. T. D., librarian.

TRENTON.

State Library—5,000 *vols.*—This library was organized in 1824, and contains 5,000 volumes. It has one volume, of about 600 pages, of letters in manuscript, most of them from men who served their country in the Revolution—a number of General Washington's.

There is an annual appropriation of $250 for the purchase of books. The library occupies an apartment in the State House. Two catalogues have been printed—the first in 1838, 36 pages 8vo.; the second in 1847, 37 pages 8vo. The library is open daily during the sessions of the legislature and the State courts, and also of the United States courts which sit at Trenton. The persons entitled to the use of the books are, officers of the executive department, members of the legislature, and members of the New Jersey bar. William D. Hart, State librarian.

Philomathean Library—300 *vols.*—The Philomathean Society of Trenton Academy has begun to collect a library, by the voluntary contributions of its members and others. About 300 volumes have already been received.

PENNSYLVANIA.

ALLEGHANY CITY.

Library of the Western Theological Seminary of the Presbyterian Church—5,000 *vols.*—The library was founded in 1827, when the institution commenced its operations, and contains (January, 1849) 5,000 volumes. The increase during the last ten years has been small. A legacy has been left, to be permanently invested and applied to the increase of the library. It will probably yield about $90 or $100 per annum, and will soon be available.

The library is in one of the wings of the seminary edifice, on the third story. The base of the library is a floor projecting some six feet from the wall, with a railing on its margin. The centre is open from the floor of the second story. It was designed, in the construction of the building, for a library-room. Its material is brick, and its dimensions are 50 by 30 feet; height, 11 feet from the floor, and 23 or 24 feet from the floor of the second story in the centre.

The books are arranged upon the shelves according to size. Around the ceiling, above the shelves, is a broad border, on which the letters of the alphabet are printed—one above each tier of shelves. On the margin of each shelf, small letters are placed in alphabetical order. On the back of each book is inscribed its number on its appropriate shelf. On the inside of the cover is this same number, together with the large and small letters, and the whole number as it advances, with the name of the institution. In the catalogue the books are arranged according to subjects; each book, under its appropriate division, having the number and letters referring to its tier and shelf. Thus, by a reference from the catalogue, every book may readily be found, and, by the marks on the book, may quickly be returned to its place. The whole number is of no further use in the plan than to indicate the number of books in the library There is as yet no printed catalogue, but a good one in manuscript.

The library is opened, statedly, once a week, and kept open one hour each time. The professors and students only are entitled to its use. By courtesy the use may be allowed to others. The faculty have the supervision of the library: they appoint one of the students annually to attend to the duties of librarian. Rev. David Elliott, D. D., senior professor.

CANONSBURG.

Jefferson College Libraries—10,000 *vols.*—The catalogue of the college for 1848 contains the following statement with reference to the libraries:

"The college library is not large, but contains a considerable number of rare and valuable books. Important additions have recently been made to it, and efficient measures taken for its enlargement.

"The literary societies are in a flourishing condition, and are probably unsurpassed by any similar associations. They are ornaments to the college, and valuable auxiliaries in the mental training of the students. Their halls are commodious and handsomely furnished, and their libraries extensive and well selected."

This college was founded in 1802, and the number of volumes in the three libraries is given in the American Almanac for 1850 as 10,000.

The Theological Seminary at Canonsburg—2,000 *vols* —This seminary went into operation in 1831, and was incorporated in 1833. It is under the direction of the associated Presbyterian church. The library is said to contain 2,000 volumes.

CARLISLE.

Dickinson College Libraries—14,550 *vols.*—The college library was founded with the college in 1782, and contains 5,050 volumes. For the last ten years the average increase has been 120 volumes per annum; the expenditure for books, $100 per annum.

The books are arranged according to subjects, following the system of Brunet. The library is open once a week for an hour, and is free to all connected with the college. There is no printed catalogue. J. U. Marshall, librarian.

There are two societies of students possessing valuable libraries, namely: the Belles-Lettres Society, 5,000 volumes; the Union Philosophical Society, 4,500 volumes.

CHESTER.

Athenæum Library—1,000 *vols.*

EASTON.

Lafayette College Libraries—5,402 *vols.*—The college library, begun in 1833, contains (January, 1849) only about 402 volumes. The libraries of the literary societies (the Franklin and ———) are larger and valuable, containing together about 5,000 volumes. The college was founded in 1832. Professor J. N. Coffin, librarian.

The Easton Library—3,751 *vols.*—This library was founded in 1811. It contains, (1850,) besides 3,751 volumes of printed books, a small number of manuscripts, maps, engravings, and coins. It increases slowly from the proceeds of a semi-annual tax upon the proprietors, amounting to about 75 dollars a year. A brick building, 60 feet by 35, forming one room 17 feet high, was erected for the library in 1811. The library is open Tuesdays and Saturdays from 3 to 5 o'clock. About 1,500 books are lent out each year. Peter Baldy, librarian.

ERIE.

The Irving Literary Institute was formed July 4, 1839, and incorporated in 1847. The library contains 1,015 volumes. The funds are raised by a semi-annual assessment of members and the loan of books. The amount will average $50 per annum. Voluntary subscriptions are occasionally made for the library. The institute occupies two rooms in the court house—a large hall for weekly meetings, and a private room for the library. A catalogue (16 pp. 8vo.) was printed in 1848. The library is open every Saturday, from 6 to 9 o'clock p. m. The members of the institute, and subscribers at $2 per annum, have free access to the books. The institute maintains a course of free lectures every winter. They have been well attended. Lucian Rust, secretary.

FALLSINGTON, BUCKS COUNTY.

The Fallsington Library Company was founded and incorporated in 1802. The 1st article of its constitution provides, that "no book or books shall ever be introduced into this library which shall have been written with an intention to discredit the Christian religion, or bring into disrepute any society or denomination thereof." Each member pays the sum of $5 entrance fee, and an annual assessment of $1. The present number of shareholders is 45. Number of volumes in the library, 1,650. Sum expended for books annually, $25. [See constitution of the F. L. Co., 12 pp. 12mo., Doylestown, 1836; and catalogue of books belonging to the F. L., 31 pp. 12mo., Newtown, 1844.]

GETTYSBURG.

Pennsylvania College Libraries—6,373 *vols.*—The college library commenced with the college in 1832, and contains (in 1849) 1,773 volumes, about 50 medals, and 400 or 500 coins. About 100 volumes are added annually. About 80 to 100 dollars are expended yearly for books. The library occupies a room in the college edifice 42 feet by 22. It is opened once a week for about an hour. Professors, tutors, resident graduates, and students, are entitled to use the books; others can borrow books through an officer of the institution. There are two literary societies (the Phrenakosmian and Philomathæan,) having libraries of about 2,000 volumes each; a scientific society, with 200 volumes; and a German society, with 400 volumes in the German language: making an aggregate of 6,373 volumes connected with the college. Professor M. L. Stoever, librarian.

Library of the Theological Seminary of the General Synod of the Evangelical Lutheran Church in the United States.—The library was begun in 1825, and contains about 8,500 volumes, and a few MSS. The additions during the last ten years amount to about 800 volumes. There is no printed catalogue. The library is opened for the use of the students every Saturday, one hour. The constitution limits its use to the faculty and students of the institution. By courtesy the professors of Pennsylvania College, located in the same town, are allowed the use of the books. The use is in all cases gratuitous. S. S. Schmucker, chairman of the faculty.

HARRISBURG.

Pennsylvania State Library—10,000 *vols.*—This library was founded 28th February, 1816, and contains, at present, about 10,000 volumes. It occupies two rooms in the capitol, each about 40 feet long by 30 wide and 20 high. A catalogue was printed in 1839, containing 168 pages 8vo. The library is open during the session of the legislature and supreme court, daily from 9 a. m to 1 p. m., and from 3 p. m. to 5 p. m. Books are lent out to officers of the State government and members of the legislature. Strangers can read in the library, but are not by law permitted to take out books. James Johnston, librarian.

HATBOROUGH.

Union Library—3,430 *vols.*—The Union Library Company of Hatborough, Montgomery county, was founded in the year 1755, and incorporated in 1787. The library contains (1850) 3,430 volumes. It increases at the rate of about 100 volumes annually. There has been no permanent fund till quite recently. Nathan Holt left by will a donation of $5,000, of which he directed $3,000 to the purchase of a lot of ground, and the erection of a suitable building thereon. The remaining $2,000 is to be placed out on landed security, and the interest devoted to the purchase of books. In 1849 a stone building was erected, for the above mentioned $3,000. It is 33 feet by 40, and finished after the plan of the Mercantile Library of Philadelphia, in one room 16 feet high. There is a printed catalogue, (64 pp. 8vo.) of which five editions have been issued. It includes a historical account of the institution, its constitution, by laws, &c. The library is statedly open two days in the week. Any person, by consent of the directors, may become a member on the payment of $10 and an annual tax of one dollar. Strangers and non-subscribers are allowed to use the books in the building, at the discretion of the librarian. Joseph Morton, librarian.

JONESTOWN.

The Swatara Literary Association has lately been formed at Jonestown, the object of which, as stated in the second article of the constitution, is "to establish a library and museum, and to encourage such exercises as will tend to spread general and useful information."

LANCASTER.

Franklin College Library.—This college has a small library of 750 volumes, including pamphlets. F. A. Muhlenberg, jr., librarian. [See Marshall College, Mercersburg.]

The Library of the Mechanics' Institute in this place contains 2,000 volumes. [See Rupp's History of Lancaster County.]

Juliana Library.—A library was established here in 1770 by Thomas Penn, and named, from his wife, the Juliana Library. [Ludewig, in the *Serapeum*.]

LEWISBURG.

Lewisburg University Library—600 *vols.*—This library was commenced in 1849. A subscription of about $10,000 has been made for the increase of the library; and it will become available, by instalments, within the next three years. Professor George R. Bliss, librarian.

MEADVILLE.

Alleghany College Libraries—8,000 *vols.*—The college was founded in 1815. It possesses in its libraries about 8,000 volumes. The college library is composed almost entirely of three bequests—the first in point of size by Hon. James Winthrop, LL. D., of Cambridge, Massachusetts, who died in 1821; the second, by the Rev. William Bentley, D. D., of Salem, Massachusetts; the third, by Isaiah Thomas, esq., LL. D., of Worcester, Massachusetts. A catalogue of the library (130 pp. 8vo.) was prepared and printed in 1828 by the Rev. Timothy Alden, who also compiled the catalogues of the libraries of the Massachusetts and New York Historical Societies. In the Alleghany Library catalogue each bequest is separately registered, under the name of its giver.

"In the catalogue, the intelligent will perceive that there is an extensive range of the best editions of the Greek and Roman Classics, and of the ancient Fathers of the Christian Church; that there are books in thirty different languages, ancient and modern, with lexicons and grammars, and elementary books for studying most of them; and that in history, ancient and modern, in belles-lettres, and other branches of literature and science, there is a most excellent collection." [See Remarks of Mr. Alden, Catalogue, p. 136.]

The Library of the Meadville Theological School—5,300 *vols.*—This institution is under the direction of the Unitarian Congregationalists. The library was founded simultaneously with the school, in 1844, and contains 5,300 volumes. For the five years since the library was established, nearly 900 volumes per annum on an average have been added to it. Somewhat more than $250 from the funds of the school have annually been appropriated for the purchase of books.

The library is open twice a week—one hour each time. Students and officers of the institution are entitled to the use of the books. A discretionary power of lending to any literary gentleman is vested in the faculty, and has always been exercised when applied for. No charge is made for the use of the library. Between 2,000 and 3,000 books are lent out annually. The number is increasing with the growth of the library.

The private libraries of the officers of the school are as largely composed of works of reference, and as freely open to students, as the public library. They contain about 3,700 volumes. Professor F. Huidekoper, librarian.

MERCERSBURG.

Library of the Theological Seminary of the German Reformed Synod of North America—6,000 *vols.*—The library was commenced with the seminary, in 1825. It contains at present (1850) about 6,000 volumes, mostly in German. The increase has been small—not more than 50 volumes per annum. No catalogue has been printed. The library is open one hour each week. A fee is charged to the students for the use of the library. John W. Nevin, D. D., senior professor.

Marshall College Libraries—7,000 *vols.*—The college library contains about 1,000 volumes. The Diagnothian Society has a library of 3,000 volumes, and the Goethean Society also has about 3,000 volumes. Each of these libraries is in a separate hall.

The college library is distributed among the professors—each professor having charge of those books pertaining to his own department. There is at present no room appropriated to the books. The institution was chartered in 1835.

Measures have been taken for uniting this college with Franklin College, Lancaster. The corporate name will be Franklin and Marshall College. The success of this plan will depend upon the raising of $25,000 for the erection of buildings in Lancaster, and $15,000 for the endowment of a professorship in Pennsylvania College, Gettysburg.

NORRISTOWN.

The Library Company—2,515 *vols.*—The Norristown Library Company was founded in May, 1796, and (in 1850) possesses 2,515 volumes, (to wit: 4 folios, 30 quartos, 872 octavos, and 1,609 duodecimos, besides phamphlets.) There is no permanent fund. There is an annual income of about eighty dollars arising from an assessment of one dollar upon each shareholder. The sum thus obtained is mostly devoted to the purchase of books. In 1835 a small wooden building was erected expressly for the library; it is 15 feet six inches square. A catalogue (40 pp. 18mo.) was printed in 1836. The library is open every day. Shareholders pay $5 for a share, and $1 annual tax. Books are lent, for a small charge, to other persons. About 200 are thus lent annually. R. Adamson, librarian.

PHILADELPHIA.

The Library Company and the Loganian Library—60,000 *vols.*—The following facts of general interest, respecting the history of this venerable and useful institution, are extracted from an article written for Waldie's Portfolio, by John J. Smith, esq., the librarian:

"The first entry in the records of the Library Company, is in the following words:

"'The minutes of me, Joseph Breintnall, secretary to the directors of the Library Company of Philadelphia, with such of the minutes of the same directors as they order me to make, begun on the 8th day of November, 1731. By virtue of the deed or instrument of the said company, dated the first day of July last.

"The said instrument being completed by fifty subscriptions, I subscribed my name to the following summons or notice which Benjamin Franklin sent by a messenger, viz:

"'To Benjamin Franklin, Thomas Hopkinson, William Parsons, Philip Syng, jr., Thomas Godfrey, Anthony Nicholas, Thomas Cadwalader, John Jones, jr., Robert Grace, and Isaac Penington.

"'Gentlemen: The subscription to the library being completed, you, the directors appointed in the instrument, are desired to meet this evening at 5 o'clock, at the house of Nicholas Scull, to take bond of the treasurer for the faithful performance of his trust, and to consider of and appoint a proper time for the payment of the money subscribed, and other matters relating to the said library.

"'JOS. BREINTNALL, *Secretary*.

"'Philadelphia, *November* 8, 1831.'

"At this meeting a treasurer, William Coleman, duly executed a bond with sureties, and Benjamin Franklin proposed that the said Coleman attend at suitable places to receive the subscription moneys; which, says our secretary, 'it was the general opinion should not be delayed, lest the directors be disappointed in sending it to England this fall to purchase books, or that other disappointments, prejudicial to the library design, should happen by delays or negligence on any hand.'

"The price of a share was fixed at forty shillings, and on the first evening of attendance for that purpose ten persons appeared and paid the amount of their subscriptions. Several individuals, however, were dilatory in meeting their engagements, and B. Franklin printed and sent them notice either to pay on a certain evening, or signify their determination to relinquish the copartnership. Much difficulty and no little forbearance appears to have been the lot of the directors and treasurer, in collecting from some of the original subscribers; but, satisfied of the utility of the project, at a meeting on the 29th of March, 1732, the sum in hand being 'above half' the amount originally intended to be raised, it was concluded to be the interest of all concerned to send for some of the books immediately. Thomas Godfrey, at this meeting, informed the directors that Mr. James Logan had heard of the plan, and would willingly give his advice in the choice of books; the minute on the subject is in these words: 'Upon this information, Thomas Godfrey was requested to return the thanks of the committee to Mr. Logan for his generous offer; and the committee esteeming Mr. Logan to be a gentleman of universal learning, and the best judge of books in these parts, ordered that Thomas Godfrey should wait on him and request him to favor them with a catalogue of suitable books against to morrow evening, which T. G. readily agreed to do.'

"With the advice of Mr. Logan the list was made out, and Robert Grace, 'to expedite the affair,' agreed to draw on Peter Collinson, mercer, in Gracious street, London, for '£45 sterling at 65 per cent. advance the current rate,' in favor of and to be remitted by Thomas Hopkinson, then about sailing for England, with directions to purchase as many volumes as he could for the money. The catalogue of this first effort evinces considerable judgment, and was very carefully prepared with a view to facilitate the acquisition of knowledge in the various departments required by the wants of a young community.

"In October, 1732, the first importation of books was received by Captain Carnock in good order. T. Hopkinson informed the directors that he had received advice from T. Cadwalader and P. Collinson in adding and omitting various books; and that 'Peter Collinson, who had given great assistance, had moreover made the company a present of two valuable books.' His claim is thus established of having been the first donor to the yet infant library.

"The importance of the step thus taken, although it was on a small scale, can be justly appreciated only by a knowledge of the fact, which is stated in the reply to Peter Collinson, that there was no manner of provision made by the government for public education, either in this or the neighboring provinces, 'nor so much as a good bookseller's shop nearer than Boston.'

"The books were taken to 'Robert Grace's chamber, at his house in Jones's alley,' and there placed on the shelves, a catalogue made out, and Dr. Franklin undertook to print the blank promissory notes for the librarian to fill up, and get subscribed by those to whom he lent books. The rules and regulations adopted were few and simple. The first librarian, Louis Timothee, gave attendance from 2 to 3 on Wednesdays, and on Saturdays from 10 till 4. He was allowed to permit 'any civil gentleman to peruse the books of the library in the library-room, but not to *lend or to suffer to be taken* out of the library, by any person who is not a subscribing member, any of the said books, Mr. James Logan only excepted.' Timothee, it appears, occupied Grace's house, and he was to receive at the expiration of three months 'three pounds lawful money certain,' and a further 'reasonable reward,' as should be agreed on in consideration of services and rent.

"In December, 1732, several new applicants presented themselves, and were admitted. Dr. Franklin produced the printed catalogue, which he presented without charge.

"The original number of fifty subscribers was not completed till the 22d February, 1733, when Joseph Growden signed the constitution, being the fiftieth member.

"William Rawle appears to have been the first American donor, having, on the 12th of March, 1733, presented 'six volumes or books of the works of Mr. Edmund Spenser.'

"On the 15th of May, of the same year, it was agreed by a committee of directors to draw up an address to Thomas Penn, proprietor, 'in order for his countenance and protection in an affair so useful and well intended as the library, and which the proprietor signified through his secretary, Mr. George, that he approved and designed to encourage.'

"Mr. Penn replied that he took the address 'kindly,' with the assurance that he should be always ready to promote any undertaking so useful.

He presented several articles to the institution, and it is to the honor of the proprietary family that they promoted the design as long as they continued to preserve any influence in the province.

"Mr. Timothee having vacated his office, Benjamin Franklin, one of his sureties, offered to take his situation for the current year, in consideration of Timothee's having been serviceable to him; he occupied the station of librarian for three months and a day, and was succeeded by William Parsons. During the period of Franklin's service as librarian, the room was agreed to be open but once a week, on Saturdays from four to eight—it having been observed that borrowers rarely came on Wednesdays, and four hours were found amply sufficient to supply all applicants. The librarian's salary was then reduced to £6.

"The increase of books was supposed to raise the value of a share annually ten shillings, and I find the price gradually increased.

"On the 12th of December, 1737, the directors were informed by the secretary that the proprietor was pleased to say that nothing remained to delay his grant of a lot of ground he intended to bestow on the company for their library. In May, 1738, a letter was received from John Penn, with a present of an air-pump. The first paragraph conveys information highly honorable to the company. It is dated London, 31st of January, 1738, and begins:

"'Gentlemen: It always gives me pleasure when I think of the Library Company of Philadelphia, as they were the first that encouraged knowledge and learning in the province of Pennsylvania.'

"A suitable reply and a vote of thanks for the lot and the air-pump were ordered to be returned to the generous donor. The pump excited considerable curiosity among the citizens—frequent notices of application to borrow it being minuted; a commitee was appointed to provide a case and frame for it, with glass lights in the door, 'to look ornamental in the library-room.'

"The first, and, I regret to add, one of the very few presents of money made to the institution, was from Dr. Walter Sydserfe, of Antigua, in 1738, who, having the sum of £58 6*s*. 8*d*. due him in this country, generously presented it to the company. In June, 1739, the number of members had been increased to 74.

"On the 7th of April, 1740, the books were removed to 'the upper room of the westernmost office of the State-house'—the use of which had been lately granted to the company by the assembly.

"In a catalogue printed in 1741, in my possession, there is a short account of the state of the institution. Shares were then granted at the price of £6 10*s*. In this year, John Penn, esq., presented a microscope and camera obscura, still in the company's possession.

"In 1746, Samuel Norris bequeathed the company £20.

"From 1748 to 1752, many of the minutes are missing, and I have only to note the reception of a telescope and a number of valuable books from Thomas Penn, esq.

"In 1752, 'a noble present of ancient medals' was received through Mr. Peters from Mr. Gray, member of Parliament for Colchester.

"In 1762 Charles Thomson, who afterwards became Secretary to Congress, was elected a director, and in April the long expected patent from the Penns for a lot of ground in Chestnut street, near Ninth, was received. The lot was enclosed with a post-and-rail fence, and continued for many years to yield a small revenue. On Dr. Franklin's return from Europe he was unanimously re-elected a director by the board, to supply the place of Samuel Shoemaker, resigned.

"On the 14th of February, 1763, the celebrated John Dickinson was elected a director. In an address to John Penn, November 21, 1763, occurs the following paragraph: 'The encouragements the library met with in its infancy have had good effects. Many other libraries, after our example and on our plan, have been erected in this and the neighboring provinces, whereby useful knowledge has been more generally diffused *in these remote corners of the earth.*

"Some dissatisfaction is noted at this period at the new regulations, by which members were prevented from coming into the library and taking down books; in consideration of which it was '*Resolved*, That the librarian should prepare a bond, which should be tendered to every member who should desire the privilege of entering the library and examining the books there, at the hours of attendance on Saturdays, by which he should bind himself to be answerable for his proportionable part of the loss that may arise from any books being lost or stole out of the library.'

"This appears to have had the desired effect; as, however anxious members might have been to consult the books, they could not be supposed willing to join in the librarian's responsibility for losses.

"1767. Mr. Hopkinson visiting England, the directors, in order not to lose his services on his return, were allowed to appoint a proxy. He brought home with him a few rare books, purchased by Dr. Franklin, with the company's money, and a present from Benjamin West, 'formerly,' says the minute, 'of this city, but now of London, historical painter: a woman's hand, taken from an Egyptian mummy, in good preservation.' This hand, which has sometimes been called Cleopatra's, is still in the building, and, notwithstanding the length of time which it has been exposed to the action of the air, is in perfect preservation.

"1768. On the 20th of February, 1768, a law was enacted for admitting new members for the sum of £10.

"1769. At a meeting of the directors, February 13th, 1769, the following gentlemen, viz: George Roberts, Jonathan Shoemaker, James Pearson, Charles Jervis, David Evans, Anthony Morris, jr., and Moses Bartram, being a committee of the Union Library Company of Philadelphia, waited on the board, to signify their approbation of the plan which had been some time in agitation, of uniting the two institutions. The directors replied, 'that they thought such a scheme might better answer the intention of public libraries, than if they were to continue in separate bodies;' and on the 13th of March a law was enacted, giving the directors 'full power and authority to admit the members of the Union Library Company,' &c.

"Of the value of this accession of books I have no data to form a judgment. The Union Company owned the house in Third street where their books had been kept, and it was for a considerable period a source of revenue, until sold. Benjamin Franklin, at this time in London, handed the orders for books to William Strahan for shipment.

"The institution having now acquired additional consequence by the accession of new members, and an increase of books, the board petitioned the assembly of the province for permission to erect on some part of the

State-house lot such a building as would prove an ornament to the city, and continue to accommodate their rapidly increasing library. This application was refused; and at a general meeting of the company, convened by advertisement, on the 5th of October, 1771, it was deemed inexpedient to build elsewhere, and the project was for the present suffered to rest. It was not till the 25th of September, 1769, that the room was opened three days in the week; these days were Tuesdays, Thursdays, and Saturdays, for four hours each, and two librarians were then appointed, viz: John de Maurengault and Ludowick Sprogell, at an annual salary of £20 each.

"1771. Another junction was formed in 1771, with the Association Library Company, but there are no data by which to judge of the extent of this institution. The Amicable Company, also admitted about this time, is only casually mentioned, and the two collections were probably of no great value.

"1773. Early in the year 1773, the second floor of Carpenters' Hall was rented, and the books removed from the room in the State-house, which was now too small for their accommodation; the library was then first opened daily, from two o'clock till seven, under the charge of Charles Cist, at an annual salary of £60. The books were here first placed behind the protection of latticed doors. The increase of the cabinet of coins seems to have been a favorite project: a great number are noted as having been presented from time to time. In October, 1773, several specimens of minerals, and 53 curious coins, were presented by Edward Pole. Unfortunately, the secretary, in reporting the gift, was obliged to add the following memorandum: 'but the library being entered by some thief (as supposed) last night, he carried off all the coins and tokens, together with some change which was left in the drawer.' Mr. Pole, however, received the thanks of the directors, and the articles were advertised, but never recovered.

"1774. On the 31st of August, 1774, it was, 'upon motion, ordered that the librarian furnish the gentlemen who are to meet in congress in this city, with such books as they may have occasion for during their sitting, taking a receipt for them.' Congress enjoyed this privilege during the whole period of its sittings in Philadelphia, and the members experienced much inconvenience from the want of a similar institution for reference after removing to Washington, before a good library had been collected in the capitol. The members of the legislature of Pennsylvania likewise enjoyed the use of the books for a long period, free of charge.

"1776. In May, 1776, an advertisement appeared in the Pennsylvania Gazette, and other journals, requesting a general meeting of the company, in order to consider of the propriety of empowering the directors to remove the books and effects of the company in case any event of the war should make that measure necessary. Two attempts to get together enough members to pass such a law failing, the books remained, and were unmolested.

"The British army had possession of Philadelphia from September 26, 1777, to June 18, 1778, but it does not appear that the company sustained any loss from those who composed it. The officers, without exception, left deposites, and paid hire for the books borrowed by them.

"1777. In 1777 the library room was occupied by the sick soldiery, and Messrs. Alison, Jones, and Hughes were 'appointed a committee, on the 11th of March, to wait on General Gates, commanding officer in this city, in order to procure, if possible, an order for their removal.' During the whole progress of the war, the importation of books was of course suspended. The funds thus accumulated were expended, on the conclusion of peace, in a large importation of the standard works which had appeared in the interval. By the will of the Honorable William Logan, the institution received this year a very handsome bequest of books of ancient authors, being a more extensive and valuable gift than any heretofore received. They may all be traced in the catalogue by the *L* attached to each.

"1779. Jno. Todd, librarian, received £100 per annum and a share.

"1781. On the 4th of May, 1781, the directors agreed to receive 30 shillings state money in lieu of a bushel of wheat, by which the annual payments were the previous year directed to be made.

"1783. The committee on importations remitted £200 sterling to London on the 10th of June, 1783, nine years having elapsed since their last order. Jos. Woods and William Dillwyn were selected as proper agents, from their well-known attachment to literature, and knowledge of books; they acted during the remainder of their lives to the satisfaction of the directors, and Jos. Woods's son is now the agent. In their letter the committee of correspondence state, 'we shall confide entirely in your judgment to procure us such books of modern publication as will be proper for a public library, and though we would wish to mix the utile with the dulce, we should not think it expedient to add to our present stock anything in the *novel* way.' This has been the uniform plan pursued, with the exception of a few of the best class of novels and romances; the consequence has been that, with the very great increase of the number of volumes, the shelves are supplied with books of real merit in most other departments, and are not lumbered with the temporary trash so greedily devoured by the sickly taste which procures its mental supplies from circulating libraries.

"1783. November, 1783, Dr. Franklin presented six volumes of the natural history of the south of France."

The erection of a building for the accommodation of the library having been long a matter of discussion, "at a general meeting, held June 1, 1789, a large number of members appeared, either in person or by proxy, and a law was passed giving the directors power to proceed, as soon as one hundred new members should be added to the list, to appropriate the money on hand, reserving sufficient for the current expenses, and to sell the ground rents and real estate owned by the company. Bishop White was nominated by the directors chairman of this meeting, at which he presided.

"All the shares requisite, except nineteen, were soon subscribed, many of which were to be paid for in labor. The directors and treasurer and secretary assuming to themselves to procure the remaining nineteen, the purchase of the lot and erection of the building was proceeded in with all convenient speed. The present site was purchased of Mary Norris and Dr. Logan. A number of plans were submitted for approval, and the one prepared by Dr. William Thornton, with some slight alterations, was adopted, for which he received a share. It may be supposed that this undertaking was not without its difficulties, and I find that, owing to the low state of the funds, the directors, treasurer, and secretary, individually, advanced sums amounting to two hundred and fifty pounds, of which Josiah Hewes advanced fifty pounds, and the others from ten to twenty-five pounds.

"1789. The first stone of the edifice was laid on the 31st of August, 1789; the minutes state, 'that, upon the suggestion of Dr. Benjamin Franklin, a large stone was prepared, and laid at the southwest corner of the building, with the following inscription, composed by the Doctor, except so far as relates to himself, which the committee have taken the liberty of adding to it:

'Be it remembered,
in honor of the Philadelphia youth,
(then chiefly artificers,)
that in MDCCXXXI,
they cheerfully,
at the instance of Benjamin Franklin,
one of their number,
instituted the Philadelphia Library,
which, though small at first,
is become highly valuable and extensively useful,
and which the walls of this edifice
are now destined to contain and preserve;
the first stone of whose foundation
was here placed
the thirty-first day of August, 1789.'

"1790. By the 30th of December, 1790, the books were all removed and ready for delivery, when it was resolved to have the room open daily, from one o'clock to sunset, and Zachariah Poulson was continued librarian, at one hundred pounds salary. During the progress of the building, more than the stipulated one hundred names were added to the list of stockholders—many apprentices having been allowed by their employers to give sufficient labor to purchase the privilege of admission. Their names are faithfully recorded; and it may, in future, be interesting to their descendants to discover that they are reaping the benefits of literary instruction from the honest labor and the sweat of the brows of their progenitors.

"Among the benefactors of the library occur the names of Robert Barclay, of London, and of Abraham Claypoole, of Pennsylvania. The former repeatedly sent presents of rare or curious books, and till his death continued to correspond with his American friends, and to mention the institution with interest. The latter left the company, by will, one hundred pounds.

"1791. In January, 1791, the directors again tendered to the President and Congress the free use of the books in the library, in as full and ample manner as if they were members of the company. President Washington, through his secretary, Tobias Lear, returned thanks for the attention in a very handsome note.

"1782. On the 18th of February, 1782, Doctor Parke informed the board that the heirs of James Logan had made a proposition to transfer to the Library Company of Philadelphia the Loganian Library, and also to convey to them, under certain conditions, a lot of ground in Philadelphia, and certain rents charge, together with the arrearages thereof, now due from estates in Bucks county. On this subject a committee was appointed to inquire into the condition of the property, and the terms intended to be annexed to the transfer.

"1792. An additional five-foot lot having been purchased of Samuel M. Fox, on Library street, a building was erected for the accommodation of the Loganian books by the Library Company of Philadelphia, for which the Loganian trustees pay an annual rent.

"On the 4th of October, John Fitch's manuscripts, respecting the steam-engine, were deposited in the library, under seal, with a request that they might be kept unopened till the year 1823. This was done, and as they have undergone an examination, I shall not here attempt their analyzation.

"1793. On the 30th of August, 1793, at a general meeting of the members, the price of shares was raised to forty dollars, at which sum they still remain.

"1799. In April, 1799, Henry Cox, of the kingdom of Ireland, presented a large number of manuscript volumes relating to the history of his native country. They consist of the original correspondence of James the First with the Privy Council of Ireland, from 1603 to 1615, inclusive, and a great variety of historical data, the value of which remains unknown. In one of the volumes is an original letter from Queen Elizabeth, dated in 1568. Several valuable printed books are also in this collection.

"1804. In this year the institution was greatly enriched by John Bleakly and the Rev. Samuel Preston. The former left, by will, one thousand pounds to the library, and the latter bequeathed a most valuable collection of rare and curious books, selected with great taste and judgment, together with two shares of United States Bank stock. Dr. Preston was influenced, in selecting this library for the reception of his own, by our countryman, Benjamin West, who painted the portrait of the donor, which was, in the succeeding year, presented by Mrs. West, as an appropriate ornament for the library rooms. To appreciate the value of Preston's library, it must be examined in detail. There are in the collection many rare books of plates, &c., of the most costly description, which the funds of the institution would forever have forbidden being purchased.

"George Campbell was now elected librarian—an office he filled for twenty three years, during which long period he was never once prevented by sickness from attending to his daily duties—a circumstance almost unprecedented in the annals of a salary officer. Under his charge, the institution continued to flourish, and was again enriched, at the period of his resignation, by the bequest from William Mackenzie of 500 rare volumes, and the purchase from his executors of the additional number of 1,466.

"Since this period, about 5,000 volumes were purchased, on very favorable terms, from James Cox, an artist, since deceased, consisting of many expensive volumes on the fine arts, and miscellaneous books. They supplied a prominent deficiency, and many rarities are among them."

From the preface to the last catalogue we take the following:

"Besides the books, the personal property consists in some available funds yielding interest, the sale of shares, the price of each of which since 1793 has been fixed at forty dollars, and the annual payments of four dollars from each member. The real estate of the company consists of the lot and buildings where the Philadelphia and Loganian libraries are kept.

"The members dispose of their shares by transfer or will; but the assent of the directors, as well in such cases as in case of an original purchase, is previously necessary—a restriction early adopted, in order as much as possible to prevent improper persons from having access to a collection of a nature peculiarly liable to injury."

The preface to the catalogue of the *Loganian Library* contains the following account of that establishment:

"This collection of rare and valuable books, principally in the learned and existing languages of the continent of Europe, owes its origin to the Honorable James Logan, the confidential friend and counsellor of William Penn, and for some time president of the council of the province of Pennsylvania. Its foundation consists of a portion of his own private library, which, having collected at considerable expense, he was anxious should descend to posterity, and continue usefully to extend to others the means of prosecuting those pursuits he had himself so successfully cultivated. With this view, he erected a suitable building in Sixth street, near Walnut, for the reception of a library, and, by deed, vested it (with the books and certain rents, for the purpose of increasing their number, and paying a librarian) in trustees, for the use of the public, forever.

"This deed he afterwards cancelled, and prepared, but did not live to execute, another, in which some alteration was made in the funds and regulations. After his death, his children and residuary legatees, with commendable liberality, carried into effect the intentions of Mr. Logan, and conveyed the building, books, and rents charge to trustees, who caused the library, consisting of more than two thousand volumes, to be arranged, and a catalogue to be printed.

"About one thousand three hundred volumes, collected by Doctor William Logan, of Bristol, England, a younger brother of James Logan, and by William Logan, of Philadelphia, son of the founder, were afterwards bequeathed to the institution by the latter gentleman, who acted for some time as librarian. After his death, in 1776, the library remained unopened during several years.

"To insure its perpetuity, the legislature of Pennsylvania, in 1792, at the request of James Logan, the only surviving trustee, passed an act annexing the Loganian library to that belonging to the Library Company of Philadelphia, under certain restrictions. This act constitutes the directors of that prosperous company for the time being trustees, together with the eldest male descendant of the founder, and two other gentlemen to be by him appointed.

"Since the two libraries were thus connected, the books of the Loganian institution have been kept in a room appropriated to the purpose, owned by the Library Company of Philadelphia, in which they were first opened for the benefit of the citizens in 1794, in accordance with the original intentions of James Logan and the act of assembly.

"Very considerable additions have continued to be made to the collection by means of the funds arising out of the sale of the lot and building in Sixth street, and from the rents of the lands in Bucks county, Pennsylvania, settled originally on the institution by the Logans, and by donations—particularly of that from the late William Mackenzie, esq., a native of Philadelphia, who bequeathed by his last will, in 1828, 'all his books printed before the beginning of the eighteenth century, and eight hundred volumes more, to be chosen by the trustees, from his French books and Latin books printed since the beginning of the eighteenth century.' This valuable bequest consists of 1,519 volumes of great rarity and value; and subsequently 3,566 volumes were purchased from his executors.* They had been accumulated by Mr. Mackenzie during a life extended beyond seventy years, which had been almost exclusively devoted to literary pursuits. During this period, one of his few intimate friends says 'he believes he never had an enemy: at least, from the purity of his principles and the correctness of his conduct, I am sure he never deserved one.'"

The Philadelphia Library contained in February, 1785, 2,764 works, in 5,487 volumes; in July, 1807, 8,074 works, in 14,457 volumes; in August, 1835, 18,762 works, in 35,221 volumes.

The Loganian Library contained, when it was annexed to the Library Company of Philadelphia, in August, 1792, 3,064 works, in 3,953 volumes; in August, 1835, 6,922 works, in 8,663 volumes.

The Philadelphia and Loganian Libraries contained in August, 1835, 25,684 works, in 43,884 volumes; in August, 1849, 60,000 volumes.

From $3,000 to $4,000 per year are expended in the purchase of books.

The income of the institution is—

From annual payments of members - - - - -	$3,800
From other sources, real estate, &c. - - - - -	2,500
Total - - - - - - - -	6,300

The books are arranged as they are received, according to size. The first catalogue was gratuitously printed by Benjamin Franklin in 1732; the second by Franklin in 1741, (56 pp. 12mo;) the third by Franklin and Hall in 1757, (132 pp. 8vo.;) others in 1764, (150 pp. 8vo.;) in 1770, (8vo.;) in 1789, (406 pp. 8vo.,) with supplements, 1793, (38 pp.;) 1794, (34 pp.;) 1796, (38 pp.;) 1798, (48 pp.;) 1799, (32 pp.;) and 1801, (23 pp.;) in 1807, (616 pp. 8vo.) The last printed catalogue was published in 1835, in two volumes 8vo., making 1,050 pages. This catalogue is classed on the system of Brunet, somewhat altered. The index is alphabetical. Under each sub-class, the titles are arranged alphabetically under the names of authors. Anonymous works are recorded after the others. In the supplements the division of belles lettres is included under that of science and arts. A supplement was published in 1844, and a second supplement in 1849. A catalogue of the Loganian Library was published in 1837, (450 pp. 8vo.) The first catalogue of this collection was printed in 1760, (116 pp. 8vo.) The library is open every weekday from 10 a. m. till sunset.

Persons entitled to the use of the library are, stockholders who pay $4 yearly; others on deposite and hire. The books are lent out in great numbers, but how many per annum is not ascertained. The number of persons who consult library without taking away books is very considerable—the exact number cannot be stated. A deposite of double the value of the books taken, will obtain most of the books of the institution, if applied for by proper persons. John Jay Smith, librarian.

Library of the American Philosophical Society—20,000 *vols.*—The American Philosophical Society, the oldest of the scientific associations in

"*The whole number of volumes received by the Loganian Library from Mr Mackenzie's library was 5,085, and by the Philadelphia Library 1,966—being a total of 7,051 volumes. The books of Mr. Logan's original collection, and those bequeathed by William Logan, are designated in the catalogue by an L.; those bequeathed by Mr. Mackenzie, by an M."

the United States, was formed in 1742. The American Society for Promoting and Propagating Useful Knowledge in Philadelphia was established in 1766. These two societies were united in 1769, and incorporated March 15, 1780, as the "American Philosophical Society held at Philadelphia for Promoting Useful Knowledge." The library contains about 20,000 volumes. The society has also an "extensive collection of manuscripts, maps, charts, and engravings, and, in its cabinet, medals, coins, &c." The precise number "cannot readily be given." The annual increase is about 200 volumes. Few books are purchased except scientific periodicals, &c., by subscription. The chief accessions to the library are by donations from learned societies and individuals abroad and in this country. The library is in the hall of the society, a brick building 50 by 70 feet, erected in 1786, on a part of the "State House Square," in the city of Philadelphia, granted to the society for that purpose by the State legislature, in 1784. The books are arranged on the shelves in numerical order, each volume having its number attached. Folios, quartos, and octavos have their respective systems of numbers. No catalogue has been printed since one in 1824. It is an 8vo. of 290 pages. The library has since that time greatly increased. A new catalogue is in preparation. The laws of the society require the library to be opened every Friday evening from 7 to 9 o'clock, and at such other times as the librarian may think proper. All members of the society are entitled to the use of the library; and facilities are afforded, at the discretion of the librarian, to well known visiters of respectable character. Books are lent out to members. A considerable number of persons consult the library at the room. Charles B. Trego, secretary and librarian.

Mercantile Library—12,232 *vols.*—The Mercantile Library Company of Philadelphia was founded in 1823. The library contained, January, 1849, 12,232 volumes, "principally of works of permanent value." "The directors have been careful to exclude from the shelves books of a frivolous character, or of demoralizing tendencies." The annual increase is about 600 volumes.

The building of the company is on the southeast corner of Delaware, Fifth, and Library streets. It was erected in 1845, at a cost, including furniture, &c., of $23,199 42. The interior of the building is divided into nineteen apartments. The entire second story is occupied as the library and reading-room, and the intermediate story of the east wing is used by the directors: all the other rooms are rented. The present librarian is James Cox.

The Academy of Natural Sciences—12,000 *vols.*—The American Academy of Natural Sciences originated on the 25th of January, 1812. It was incorporated in 1817. The library contains about 12,000 volumes. It had 435 separate maps and charts in 1836, when the catalogue of the library was printed; since which date the additions have been few. For the last three years the annual increase has been about 700 volumes. This is exclusive of periodicals, *serials*, and pamphlets. There is no permanent library fund. The increase is mostly from donations, deposites, and occasional purchases. The library occupies an apartment on the ground floor of the hall of the society. It is about 45 feet by 28, and 14 feet high, with a gallery on all its sides. The books are arranged according to subjects. A catalogue was printed in 1836, containing 300 pages 8vo. At that time the library contained 6,890 volumes. An appendix will soon be prepared. The library is open daily, Sundays excepted, from 11 a. m. till sunset. The members alone are entitled to the use of the books. The friends of members, however, are by courtesy allowed access to the library. William S. Zantzinger, M. D., librarian.

The cabinet is the best in the United States. The collection of birds is said to be the largest in the world, containing about 25,000 specimens, many mounted in skins. The collection of eggs and nests of birds is also the most extensive ever made. The collections of mammalia, fishes, reptiles, crustacea, insects, and plants, are superior to any others in this country.

The library is rich and valuable in all departments of natural history. In ornithology it is quite complete.

For these magnificent collections the academy is mainly indebted to the munificence of three gentlemen—William Maclure, esq., Dr. R. Eglesfield Griffiths, and Dr. Thomas B. Wilson. Mr. Maclure presented 5,233 volumes. Among them is a curious and important collection of pamphlets and books published in France during the first Revolution. The donations of Dr. Wilson, if less in number, are not inferior in value to those of Mr. Maclure. His valuable gifts are still continued. They are presented with the wise condition that they shall never be taken from the building.

The new building was commenced in 1839, on a vacant lot, corner of Broad and George streets. The edifice is entirely fire-proof. It is well adapted to its purposes; but, although ten years ago it was considered large enough to accommodate the collections for half a century, it is now crowded to excess.

The Apprentices' Library—11,700 *vols.*—The Apprentices' Library Company was incorporated April 2, 1821. In 1841 a separate department was established for girls. The boys' library contains about 9,000 volumes; the girls' library about 2,700. For the last three years the average annual increase of both libraries has been 900 volumes; the expenditure about 400 dollars per annum. The annual income of the institution is: from members, $550; from investments, $450. There is a catalogue for each library. For the boys' library the last catalogue (143 pages 12mo.) was printed in 1847; for the girls' library in 1849, (52 pages 12mo.)

The library is opened, for boys, on Monday, Wednesday, Friday, and Saturday evenings, about 2½ hours each; for girls, on Thursday afternoon from 3 to 7, and on Saturday afternoon from 3 to 6.

Apprentices and others under 21 years of age are allowed the use of the books gratis. About 24,000 books are annually lent to boys, and 7,000 to girls. The library is used regularly by about 800 boys and 250 girls.

Members pay $2 per annum, or $25 for life. The library is situated at the southwest corner of Fifth and Arch streets.

From the annual report of the managers, presented March, 1848, we gather the following additional statements:

"Mr. Thomas W. Goldtrap has bequeathed to the company one thousand dollars for the increase of the library.

"It is not the object of this company to swell the number of volumes in its libraries, for effect either at home or abroad. The sale, a year or two since, of about 2,000 volumes, will probably be followed by another when the present catalogue is disposed of. It is desirable that the libraries be kept fresh and attractive. Books as they are now prepared have a charm for youth, which the more ancient tomes do not possess; but it has been the care of your board to reject that spurious literature with which the market has been inundated by persons whose object appears to have been to make a book, regardless of historical accuracy. No work of a known immoral tendency is ever admitted."

About 600 copies of a work published by the company, were, in 1847, distributed among the apprentices using the library.

The Athenæum Library—10,000 *vols.*—We are indebted to an address, delivered at the opening of the new hall of the Athenæum, October 18, 1847, by Thomas J. Wharton, esq., for the following facts respecting this institution: It was founded in 1813 by a few young men, "who, feeling the want of a convenient place of common resort in which their leisure hours could be passed without danger to morals or tastes, came together and arranged a plan for the establishment of reading rooms." On the 9th of February, 1814, when the articles of association were adopted, the number of subscribers amounted to 200; and on the 7th of March following the institution was first opened to the public, in the room over the book-store of Mr. Matthew Carey, at the southeast corner of Chestnut and Fourth streets. Chief Justice Tilghman and Mr. Du Ponceau each bequeathed to the Athenæum $200.

Dr. William Lehman, who died in 1829, bequeathed to the Athenæum the sum of $10,000 for the erection of a suitable building. This legacy, by the prudent management of the treasurers, amounted, on the 1st of January, 1847, to $24,845 45. It is now invested in the beautiful building occupied by the Athenæum, the Historical Society, and the controllers of the public schools. The society derives a permanent income of $2,000 from the rent of the rooms. The entire cost, including fitting up, &c., will be less than $50,000, leaving a debt, to be secured by mortgage, of less than $14,000.

"The whole structure is 50 feet front on Sixth street, 125 feet on Adelphi street, and 58 feet high. It is an excellent specimen of the Italian style of architecture, treated with spirit and taste. The first story is divided into offices, and a large room of 37 by 60 feet, 14 feet high, for the comptrollers of the public schools. The second story is arranged for the uses of the Athenæum, and is divided into a news-room, library, and chess room. The news-room is on the Sixth street front, and is 37 by 47 feet, and 24 feet high; it will be finished in pilasters, with an enriched cornice and cone to the ceiling. The library is 37 feet wide, 65 feet long, and 24 feet high, and will be finished with a columnar ordinance of the Corinthian order, advanced from the sides of the room, forming a centre cell or nave and aisles; the latter will be filled up with bookcases, set laterally from the pillars to the wall, and is designed at some future time to be finished with a gallery, as the library extends; the cornice will be enriched with modillions and ornament, the ceiling being in panel. The chess room is 18 feet square, and is an ante room between the two large rooms; a room of the same size over this is intended for the directors' room. The third story is divided into 8 rooms (three of large size;) one of them, to be occupied by the Historical Society, is 26 feet by 37 feet, and 14 feet high."

"A feature (says Mr. Wharton) of this institution, to which I would advert with complacency, but certainly without boasting, is the free admission which it has always afforded to strangers; meaning by this term, persons not permanently residing in the city, or within ten miles of it, introduced by members. It may be worthy of remark and remembrance, that, according to a register kept by our worthy and attentive librarian, more than 30,000 strangers have visited the rooms, and availed themselves of the facilities and conveniences which they afford. During certain years the number has exceeded 1,000 annually, including representatives of every civilized country and community.

"Whatever may be the deficiencies of our catalogue, in respect to the standard works of English literature, I believe it will not be easy to find, in this country, a more complete or various collection of periodical literature, from the daily journal, through the various monthlies and quarterlies to the annual registers. Our library consists now, (October, 1847) I am informed, of nearly 10,000 volumes. We receive 24 foreign journals, scientific and literary; and 25 American. We take 5 foreign newspapers, and 62 American; one at least, I believe, from every State.

"Among the curiosities of literature in our rooms is a large collection of pamphlets, bound into 148 volumes, which belonged to Dr. Franklin, some of them containing his manuscript notes and marginal remarks; and a regular series of the Journal de Paris, bound in volumes, and continued during the whole eventful period of the French revolution."

The Library of the Pennsylvania Hospital—10,000 *vols.*—The hospital was established in 1750. The first medical book possessed by this institution appears to have been a present, in 1762, from Dr. John Fothergill. It was Lewis's History of the Materia Medica. The next year it was determined to demand a fee from students attending the wards at the time of the physicians, visiting the patients, and to appropriate the money arising from thence to the founding of a medical library.

Prior to the Revolution about 100 volumes had been presented, and two orders for books had been sent to London. Only 11 volumes were added to the library from 1774 to 1787. One of these was a pamphlet; another, "Cullen's First Lines of the Practice of Physic, 2 vols. 8vo." "cost the apparently enormous sum of £135 5*s*. This, however, when subjected to the talismanic operation of Richard Wells's scale of depreciation, shrinks to the comparative trifle of £1 15*s*. specie!"

In the years 1787–'9 the amount paid for books was £266 5*s*. 11*d*. The total expenditure for books previous to 1790, was equal to $886 48. The first catalogue, published in the year 1790, contains of folios 21, quartos 77, octavos 341, duodecimos 89; total, 528 volumes.

The increasing number of students from this time has afforded a fund for the steady increase of the library. For several years the books were selected and purchased by the celebrated Dr. Lettsom, who enriched the collection with many valuable donations.

In the year 1800 Sarah Lane presented 142 volumes of medical books, some of them very rare and valuable. A supplementary catalogue was printed in 1793, and a new catalogue in 1806, containing 127 pages 8vo.

On the decease of Dr. Benjamin S. Barton, his extensive and rare collection of works on natural history was purchased of his widow for $2,270.

A supplement to the second catalogue was printed in 1818.

Another, and the last catalogue of the library, was printed in 1829, containing 324 pages 8vo. At this time the library contained 5,828 volumes. A supplement, paged continuously with the catalogue, from page 325 to page 426, was printed in 1837, at which time the library contained 7,300 volumes.

The catalogue is thus divived: Alphabetical catalogue of authors, pages 1–202; alphabetical catalogue of editors and translators, 203–211; inaugural theses, in two parts—1st, an index to the universities, and names of graduates; 2d, a general catalogue in the order of subjects, 213–241—periodical literature, memoirs of societies, under the names of places where printed, 243–257; anonymous publications, arranged under classes, 259–268; index to subjects—part 1, medical, surgical, and chemical, (alphabetically arranged) 269–308; part 2, natural history and miscellaneous, &c., 309–322.

The library at present contains about 10,000 volumes, and occupies a large and elegant room in the hospital. The books are mostly medical, and pertaining to kindred sciences. In these departments it is probably the most extensive and valuable collection in this country.

Library of the Law Association of Philadelphia—5,100 *vols.*—"In the year 1802 a few gentlemen of the bar associated themselves for the purpose of forming a law library, for the use of the profession in this city; and, partially by donations which they made, and partially by payments from members of the company, succeeded, by degrees, in forming a collection, which, with the small number of books formerly known, was all that was needed. With the increasing number of reports in modern times, the library, as originally organized, fell very far behind the professional requirements of the day; and in September, 1841, an effort was made by a number of gentlemen to enlarge the collection, and to place it, generally, upon such a basis as should make it more worthy of the bar to which it belonged. Between the 15th of October, 1841, and the 1st March, 1850, there has been laid out by the association, in the purchase of new books, the sum of $9,583 72, exclusive of $865 87, in which last sum is embraced the cost of binding such of them as were bought in sheets."

"The collection, we are happy to believe, is now complete in all those departments usually required in the practice of the law. There exists in it a series of all the English, Irish, and American reports—a department in which we believe that no other library, either in Great Britain or the United States, is equally perfect. The department of text books is also reasonably good; and, in addition to complete collections of the British statutes at large, and of the acts both of our State and federal legislatures, in their authoritative, unabridged condition, there will be found upon the shelves of this library such digests and works of general jurisprudence as have obtained, with the profession, any title to authority. As a means of professional culture, and of extending among the bar a knowledge of the judicial decisions of England and of the United States, the collection affords all that as yet is practicable, and much of all that can at any time be desired.

"In the course of nearly fifty years which has passed since this library was founded, neither the State, the county, nor the city, have contributed a dollar to its increase; and while, even in its present condition, the payment of a sum merely nominal makes the least opulent practitioner among us the possessor of a library larger than any which the most wealthy owns, it is yet certain, that as a public library, answering all the demands of a numerous and intellectual profession, stimulated by the keen spirit of ambition and reward, and pushing its investigations through every avenue of knowledge, the collection is yet far in arrear of what it might be. There are some departments in which it is entirely wanting, and others where it is very imperfect. The civil law has no place in it at all, and the canon and ecclesiastical law have much too small an one. There is also a large class of books which do not come exactly within the title of law books, that yet belong to the law, considered as a philosophic science, or as a system of lofty morals. They are sometimes cited in courts, and would form, at any rate, a graceful addition to a library which represents in its corporate dignity an intellectual and elevated profession." [See circular letter of a committee of the Law Association.]

About 2,000 dollars a year are expended in the purchase of books. There is no vested fund. The income is derived from assessments of members and occasional contributions.

The library occupies a room 50 feet square, in the county court-house. The last catalogue, containing 64 pages 8vo., was printed in 1849.

The following are the most important rules of the library:

"The library is open from 10 o'clock a. m. till 3 p. m., and from 4½ till sunset, daily throughout the year, excepting during the months of July and August, on Christmas and New Year's day, the 22d of February, and on Saturday afternoons and Sundays; at which times it is closed.

"The following persons are allowed to use the library:

"1, members of the association and subscribers to the library; 2, judges of the court sitting within the city; 3, members of the bar from the country, attending the sessions in this city of the supreme court of Pennsylvania, or of the circuit court of the United States.

"Persons desirous of using this library can have the use of it for life, free of any annual charge, by paying the sum of $100. Or they may become members of the association by paying $30 in the first instance, and afterwards an assessment of $10 a year.

"Gentlemen of the bar who are not members of the association, nor subscribers for life to its library, may become subscribers to it annually by paying, during the first two years after their admission to the bar, $6 a year; during the ensuing two years, $8 a year; and afterwards, $12 a year.

"No book can be taken from the library-room by any person whomsoever, except for the purpose of being used in the court rooms. The present librarian is John William Wallace, esq."

The Library of the Franklin Institute, of the State of Pennsylvania, for the promotion of the mechanic arts, was founded about the year 1830, and contains 4,300 volumes, not including pamphlets. The apartment occupied as the library and reading-room of the society is 45 feet by 44. A catalogue was printed in 1847, containing 117 pp. 8vo. The library is open every day, except Sunday, from 9 o'clock a. m. till 10 p. m. It is intended primarily for the use of the members of the institute. The books are lent out. Not less than 1,000 annually consult the library without taking away books. The library is but an auxiliary means of producing the effects desired by the institute—the improvement of its members—and is not made or considered a separate branch or department. It is intended, like the collections of models, machines, &c., to be open for constant reference to the members and their friends. William Hamilton, actuary and *ex officio* librarian.

Library of the German Society—7,341 *vols.*—This library contains both German and English books. A catalogue (218 pp. 12mo.) was printed in 1839. [Ludewig.] It is now said to contain nearly 18,000 volumes, (January, 1851.)

The Library of the four monthly meetings of Friends, of Philadelphia, was founded in 1741, by a bequest of Thomas Checkley. A catalogue (150 pp. 8vo.) was printed in 1831. [Ludewig.]

College of St. Thomas of Villanova, near Philadelphia.—This is a new institution, chartered in 1847. It has no regularly organized library, but possesses about 2,000 books of all kinds. J. P. O. Luzen, O. S. A., president.

Library of the University of Pennsylvania—5,000 *vols.*—The University was founded in 1750. The library at present contains about 5,000 volumes. A catalogue (103 pp. 8vo.) was prepared and printed in 1829, by Judah Dobson. The following facts are stated in the preface:

"This library was begun by private donations of the friends of the institution; among whom the Rev. William Smith, the first provost of the college and academy, and Dr. McDowell, one of his successors, deserve to be particularly noticed. During the revolutionary war our little collection was enriched by a donation in books from his Majesty Louis the Sixteenth. Those books, printed at the royal printing office, consist chiefly of mathematical works; of works on natural history, among which is a collection of M. Buffon's; and some of the Byzantine historians. They have been all carefully preserved, and will, it is hoped, long remain a memorial of the liberality of that great and unfortunate monarch."

The Philomathean Society of undergraduates, founded in 1819, possesses a library of about 3,000 volumes. The Zelosophic Society, founded in 1829, has a library of 1,250 volumes.

Library of the American Baptist Publication Society—1,032 *vols.*

The Library of the Historical Society—1,728 *vols.*—The Historical Society of Pennsylvania was founded in 1825. The library contains 1,728 volumes, including 47 volumes of bound manuscripts. The society also has collections of medals and coins. Most of the books have been received within the last five years, and principally by donation. The library is kept in the hall of the society, a room in the third story of the Athenæum, about 29 by 42 feet in size. The books are arranged according to subjects. The shelves are distinguished by letters, A, B, C, &c., and each shelf has a distinct series of numbers, commencing with No. 1. The first part of the catalogue was printed in 1849. It contains 36 pages 8vo., and comprises the departments of history, biography, and manuscripts. The library is open on the evenings of the meetings of the society, namely, the second Monday of each month, and is accessible to the members of the society, and only by courtesy to others. No record has until lately been kept of the use of the library. William Duane, librarian.

The following notice prefixed to the published catalogue gives some additional facts respecting the library:

"The Historical Society of Pennsylvania was founded in 1825. It met for nineteen years in one of the rooms of the American Philosophical Society, and had the use of a small closet in this room to contain its books. In the year 1844 the society removed to a room rented by itself for its exclusive accommodation. Its collection of books then amounted to about sixty volumes, in addition to some boxes of public documents from Washington, which had not been opened, as the society had no place in which to place the books. Immediately after the removal, the library increased rapidly, and a still further increase has followed its removal to their present location in the Athenæum building, south Sixth street. The library now amounts to about 1,750 volumes, divided into ten classes: history, biography, manuscripts, pamphlets, periodicals, voyages and travels, newspapers, public documents of Pennsylvania, public documents of the United States, and miscellaneous. These observations have been considered necessary to explain why a society twenty four years in existence has not a larger collection of books. Had it not been for the cramped position it was compelled to occupy before it had a room of its own, it would doubtless have long since reached its present size.—*January* 10, 1849."

An address before the society, delivered by William B. Reed, on the occasion of opening the hall in the Athenæum, January 28, 1848, has been printed, and contains some interesting facts concerning the society, besides valuable remarks and suggestions respecting the objects of such an institution.

PITTSBURG.

The Young Men's Mercantile Library and Mechanics' Institute—1,188 *vols.*—Founded September, 1847; incorporated March, 1849. The library contains (January 1, 1850) 1,188 volumes, a small collection of engravings, and about 353 mineralogical specimens. A reading-room of valuable journals is connected with the library. Since the establishment of the institution, about 500 volumes have, each year, been added to the library, and about 450 dollars been expended in the purchase of books. The association occupies two rooms, each 29 by 55 feet, forming the 2d and 3d stories of a well-built brick building. A catalogue is in preparation.

The library is open daily from 8 a. m. till 10 p. m.

The persons entitled to the use of the library are: members by the payment of $4 per annum ; life members by the payment of $35 at one time; and honorary members elected by the directors.

About 2,200 books were lent out during the last year. J. Finney, jr., president.

Theological Seminary Library—1,500 *vols.*—This seminary was incorporated in 1828. It is under the direction of the Associate Reformed Church.

Washington College Libraries—3,300 *vols.*

WESTCHESTER.

The Chester County Cabinet of Natural Sciences, at Westchester, Pennsylvania, was founded in March, 1826, and incorporated in 1831. Its library contains 450 volumes, of which 150 are works on the natural sciences, chiefly botany, zoology, and geology; and 300 miscellaneous, general science, languages, and literature. It has a collection of original letters, from the principal general officers of the American army of the Revolution; and also the autograph signatures of 103 distinguished patriots of the Revolution, military and civil, cut from their letters to Gen. Anthony Wayne—all presented by his son, the Hon. Isaac Wayne. It also has several charts of the coast survey from Professor Bache; a very few engravings and medals, and about 400 coins, (300 copper and 100 silver,) among which are 86 silver and 59 copper coins from 21 different governments, collected during the circumnavigating cruise of the United States ship Peacock, in 1835-'37, by the late Lieutenant Darlington, United States navy, and presented by him. The additions to the library have been made very irregularly, and probably do not average more than 15 or 20 volumes annually. There is no regular expenditure for books. The greater portion of the books has been obtained by donation. A three-story brick hall, roofed with tin, was erected in 1836 for the use of the "Cabinet," and to contain its library and museum. The cost of the building was upwards of $5,000. The hall of the "Cabinet" is 40 feet front by 50 feet deep; the lower story is fitted for a lecture room, with a larboratory in the rear. The second story is a large room calculated for an athenæum, or reading-room; and the third story contains the museum and library of the "Cabinet." There is no printed catalogue. The library is accessible to all the members at each meeting of the "Cabinet." The books are lent out to members, when applied for.

The Chester County Cabinet of Natural Science, in addition to the library, &c., possesses one of the best and most extensive collections of minerals in Pennsylvania; a splendid collection of *shells*, and of English and American *birds;* a *herbarium* of *seven thousand species of plants*, duly arranged, labelled, and catalogued; with various curiosities in nature and art. William Darlington, M. D., president.

The Chester County Athenæum was founded February 9, 1827, and incorporated in 1828. The library contains 1,431 volumes, consisting of works on history, biography, natural science, travels, and the usual assortment of books proper for a village library. Until within the last six years the institution was neglected; within that time, by the exertion of some public-spirited individuals, it has been resuscitated, and the annual increase is now from 130 to 160 volumes, and the annual expenditure for books from 110 to 140 dollars. There is a written, but not a printed catalogue. The library is open every day, at all hours till 8 o'clock in the evening. The members and subscribers are entitled to the use of the library on the following terms:—stockholders pay each $2 per year; subscribers $2 per year; minors $1; transient subscribers 6 cents per week for duodecimos, 8 cents for 8vos. The number of books taken out for the last three years has ranged from 1,300 to 1,600 annually, and is increasing each year. Any respectable person can have the opportunity of consulting the library, or taking home the books. William Darlington, librarian.

DELAWARE.

DOVER.

The State Library, and the Law Library, contain, together, about 4,000 volumes. Since 1837 a room in the capitol has been devoted exclusively to the use of the library. Occasional appropriations are made by the legislature for the increase of the collection. About 100 volumes have been added annually for the last ten years. Books may be freely used by any citizen who subscribes the rules. Samuel C. Letherbury, librarian.

NEWARK.

Delaware College Libraries—8,700 *vols.*—The college was founded in 1833. The college library contains 2,500 volumes. There are two societies of undergraduates, with libraries of 1,500 volumes each. The private library of the president contains 2,000 volumes; and the private collections of two other members of the faculty contain 1,200 volumes. These are all in the college building, and form an aggregate of 8,700 volumes, accessible to all persons connected with the college; and indeed to others who may wish to use them for literary purposes. An effort is making to enlarge the college library. Rev. James P. Wilson, president.

NEWCASTLE.

Public Library—4,000 *vols.*—The Newcastle Library Company was founded in 1812. The library contains about 4,000 volumes. It is sustained by an annual assessment of $2 on each share. The price of a share is $20. The library at present occupies a room in the town academy. Samuel Guthrie, librarian.

MARYLAND.

ANNAPOLIS.

The State Library—15,000 *vols.*—The State Library of Maryland was founded in 1827, and contains 15,000 volumes, besides 59 volumes of manuscripts, 108 maps, 19 charts. The yearly average number of volumes added to the library for the last ten years is 580. There has been an annual appropriation by the legislature of $500. There is also in operation a system of exchanges with other States. The library occupies a room in the State-house. A catalogue (132 pages 8vo.) prepared by David Ridgely, then librarian, was published in December, 1837, at Annapolis. The titles are classified under 37 chapters. The arrangement of the books upon the shelves corresponds with the divisions of the catalogue. The library is opened daily (Sundays excepted) during the sessions of the legislature, from 9 o'clock a. m. to the time of the daily adjournment of both houses, and from 5 to 9 p. m., except during night sessions, when it is kept open till the adjournment. The governor, chancellor, judges, State officers, members and ex-members of the legislature, lawyers practising in the court of appeals, and officers of the army and navy stationed at Annapolis, can take out books. Any person may consult the library in the room. No record has been kept of loans or of visitors. Richard Swann, librarian.

St. John's College Library—3,292 *vols.*—The library dates, with the college, from 1784, and contains 3,292 volumes. Occasional appropriations are made by the board for the increase of the library. The collection is in a room of the new brick college, 36 feet by 15, in 7 alcoves. The books are arranged according to subjects; only one catalogue has been printed—date 1847, pp. 38. The library is opened one hour every Saturday. All persons connected with the college are entitled to use the books; and they are occasionally lent, by courtesy, to others. About 800 volumes are lent in a year. William D. Greetham, librarian.

BALTIMORE.

The Baltimore Library—15,000 *vols.*—The Library Company of Baltimore was founded in 1796, and possesses 15,000 volumes of printed books and five volumes of manuscripts: among them "Aristotelis Physica," 1312, and "Nic. de Lyra, *Matth.*" of the middle of the 14th century, with beautiful illuminations; 20 collections of maps and charts; 100 volumes of engravings. The income of the institution is derived from the annual payments of stockholders (about 265) and annual subscribers, and amounts to about $1,100 per annum. The building was erected in conjunction with the Maryland Historical Society and the Mercantile Library Association, and was a gift from the citizens of Baltimore. (See Maryland Historical Society.) The rooms of the Library Company are upon the second story of the edifice, and consist of a library 47 by 53 feet, height 20 feet, with a gallery. Adjoining, at one end, is a directors' room, 14 by 16 feet; at the other end is a reading-room, 26 by 47 feet; and beyond that another, 14 by 32 feet. A catalogue was printed in 1798; a second in 1802; and a third in 1809. The last mentioned contains 196 pages 8vo., and has been continued by supplements—the first in 1816, of 36 pages; the second in 1823, of 40 pages; the third in 1831, of 21 pages; the fourth in 1841, of 28 pages. The library is open daily, except Sundays and certain holidays, in summer from 8 a. m. to 6 p. m., in winter from 9 a. m. to 4 p. m. Persons entitled to the use of the library are: stockholders paying $100 for a "free" share, or $30 for a share and $5 per annum, and subscribers at the rate of $8 per annum, or $1 per month. About 5,000 books are lent out each year. Perhaps 100 persons, each year, consult the library without taking away books. About 400 visitors each year. John S. Sumner, librarian.

St. Mary's College Library—12,000 *vols.*—The library was commenced with the institution in the year 1809, and contains about 12,000 volumes; a few manuscripts, among them a modern 4to. MS. entitled "Tableau présent des Etats Unis par George Novion," in 369 elegantly written pages, with statistical tables: date, about 1791–2; some valuable maps, charts, and engravings. The annual increase is about 500 volumes. The library occupies two large rooms in the college edifice. The librarian is engaged in classifying the books according to subjects. There is no printed catalogue. A complete MS. catalogue is in preparation. There is no stated time for opening the library, but it is accessible at all times on application to the librarian. All persons connected with the institution are entitled to the use of the books, and others are allowed the use on application. Books are sometimes lent out to read, but the practice is discountenanced at present on account of former abuse of the privilege. With the permission of the superior, books may be lent to persons at a distance. Rev. M. Feller, librarian.

This is a very excellent library, composed for the most part of theological and classical books, but not deficient in other departments.

There is a small library of some 600 volumes belonging to a society of students.

The Mercantile Library—9,000 *vols.*—The Mercantile Library Association of Baltimore was established November, 1839, and incorporated January, 1842. The library contains (June, 1850) 9,000 volumes of books, 1 volume of autographs, 20 maps, 15 framed engravings, 25 volumes of engravings. The yearly average increase is about 700 volumes; the annual expenditure for books $700. The library occupies the ground floor of the Baltimore Athenæum. (See Maryland Historical Society.) Its rooms correspond with those of the Library Company. A short catalogue, alphabetical, was printed in 1842, and a supplement in 1844. Another catalogue (118 pages 12mo.) was printed in July, 1848. The library is opened every day from 11 a. m, to 2 p. m., and from 3 to 10 p. m. Active members (who must be clerks by profession) pay for the privileges of the library $5 for the first year, and $3 for each succeeding year. Honorary members (all persons other than clerks) pay $5 per annum. James Green, librarian.

The following table, compiled from the first six annual reports of the association (all that have been printed,) exhibits the early progress of the institution. The last line shows its present condition:

	No. of volumes in library.	Dollars expended during year for books.	Honorary members.	Active members.	Use of library.
					Volumes.
November, 1840...	1,400	1,400	141	125	2,314
Do....1841...	2,100	800	150	262	4,204
Do....1842...	2,839	890	122	312	....
Do....1843...	3,610	640	....	303	5,805
Do....1844...	4,393	854	112	361	7,800
Do....1845...	5,221	544	....	571	8,500
June, 1850........	9,000	700	250	450	10,000

The Maryland Historical Society was founded in 1843, and incorporated March, 1844. The library contains 1,500 volumes, principally historical, and 270 volumes of newspapers, published mostly in Maryland. The set of the Maryland Gazette commences in 1728, and, though this is imperfect, a complete series of papers printed in Maryland from that time to the present, exists in the library. The collection of manuscripts, though not large, embraces many of value and interest, especially those placed under the care of the society by the State legislature, as the journals of the old council, and letters to and from the governors and the proprietors. Among the MSS. are also several unpublished orders of General Washington, and some valuable letters from officers of the Maryland line, with regard to the southern campaign. A large and commodious building has been erected for the joint accommodation of the Maryland Historical Society, the Library Company of Baltimore, and the Mercantile Library Association. The Maryland Historical Society holds in fee the third floor of the Athenæum building; and this floor is divided into four inter-communicating apartments: a room for the use of the officers of the society, which is 14 feet by 23; a meeting-room and library, 26 feet by 47 and 23 feet high; a gallery of fine arts, 47 feet by 53, with a ceiling 23 feet high at the apex and sloping to 20 feet at the walls, lighted by a skylight in the roof, affording 400 superficial feet of glazed surface; and a gallery for sculpture and casts from the antique, 14 by 23 feet. The rooms of the society are furnished in an elegant manner, with solid oak cases, tables, and chairs. The whole cost of the building was $28,182. The furniture is valued at $8,000.

As yet no regular catalogue of the library has been prepared for printing. The library is open daily from 10 in the morning until 6 o'clock in the afternoon. The regular meetings of the society are held upon the first Thursday evening of every month. The members of the society are, of course, entitled to the use of the library; but as the object of the institution is not only to collect valuable material, but to make it as generally useful as possible, the books, original papers, &c., are at all times open to the examination and perusal of all who may wish to refer to them, subject only to the observance of such rules as are essential to their preservation. The books are not allowed to be taken from the rooms, except under circumstances which appear to justify a departure from the rule; because, the library being chiefly valuable for purposes of reference, it is thought desirable that investigations should be conducted in the rooms as much as possible; and much inconvenience would result to the many from this partial accommodation of the few. The number consulting the library is large, though it cannot be exactly stated.

One of the prominent features in the plan of the society was the establishment of chapters in the different counties of the State. It is hoped that this novel but admirable project may, ere long, be realized. Francis B. Mayer is the acting librarian.

From a letter of J. Morrison Harris, esq., corresponding secretary of the Historical Society, besides the foregoing statements, we quote the following passage, explanatory of the views of this energetic association, in the establishment of the gallery of art:

"The gallery of fine arts is intrusted to a committee who are elected to serve for one year, and who make all the arrangements connected with exhibitions, &c. As this feature is not exactly connected with the purposes and legitimate plan of an historical society, it may be well to say something in explanation of its connexion with our society. The idea was first suggested by an effort which the society made, some years since, and still continues, to procure the originals or copies of the portraits of distinguished men connected with the founding of the colony, the events of its early history, and eminent in their associations with its annals down to the present time. Our plan is to raise, by yearly exhibitions of good pictures, a fund which will, by degrees, enable us to build up a gallery of our own, consisting of good copies of the best pictures of the old masters, and original pictures of merit by native artists; and we cherish the confident hope that, while the prosecution of this scheme will in no way interfere with our historical labors, it will enable us to throw open, hereafter, to the man of taste and to the student, a well selected collection of paintings, which will produce upon the community those good effects inseparable from an elevated appreciation of art."

The following is from the annual report made in February 1, 1849, by J. Spear Smith, esq., president of the society:

"In the original project of the Athenæum, it was deemed not only proper, but essential, to embrace within it a gallery of fine arts. Various attempts had previously, and at different epochs, been made, to form and sustain societies connected with the subject, and in the hope of introducing the desirable accompaniment of a permanent gallery; but, notwithstanding the zeal and talent with which these meritorious essays were made, they failed of being attended with commensurate success. If, therefore, such an opportunity as was now offered were permitted to escape, the day seemed distant when Baltimore would be in the enjoyment of so attractive an addition to her public institutions. There existed also a confident belief that, under the strong protection of the society, it could be alone instituted and successfully maintained. It was, consequently, no accidental circumstance which led to the union of a gallery with the society, nor did it arise from any difficulty in the disposition of the space allotted to it. Being thus an element in the primary scheme, the architect was instructed to incorporate in the plan an apartment adapted in its proportions, and in the proper admission of light, to this object. This was successfully accomplished, and with so much judgment as to have elicited the decided approbation of connoisseurs, and others versed in such matters. In accordance with the original design, the gallery fell under the administration of this society. This disposition of it seemed appropriate for many reasons, not the least of which was the connexion, for the most part, of the productions of the painter and sculptor with historical persons or events. It was intended, also, to increase the attractions and popularity of the society, by affording an agreeable and tasteful relaxation to its members."

The Odd Fellows' Library—3,541 *vols.*—The Odd Fellows' Library was established in 1849, though some books had been collected for the purpose several years before. Last year, upwards of a thousand dollars were expended for books. An appropriation is regularly made from the funds of the different lodges, but no member is taxed additionally for the support of the library; yet every one has the full use of it. The Grand Lodge has appropriated a large room—about 60 feet by 20—on the first floor of the hall, for its use; but it is hardly large enough to accommodate the numerous visitors. The hall is soon to be enlarged, and then, it is supposed, a fine suite of rooms will be assigned to the library. The only catalogue published, as yet, is one of the German books, (812 in number.) The library is open every evening, except Saturday, from half-past 7 to 11 in summer, and from half-past 6 to 10 in winter. All the members of the Order in Baltimore (about 8,000 in number) are allowed the use of the books without charge. The circulation for one quarter ending July, 1850, has been 2,331 volumes. John Shotton is librarian.

Baltimore Female College.—This institution was incorporated in 1850, with power to confer degrees; it is located in St. Paul's street. It possesses a well-selected library of 2,800 volumes, to which the older pupils have access. There is also a valuable collection of minerals, and a cabinet of ancient and modern coins. Of ancient coins there are more than 500. [See catalogue of the B. F. C. for 1850.]

Library of the Medico-Chirurgical Society—2,000 *vols.*

Library of the Medical Department, University of Maryland—1,000 *vols.*

Law Library—1,000 *vols.*

Several of the Fire Companies in Baltimore possess valuable collections of books. The libraries of the Mechanical Fire Company and of the Patapsco Fire Company number about 1,000 volumes each.

Mechanics' Institute Library—1,000 *vols.*—"The Maryland Institute for the Promotion of the Mechanic Arts" was founded in 184–, and incorporated in 1849. It receives an annual grant of $500 from the State. It has held three annual exhibitions of American manufactures. It supports a course of lectures during the winter months, and has established a school of design, which promises to be an important and highly useful branch of the institute. Among the objects of the association is the collection of a library. About 1,000 volumes have already been obtained, and vigorous efforts are making to increase the number. The institute is contemplating the immediate erection of a building for its purposes.

CHESTERTOWN.

Washington College Libraries—1,100 *vols.*—The College Library was founded in 1783. In 1827 the college was burned down, and only 170 volumes rescued from the flames. In 1844 the college was revived, a new building erected, and 380 new volumes added. These, together with the valuable present of State papers, and other documents, by Hon. J. A. Pearce, form an aggregate of 1,000 volumes, with some good collections of maps, &c. No yearly appropriation of money for the increase of the library has, as yet, been made, in consequence of the determination of the board to erect new buildings. After these are finished, a liberal sum will be set apart for the purchase of books. There is a manuscript, but no printed, catalogue. Persons connected with the college are allowed the use of the books without fee. Strangers are sometimes, by courtesy, permitted to use the library. S. S. Rogers, librarian.

The Mount Vernon Society of Students, founded in 1847, has about 100 volumes.

EMMETSBURG.

Mount St. Mary's College Library—4,000 *vols.*

HAGERSTOWN.

St. James College Libraries—3,500 *vols.*

The College Library contains - - -	2,500 volumes.
The Library of the Belles Lettres Society contains	500 "
The Irving Society Library contains - -	500 "

ROCKVILLE.

The Montgomery County Library Association, founded in 1849, has a commencement of a library (115 volumes.) The money received by annual subscriptions will be devoted to the increase of the collection. Arrangements have been made for fitting up a room in the building formerly occupied as the county clerk's office for a library and reading room. The library is open daily from 9 to 3 o'clock. Persons become members of the association by subscribing to the constitution, and paying a small initiation fee. O. W. Treadwell, librarian.

The *Academy* at Rockville has a small library, containing about 150 volumes, for the use of the students.

SANDY SPRING.

Sandy Spring Library Company.—This library, founded in 1841, contains about 500 volumes. About 70 volumes are added each year, and about 40 dollars expended for books. A catalogue was printed some six years ago, containing 12 pages 12mo. The library is open daily from 6 a. m. to 10 p. m. It is restricted to members of the company, who pay five dollars for a share, and $1 50 annual subscription. Joseph Gilpin, librarian.

DISTRICT OF COLUMBIA.

GEORGETOWN.

College Libraries—26,100 *vols.*—The library of Georgetown College dates from the foundation of the college, in 1792, and contains at present 25,000 volumes. Many duplicates have been given to kindred institutions, and a valuable collection of astronomical works has been taken from the library and placed in the observatory attached to the college. About $350 a year are expended for books. The library is kept in a room 33½ by 26 feet, most tastefully arranged with shelves of Brazilian wood, birds'-eye maple, curled maple, &c., the work of one of the members of the institution. There is also an octagonal room for state papers, journals, &c. No catalogue has been published, but one will soon be put to press. The books are arranged according to subjects. Only the faculty and students of the higher branches are entitled to take books from the library, and the person borrowing the book is strictly prohibited from lending it to any person, *even in the college.* Books are very seldom lent out of the college; owing to the loss of several works, great caution is exercised in lending. Rev. J. M. Finotti, librarian.

The Philodemic and Philonomosian Debating Societies have libraries of books in general literature, in all upwards of 1,100 volumes, purchased with the subscriptions of members, or presented by members on their admission to the societies.

The college library is one of the most valuable in the country, particularly in theology and the classics. It contains a complete set of the Acta Sanctorum, the Church Fathers in the Benedictine editions, and many works of great value and rarity, at least in this country.

WASHINGTON.

The Library of Congress—50,000 *vols.*—The first Library of Congress was founded April 24, 1800. It was collected under the direction of Dr. Mitchell, Mr. Gallatin, and others, and consisted of about three thousand volumes, when it was destroyed by the British army on the 24th of August, 1814. It was a valuable collection, and was much resorted to in the early days of the city. The total loss of the library induced Mr. Jefferson to offer his collection to Congress. It was purchased in 1815. It consisted of about 7,000 volumes, for which Mr. Jefferson received $23,000. It formed the nucleus of the present library, which contains (January 1, 1850) about 50,000 volumes, a few manuscripts, a series of medals designed by Denon and executed by order of the French government, commemorative of events during the reign of Napoleon; some valuable maps and charts, and busts of several of the Presidents, with a few paintings of interest. The yearly average increase is about 1,800 volumes. $5,000 per annum are appropriated by Congress for the purchase of miscellaneous books, and $1,000 for law books.

The library occupies three rooms in the Capitol, only one of which was originally designed for the purpose. The principal library-room is 92 feet in length, 34 feet in width, and 36 feet in height. It contains 12 alcoves—6 on each side—divided by a gallery. The books are arranged according to subjects, on the system of Bacon. Catalogues have been published as follows: In 1802 (10 pp. 8vo.;) supplement, 1803 (3 pp.) and 1808 (41 pp.;) in 1812 (101 pp. 8vo.;) in 1815 (170 pp. 4to., containing Jefferson's library;) supplement, 1820 (28 pp.;) and in 1830 and '31 (362 pp. 8vo.)

The last catalogue was printed in 1840 (747 pp. 8vo.) The additions since that time are in annual supplements. A new catalogue is in press.

The library is open every day during the sessions of Congress. During the recess it is opened on Tuesday, Thursday, and Saturday of each week, six hours each day. Members of Congress, the President and Vice President of the United States, Heads of Departments, Judges of the Supreme Court, Secretary of the Senate, Clerk of the House, agents of the Library Committee, and Foreign Ministers, are entitled to the use of the library, and are allowed to take out books. The number of books annually lent out is not known, nor can the number of persons consulting the library be stated. It is very great during the sessions of Congress. John S. Meehan, librarian; E. B. Stelle and C. H. W. Meehan, assistants; Robert Kearon, messenger.

In the catalogue the works are classed according to the system of Lord Bacon. This system was introduced by Mr. Jefferson, and, unfortunately, has been continued here, after its abandonment in most other libraries. It was not intended by its author as a bibliographical system, nor has any improvement which it has received rendered it convenient or useful for that purpose.

The Library of Congress is one of great value. It is worthy of a minute and accurate catalogue. It would be comparatively useless without one, were it not for the catalogue of its contents written upon the memory of the librarians. In a catalogue of the Library of Congress every book, pamphlet, map, handbill, speech, and important article in a review or magazine, should be entered carefully and accurately under the name of its author, and alphabetical and analytical indexes of subjects should be made. The catalogue should be a model performance. Such an one should not, of course, be required from the present force employed in the library, which is not sufficient for the regular work of the establishment. The making of a catalogue should be a separate affair.

The librarian is appointed by the President of the United States, and is governed by rules adopted by the President of the Senate and the Speaker of the House of Representatives. A joint committee of the two houses is charged with the purchase of the books.

Library of the House of Representatives—12,000 *vols.*—Besides the Library of Congress, there is in the Capitol a library for the use of the members of the House, consisting mostly of public documents, and containing several sets, nearly complete, from the first commencement of the government. The aggregate number of volumes is at present upwards of 12,000. The annual increase is about 400 volumes. The library occupies a series of closets, triangular rooms, and attics, near the hall of the House. It is open daily while the House is in session, and is the constant resort of members, who alone are entitled to the use of it. There is no printed catalogue, but one in manuscript. Philip Williams, librarian.

Library of the State Department—7,000 *vols.*—The library commenced with the "Department of Foreign Affairs," in 1781. It contains at present about 7,000 volumes and 500 pamphlets. The number of maps and charts unbound is about 1,500. The annual increase is about 50 volumes. About $100 are expended for books. The library is in the building of the department, and occupies two rooms. The larger is 36 feet long, 15 feet 9 inches wide, and 14 high, divided on one side into seven alcoves. The smaller room is 17 feet by 15 feet 9 inches. A catalogue was printed in 1825, (small 8vo.. 67 pp.,) and another in 1830 (small 8vo., 150 pages.)

Besides the public library of the State Department, there is a large collection of manuscripts relating to the history of the country, in the archives of the department. The number cannot now be accurately stated.

Copyright books—State Department.—Since May 31, 1790, when the first copyright act was passed, books and other articles have been accumulating in the State Department, deposited there in accordance with the provisions of the law. They number at present about 10,000 volumes, besides maps and charts; over 3,000 pieces of music, and more than 800 lithographic prints and engravings.

The average annual increase of books for the last ten years has been about 400 volumes. These articles are kept in two rooms in the State Department, each about 18 by 21 feet and 12 feet high. They are arranged in close presses, according to their subject-matter. There is no complete catalogue. The rooms are open from 9 o'clock a. m. to 3 p. m. on office days. The books are not lent out. But few persons consult the library—probably not more than 50 a year. Charles E. Weaver, librarian.

The Library of the War Department, Washington, was organized about the year 1832, when Lewis Cass was Secretary of War. It contains about 7,000 or 8,000 volumes, all the government medals, (50 or 60 in number,) and is well supplied with maps and charts. About $2,000 has for the last ten years been the average annual expenditure for the purchase of books. The library occupies a room in the War Department 50 by 18 feet, handsomely furnished. It is open every day, excepting Sunday, from 9 to 3 o'clock. The heads of departments and bureaus, officers of the army and navy, foreign ministers, and the clerks of the War Department, are entitled to the use of the books, and are allowed to take them from the library. Charles Lanman, librarian.

Columbian College Libraries—6,200 vols.—The library of the Columbian College was founded in 1821. It contains (January, 1850) about 4,500 volumes, and some maps, charts, and engravings. The yearly average increase is about 50 volumes. The collection of a fund for the library has been commenced. The librarian is now preparing a catalogue for the press. The library is opened once a week, and kept open several hours. Officers, students, trustees, and such other persons as they may recommend, may use the books.

There are two societies of students connected with the college, possessing in their libraries about 1,700 volumes.

Library of the Navy Department.—The Navy Department has no regularly organized library. There are, however, valuable collections of books in the office of the chief clerk, in the Bureau of Ordnance and Hydrography, in the Bureau of Yards and Docks, and in the Bureau of Construction. In all there are not less than 3,000 volumes, including Congressional documents.

The Library of the Patent Office contains about 6,000 volumes. A catalogue was printed in 1847, (34 pages 8vo.) The library has greatly increased since that time. It contains a valuable collection of works on chemistry, agriculture, technology, engineering, &c.; complete series of many valuable scientific periodicals; the best encyclopedias, English,

French, German, &c. It is in a room in the Patent Office, and under the care of a librarian appointed by the Commissioner of Patents.

Treasury Department—2,000 *vols.*—Books have, from time to time, been procured by occasional appropriations by Congress, for a library of the Treasury Department. Until the present year, however, no such institution has been regularly organized. Very recently Mr. John Taliaferro, of Virginia, has been appointed librarian; a room in the Treasury building, 60 feet by 20, has been appropriated and fitted up for the collection; and measures have been taken for establishing a library upon a permanent foundation, and procuring for it books important to the officers of the department, for whose use the library is principally designed.

The Library of the Engineer Department contains about 1,700 volumes, including Congressional documents, of which the sets are nearly complete since 1805, many manuscript official reports, and a large number of maps and charts relating to the defences of the country. The yearly average increase is about 50 volumes. Books are purchased out of the contingent fund of the department, annually granted by Congress. The library is in the office of the Chief Engineer, Winder's building, and is open every day from 9 to 3 o'clock. Books are lent to the officers of the department, the clerks, and to other persons by courtesy. The assistant to the Chief Engineer is *ex officio* librarian. The present officer is Captain Frederick A. Smith, United States engineers.

Washington Library—5,000 *vols.*—The "Directors of the Washington Library Company" were incorporated by act of Congress, approved April 18, 1814. The library contains about 5,000 volumes, and increases at the rate of about 50 volumes per annum. The price of a share is $12, subject to an annual assessment of $3. The library is open daily from 3 o'clock till 6 p. m. A catalogue was printed in 1835, containing 75 pages 12mo.

The Library of the Smithsonian Institution—6,000 *vols.*—The Smithsonian Institution was established by act of Congress, 10th August, 1846, upon a fund bequeathed by James Smithson, esq., of England. The act of Congress provides that the Board of Regents, to whom is intrusted the management of the institution, shall make an annual appropriation, not exceeding $25,000 a year, for the collection of a library. By a resolution of the Regents the whole income of the institution is to be perpetually divided into two equal parts; one half to be devoted to the publication of memoirs, reports, &c., the instituting of researches, and the support of lectures, &c.; the other part to collections in science, literature and art. Common expenses are to be divided equally between the two departments. As the museum and cabinet will require but small annual appropriations, the greater part of the half of the income devoted to collections will be expended for a library. From this provision, and from gifts, exchanges, and bequests, we may justly hope to see, ere long, upon this foundation a library worthy of the United States of America—one which shall release us from a provincial dependance in literary matters upon the libraries of Europe. As a full account of the collection at present belonging to the institution will be found in the librarian's report (to which this is an appendix,) it is unnecessary to give further details in this place. The library is open daily, during business hours. The books are accessible to all who wish to use them in the room. The use of the library is already considerable. The number of visitors is very great. C. C. Jewett, librarian.

The National Institute for the Promotion of Science was founded at Washington in May, 1840, and incorporated by act of Congress, approved 27th July, 1842. The library contains 3,173 volumes and pamphlets. It has three manuscripts, viz: two Arabic, and one illuminated Latin. There are, also, considerable collections of maps, charts, and engravings. In the cabinet are many medals, coins, &c. The library has been received entirely by donation and exchange. It is of course quite miscellaneous; but it contains many valuable scientific and historical works, and transactions of learned societies. Many useful and costly books have been obtained for the institute by Mr. Alexandre Vattemare, the well known advocate of the system of international exchanges. The library occupies, temporarily, a room, 22 feet square, in the Patent Office of the United States. There is no printed catalogue, but one in manuscript. The library is always opened when calls are made especially for books; but there are no stated times for opening it. No rules have been adopted respecting the use of the library. Members of the institute are entitled to visit the library, and there consult books as they wish; but they cannot take them away. Dr. James H. Causten, jr., librarian.

Jefferson Apprentices' Library—2,000 *vols.*

Library of the Observatory—500 *vols.*—The observatory (depot of charts and instruments) was established in 1842, under the Navy Department. Its library is composed mostly of mathematical works.

VIRGINIA.

BERRYVILLE.

The Academy Library—1,000 *vols.*—The president and trustees of this institution, in their report to the president of the literary fund, in 1835, state: "About 25 years since a lot of ground, containing about two acres, was procured in the town of Berryville, and a building erected thereon by private contribution, at an expense of about $3,000, which has since been constantly occupied as an English and classical academy. A few years since further subscriptions were entered into for the gradual purchase of a library of about 1,000 volumes, to be attached to the academy; which library is also in successful operation, and promises to be extensively useful, both to the students of the academy and to the residents in its immediate neighborhood."

BETHANY.

College Libraries—2,280 *vols.*—The library of Bethany College was founded in 1840, and contains 1,224 volumes, 12 maps and charts, and 21 engravings. One-half of the matriculation fees received from students is devoted to the library. The fund consequently fluctuates with the number of new students each successive session. The library is opened one hour each week. All persons connected with the institution are entitled to the use of the library. Books are not lent to other persons. There are two literary societies connected with the college. The Neotrophian Society, founded in November, 1841, has a library of 562 volumes. The American Literary Institute, founded in December, 1841, has a library of 494 volumes. J. D. Pickett, librarian.

BOYDTOWN, MECKLENBURG COUNTY.

Library of Randolph Macon College, near Boydtown—6,000 *vols.*—This institution was incorporated in 1832. Its library and mineralogical cabinet are valued, in the report to the president of the literary fund, in 1835, at $2,500. The number of volumes in its libraries is stated in the American Almanac, for 1850, at 6,000.

BRUNSWICK COUNTY.

Ebenezer Academy, incorporated in 1795, reports to the president of the literary fund, in 1835, "a small library."

CAROLINE COUNTY.

Rappahannock Academy.—Incorporated 1809–'10. The trustees in their report to the president of the literary fund, in 1835, say: "Connected with the institution is a library, selected, for the most part, by the late Colonel John Taylor, who may be regarded as the father of the institution, and purchased with funds obtained by the sale of the organ belonging to Mount Church. The library contains works on law, medicine, theology, history, biography, science, geography, political economy, &c., &c. It is, however, very inadequate to the wants of the academy; but such additions are made to it, from time to time, as its feeble means will allow."

CHARLOTTESVILLE.

Library of the University of Virginia—18,378 *vols.*—The library was founded in 1825, and contains 18,378 volumes, 24 maps and charts, and 2,000 engravings. The yearly average increase for the last ten years has been 413 volumes. The yearly average expenditure, prior to 1848, $500; for 1848, $1,000. The regular annual appropriation, out of the revenues of the university, is $500. The Madison legacy of $1,500 yields $90 per annum, for the increase of the collection. The library occupies the third story and dome of the rotundo—a circular brick building, 75 feet in diameter, erected in 1825, expressly for a library, for $70,000. The two lower stories are used for lecture-rooms, laboratory, museum, &c. A catalogue was printed in 1828 containing 116 pages 8vo. The library is open daily for an hour and a half. The rector, visitors, professors, and students of the university, and no others, are entitled to the use of the library. To these persons books are lent out under certain prescribed limitations. About 3,000 are taken out annually. About 275 persons, in a year, consult the library without taking away books. William Westenbaker, librarian.

"This library was originally selected and arranged by Mr. Jefferson. It has since been augmented by several valuable donations, among which are the legacy of Mr. Madison, amounting to 587 volumes; that of the late Christian Bohn, esq., a generous and enlightened citizen of Richmond, amounting to 3,380 volumes; and a donation of 234 works by an unknown and benevolent lady, through the Rev. Dr. Alexander, of Princeton. It contains an unusually large proportion of standard literary and scientific works in the principal European languages, together with a rich and extensive collection of engravings." [Annual catalogue, 1848–'9.]

EMORY, WASHINGTON COUNTY.

Emory and Henry College Libraries—8,001 *vols.*—The college library was founded in 1839, and contains 2,591 volumes, 51 maps and charts, and 63 coins. The yearly average increase, for the last ten years, has been 250 volumes. The average annual expenditure about $75, raised by a tax of $1 a year on each person using the library. A catalogue (28 pages 12mo.) was printed in 1846. The library is open one hour and a half each week. Any person paying the fee, and conforming to the rules, may borrow the books. E. Longley, librarian.

There are two societies of students possessing libraries: the Hermesian Society, 2,693 volumes; and the Calliopean Society, 2,717 volumes.

FAIRFAX COUNTY.

The Episcopal Theological Seminary of Virginia—4,995 *vols.*—The library, founded ——, contains 4,995 volumes, besides a considerable number of unbound periodicals and pamphlets. There is no permanent fund for the library. About $50 a year are appropriated by the trustees for the purchase of books. The library-room is about 30 feet by 15. The library is opened twice a week. Those connected with the institution, and a few gentlemen in the neighborhood, are entitled to the use of the books. About 650 books are lent out in a year. There is a small library (200 volumes) belonging to the Rhetorical Society. Professor Packard, D. D., librarian.

LEXINGTON.

Washington College Libraries—4,997 *vols.*—The college library was founded in the spring of 1776. On October 13, 1774, a resolution was passed by the Hanover presbytery, appointing a committee to raise subscriptions for this purpose. In 1837 the library, though more than 60 years old, scarcely contained 700 volumes, and those were in a very shattered condition. It had no fund or other means of increase. A small fee has, for several years, been imposed upon every matriculate, which is devoted to the library, and yields from $125 to $150 per annum. Since 1837, about 230 volumes of public documents have been received from Congress, and about 420 volumes, "of a solid and substantial character," have been added by purchase. The library now contains 1,397 volumes. The college laws provide only for its use by students and professors, who can have access any day for consultation, and can take out books on the regular days twice a week. Other persons would doubtless be allowed the use of the books on applying for permission.

There are, besides, two literary societies connected with the college, possessing libraries of 1,800 volumes each. Rev. P. Calhoun, librarian.

Virginia Military Institute.—The library, founded in 1841, contains 2,500 volumes. The average annual increase has been 250 volumes. For the last five years, the State legislature has appropriated $500 per annum for the library. This is the only permanent resource. A room,

20 by 20 feet, in the public building, is appropriated to the use of the library. The library is open half an hour each week. The use of it to officers and cadets is gratuitous. About 1,500 volumes a year are lent out. Any person of respectability can always procure a book on application. Col. Francis H. Smith, librarian.

MADISON COURT-HOUSE.

Library Association—353 *vols.*—Founded January 1, 1842. The library contains 353 volumes, 2 manuscripts, 25 maps, 6 charts. It is opened once a week, and kept open two hours. A person may become a member by paying $1 per annum. T. J. Humphreys, librarian.

NORTHUMBERLAND COUNTY.

Academy Library—150 *vols.*—Founded in 1819. The trustees in their report to the president of the literary fund, in 1835, state: "The trustees have commenced a library, and have procured about 150 volumes of books, a set of globes and surveying instruments, and some maps; and for the want of funds, are unable to proceed further in this way."

PARKERSBURG.

Literary Association—360 *vols.*—Incorporated January 11, 1844. The library was commenced in the autumn of that year, and contains 360 volumes. About $40 a year are expended for books. The library is open every week-day during business hours. Persons entitled to the use of the books are: 1. Members of the association, who pay three dollars per annum; 2. Subscribers, who pay $2 per annum; 3. Apprentices, wards, and children of members or subscribers (they being responsible,) at $1 per annum. The average annual issue of books is about 225. Non-subscribers may obtain the use of books by depositing their value. S. C. Shaw, librarian.

PRINCE EDWARD COUNTY.

Union Theological Seminary—4,306 *vols.*—This institution is under the direction of the Presbyterians. It was founded in 1812. The library was founded in 1828, and contains 4,306 volumes and some manuscripts. The increase is slow; less than 100 volumes a year. Efforts are in progress to raise a fund for enlarging the library. The books are kept at present in the gallery of the seminary chapel. There is a catalogue, printed in 1833, of 107 pages 8vo. The library is open on Tuesdays and Fridays, one hour. All persons connected with the seminary and the faculty of Hampden Sidney College are entitled to the use of the books. The collection is a very valuable one, and is often consulted; but books are not lent out to others besides those mentioned, except on the personal responsibility of the librarian. The Society of Inquiry on Missions has 200 bound volumes and a multitude of papers and pamphlets. Rev. Samuel S. Graham, librarian.

Hampden Sidney College Libraries—8,000 *vols.*—This college was chartered in 1783. In 1835, the president and trustees, in their report to the president of the literary fund, say: "The college has a few books, scarcely deserving the name of a library. The two societies have each a respectable library." "By the census of 1840, this institution had 65 students, and 8,000 volumes in its library." [Howe's Hist. Coll.] This number probably includes the books in the society libraries.

PRUNTYTOWN, TAYLOR COUNTY.

Rector College Library—2,000 *vols.*—This college was chartered by the legislature in 1838. It was opened for the reception of students in 1839. The library was founded in 1840. It is a "valuable collection of more than 2,000 volumes, containing the Latin and Greek classics, a choice selection of works of modern authors, English, French, German, Spanish, &c. In the departments of theology, anatomy, mathematics, history, and moral science and law, are many standard authors." The whole library was collected in contributions from a great number of clergymen, officers of colleges and seminaries, and individuals in the New England States, but mostly in Massachusetts. The room occupied by the library is 25½ feet square, in the third story of the brick building erected for the college in 1838–'39. The library is open one hour a week. All the officers and students are entitled to the use of the library; the latter pay fifty cents a year for the privilege. Books are also lent to persons living in the town and vicinity. Besides the college library, the principal has a private library of 1,000 volumes, acessible to all the students. Charles Wheeler, principal.

RICHMOND.

State Library of Virginia—14,000 *vols.*—Founded in 1828, and contains about 14,000 volumes. There is a permanent fund derived from sales of books and maps published by the State, devoted to the increase of the library. It will yield about $2,000 per annum. The library occupies two rooms in the capitol; the larger 35 feet square, with a gallery containing an upper range of shelves; the smaller room is about 30 feet by 15. Several catalogues have been printed. The last is "A Catalogue of the Library of the State of Virginia, arranged alphabetically, under different heads, with the number and size of the volumes of each work specified; to which are prefixed the rules and regulations provided for its government"—157 pages 8vo.: Richmond, 1849; it is a handsomely printed catalogue, in which the books are arranged under twelve divisions. The departments best supplied are those of law, politics, and history. The general collection is very good. About 200 volumes have been received through M. Vattemare's system of exchanges. The library is open daily, Sundays and holidays excepted, from 9 a. m. to 3 p. m. Officers of government, judges of the courts, and members of the legislature are entitled to the use of the library. The customary courtesies are extended to visitors and to persons engaged in literary or scientific research. A note payable to the governor for double the value of the book, o rset to which it belongs, must be given by any person taking a book from the library, conditioned upon its prompt and safe return. The note is to contain a further forfeiture for every day's detention of the book beyond the specified time. W. H. Richardson, librarian *ex officio.*

The Virginia Historical and Philosophical Society—1,200 *vols.*—This society was formed 29th December, 1831. The General Assembly, by an act of the 10th March, 1834, incorporated the society, and by resolution of the 6th February, 1835, directed to be presented to it a copy of the large map of Virginia, and such books and papers belonging to the library fund as the joint committee on the library may designate. A leading object of the society was to collect and preserve books and papers, both in print and manuscript, relating to the history of America, and especially of Virginia; to make its library a repository of everything of the kind, as far as practicable. [See preface to C. Robinson's "Voyages to North America, 1520 to 1573," 8vo.: Richmond, 1848. Prepared for the society.]

The library of the society now contains about 200 volumes, and about 50 manuscripts, relating chiefly to the history of Virginia, and a few medals, coins, and relics. But few purchases have been made. The library is kept in a large room in the law building, in which the meetings of the society are also held. It is open for consultation daily at all hours. Members of the society can introduce others. No books are allowed to be taken from the room. Perhaps 100 different persons consult the collection in a year. William Maxwell, corresponding secretary and librarian.

The private library of Mr. Maxwell, lent to the society and deposited in their rooms, contains about 1,000 volumes.

Richmond College Library—1,200 *vols.*—This library, founded in 1843, contains 1,200 volumes, a few maps, and about 40 diagrams for illustrating natural philosophy. The library occupies a room (12 by 18 feet) in the college building. It is opened once a week for half an hour, and frequently at other times, by request. Students who have the gospel ministry in view, pay nothing; other students pay $1 per annum for the use of the books. The Mu-Sigma-Rho Society has 60 volumes of books and a reading-room, with 6 periodicals, accessible by paying 6¼ cents per month. Robert Ryland, president.

The Library Association—1,600 *vols.*—This association published in 1841 a catalogue of its library, in 22 pp. 8vo.

ROMNEY.

Library of the Literary Society—1,000 *vols.*—The "Literary Society of Romney" was founded on the 4th of February, 1819, and incorporated by an act of the General Assembly of Virginia, passed January 3, 1823. A leading object of its institution was the purchase of a library of valuable standard authors, by the annual subscription of its members—an object which has been since steadily pursued, its present library of 1,000 vols. having been acquired solely by this means. By the liberality of the legislature (acts of the 6th of January, 1832, and of 15th of February, 1844,) the society, having then become possessed of considerable means, procured an act to be passed on the 12th of December, 1846, conferring upon it authority "to establish at or near the town of Romney a seminary of learning, for the instruction of youth in the various branches of science and literature." Immediately after the passage of this last act the "Romney Classical Institute" was founded under the auspices of the society, and is in a very prosperous condition. After 1853 the society will have received an endowment of $20,000; and will possess a permanent fund of

$12,000, yielding $720 per annum; one-half of which is devoted to the support of the Romney Classical Institute, and the remainder to the purposes of the Literary Society—the purchase of books, philosophical apparatus, &c. In 1845 a handsome brick building (two stories high, main building 54 feet by 40, with a wing forming a convenient residence for the principal of the institute) was built by the Literary Society, for its own use, and for an academy. The building and grounds cost about $8,000. The upper story of the main building is devoted to the use of the society, and is divided into two rooms—a hall for meetings, and a library. The meetings of the society are held in public, semi-monthly, for the discussion of questions literary, moral, &c.; and lectures on various subjects are occasionally delivered before it, by its own members or others, on the invitation of the society. By resolutions of the society, the use of its library is extended to ministers of the gospel of all denominations *gratis*, and to citizens generally on the same terms as those on which it is enjoyed by its own members. A "catalogue of the members and library" was printed at Romney, June 1, 1849: 16 pages 16mo. There are at present twenty regular members, who pay $3 each per annum to the library fund; and eight library members, admitted under certain regulations of the society, and paying the same fees. Persons having the use of the library are furnished with keys, and may enter at any time. Clergymen of the village, or vicinity, and the principal of the institute, are the only persons to whom the privileges of the library have been gratuitously extended. The librarian is A. P. White, of Romney. The principal of the institute is E. J. Meany.

WILLIAMSBURG.

William and Mary College Library—5,000 *vols.*—This college, next to Harvard the oldest in the country, was founded in 1692. It is not known with certainty when the library was commenced. It now numbers about 5,000 volumes. It is supported by a matriculation fee, or tax, of $5 a year from each student, amounting to about $400 a year. The library is opened one hour a week. There is no printed catalogue. Professor M. J. Smead, librarian.

NORTH CAROLINA.

CHAPEL HILL.

Libraries of the University of North Carolina—11,847 *vols.*—The University of North Carolina was incorporated December 11, 1789. The business of education was commenced early in the year 1795. At that time the library was begun. (See History of the University of North Carolina, American Quarterly Register, November, 1842.) It now contains 343 folios, 357 quartos, 2,536 octavos, and 265 duodecimos; in all, 3,501 volumes, besides a collection of manuscripts, principally relating to the history of North Carolina. The shelves of the room occupied as a library have been for some time more than full; and for this, among other reasons, little effort has been made to increase the library. A separate building is in contemplation, and will probably be erected during the ensuing year; and, when this is completed, it is expected that systematic arrangements will be made for the increase of the library. The library is open five times a week, an hour at a time. The faculty and the students use the library without fees. Ashbel G. Brown, A. M., librarian.

There are two literary societies connected with the college which have valuable libraries. The *Dialectic Society* has 26 folios, 93 quartos, 2,478 octavos, and 1,938 duodecimos; in all, 4,535 volumes. A catalogue was printed in 1821, (21 pp. 12mo.,) containing 1,673 volumes; another in 1835, (26 pp. 8vo.,) containing 3,060 volumes. The *Philanthropic Society* has 26 folios, 167 quartos, 3,314 octavos, 804 duodecimos, *et inf.;* in all, 4,311 volumes. A catalogue was published in 1822, (18 pp. 8vo.,) containing 1,473 volumes. These libraries are in buildings apparently connected with the wings of the other college buildings; separated, however, by a wall and copings of some four feet high. They were erected in 1847, of brick, at an expense of $10,000. The rooms are fitted up with alcoves 8 by 8 feet on each side. The central aisle is 20 feet wide; the length of the room 37 feet. All residents on the Hill who seem to be proper persons to have books, are allowed to use them without charge. The libraries are opened twice a week for an hour. The books in both are well selected, and in fine condition: they are much used.

MECKLENBURG COUNTY.

Davidson College Libraries—1,200 *vols.*

RALEIGH.

State Library—3,000 *vols.*

SALEM.

The Fayette Academy possesses a library, founded in 1804, containing about 1,500 volumes. The library is for the use of the teachers and pupils of the academy, which is an unincorporated institution of the Moravian Church. E. A. de Schweinitz, principal.

VALLE CRUCIS, WATAUGA COUNTY.

Mission School Library—1,500 *vols.*

WAKE FOREST.

Wake Forest College Libraries—4,700 *vols.*

SOUTH CAROLINA.

CHARLESTON.

The Library Society—20,000 *vols.*—The library was founded in 1748. On the 15th of January, 1778, it was nearly destroyed by fire; only 185 volumes of 5,000 or 6,000 being saved. It now contains 20,000 volumes. Its average annual increase for the last ten years has been 180 volumes, besides pamphlets. Average annual expenditure for the same period, about

$1,000. The income of the institution is derived from an annual assessment upon the members of $10 each; from rents of rooms and buildings belonging to the society, and from admission fees of new members, $25 each. It of course varies with the rise or fall of rent, and the number of new members admitted. It is at present about $2,500. A brick building, erected and long occupied by the Bank of South Carolina, was purchased about ten years ago by the society, and the upper story, consisting of one room 40 feet by 35, and two others, each 20 feet square, was fitted up at an expense of $2,000 for the library. The rooms on the first story are rented as offices. A three-story brick building belonging to the estate is rented as a dwelling-house.

"A catalogue of the books belonging to the Charleston Library Society, published by order of the society," containing 375 pages 8vo., was printed at Charleston in 1826. This is a classed catalogue, with an alphabetical index of authors and the titles of anonymous works. The preface contains a minute history of the society, with some excellent remarks on the arrangement and cataloguing of a library.

Volume two of the catalogue, containing books purchased since 1826, in 144 pp. 8vo., was printed at Charleston in 1845. This volume is classified, but the classification is different from that of the first volume. It has no index.

"A list of books obtained by the Charleston Library Society since the publication of the second volume of the catalogue of books, being the first supplement to the same, prepared by the librarian, and printed by order of the society," was published in 1847, at Charleston. It is alphabetical, and contains 23 pages 8vo. Several catalogues were printed before the destruction of the first library: in 1790, in 1802, in 1806, another in 1811, when the library contained 7,000 volumes. Some supplementary pages were printed in 1816 and 1818.

The library is open every day, Sundays and holidays excepted, from 10 o'clock a. m. to 3 o'clock p. m. About 5,000 volumes are lent out annually to members of the society or to their orders. The book committee may extend the privileges of the library occasionally to others. William Logan, secretary and librarian.

The following interesting sketch of the history of this important institution is taken from the preface to the catalogue of 1826:

"The Charleston Library Society owes its origin to seventeen young gentlemen, who, in the year 1748, associated for the purpose of raising a small fund to 'collect such new pamphlets' and magazines as should occasionally be published in Great Britain. They advanced and remitted to London ten pounds sterling as a fund to purchase such pamphlets as had appeared during the current year, acting at first under a mere verbal agreement and without a name. Before the close of the year their views became more extensive; and on the 28th December, rules for the organization of the society were ratified and signed, when they assumed the name of a *Library Society*, and made arrangements for the acquisition of books as well as of pamphlets.

"Officers were first elected on the 1st of April, 1749, and a few members were added during the spring and summer of that year. But as soon as the benefits of such an association were distinctly understood, the society became popular, and before the close of the year 1750 numbered more than 160 members.

"Efforts were made at an early period to obtain an act of incorporation. In the spring of 1751, through the influence of some of its members, a bill for incorporating the society was passed through both houses of Assembly, but was defeated by the governor, who refused his assent and signature. In the spring of 1752 another bill was passed through the legislature, which shared the same fate; and in 1753 the agent of the colony in London was requested to make every exertion in his power to obtain from the Privy Council in Great Britain a charter for the society, or instructions to the governor to ratify the act which both houses of the Colonial Assembly had passed. Upon an application to the Board of Trade by the agent, and some gentlemen who interested themselves in behalf of the society, they were informed that the measure was not considered as contrary to his Majesty's instructions, but that it was unprecedented to ratify in England a bill to which the governor of a province had refused his assent.

"It is difficult now to ascertain the causes which created these obstructions to the incorporation of a literary society. But the effect was injurious, and had nearly produced a dissolution of the association. The members finally resolved to place their funds at interest, and make no further purchases until a charter could be obtained. A third bill, however, was passed in 1754, to which Governor Glen finally gave his assent, and on the 24th June, 1755, it was confirmed by the Crown.

"From this time the progress of the society was rapid and satisfactory. The members continued to invest a portion of their income in bonds, and soon began to embrace in their views the establishment of an institution for education in connexion with their library.

"Such was the increase of their funds, that in January, 1775, the amount in bonds was £18,000, and between two and three thousand pounds were added to this sum between this period and the 1st of January, 1778.

"The library of the society, at the same time, was receiving regular additions from annual purchases and the donations of individuals, which were then frequent. Great attention appears, from the minutes of the society, to have been paid at this period to classical literature, and many discussions took place as to the portion of the funds which should be annually applied to this department of literature. The collection of classical authors and of commentators on the classics was not only respectable from its number, but valuable for the selection; for some excellent scholars then superintended this portion of its labors.

"It was in all probability this steady adherence of the society to the future establishment of an academy or college, (for the professors indicated in the report of the committee were adapted to a collegiate course of studies,) and the complexion of the library, that induced Mr. John M'Kenzie, a lawyer of eminence in Charleston, who died in the summer of 1771, to bequeath a valuable library to the society for the use of a college when erected in this province. These books were received, distinctly marked, and always kept apart from the books of the society.

"The commencement of our revolutionary struggle suspended all schemes of improvement. It soon became difficult for the society to collect its funds—it became more difficult to invest them; a large sum was placed in the treasury of the State, and the certificates of this debt were for a long time unproductive memorandums.

"But a heavier calamity awaited the society. The fire of the 15th

January, 1778, which destroyed nearly one-half of Charleston, broke out a little after midnight in the immediate vicinity of the library. From the hour, the violence of a north wind which unfortunately blew, and the combustible materials with which our houses were usually built, the neighborhood was enveloped in flames before any effectual assistance could be rendered. The library, which then contained, according to the statement of Dr. Ramsay, who was a member at the time, between five and six thousand volumes, almost totally perished. A melancholy record on the journals states that only 185 volumes were saved, and many of these were volumes of mutilated sets.

"M'Kenzie's library, from some circumstance, probably accidental, fared better than that of the society: about two-thirds of the books were saved, though many of the sets were broken.

"This loss could not at that time be repaired. The war closed our communication with England, and the British maritime force intercepted our intercourse with Europe. A few books were procured in the city, but Charleston itself fell into the possession of the British in the spring of 1780.

"From a report made to the society in October, 1786, it appears that Fr. J. Fariau, who had been elected librarian in January, 1780, remained in Charleston during the time that this city was occupied by the British troops; that he took charge of the library, removing it with him from place to place as circumstances compelled him to change his habitation, and that it was owing to his assiduous care that the remnants of these libraries were saved from entire destruction.

"Immediately after the peace the society was reorganized, officers were appointed, and its meetings regularly resumed. But its funds were in a ruinous condition. Its members had been widely scattered by the accidents of war. Some had perished, many left the country, and those that remained could render but little effectual aid to its treasury. The country had been rendered desolate. The fortunes of individuals were prostrated, and where the bonds remaining to the society were eventually good, it was difficult to collect either the principal or the interest. For several years, although some few purchases of books were made, the society seemed to exist rather as a social club than as a literary association.

"If a catalogue entered on the books on the 3d November, 1790, is faithful—and there seems no reason to doubt its correctness—the library of the society then contained only 342 volumes, and M'Kenzie's books were reduced to 403 volumes. The librarian's minutes corroborate this statement, for they show that, in 1790 and '91, it was uncommon for more than three persons to take out books in the course of a month, and in some months none were borrowed.

"At length, in 1790, some debts due the society were put in a train for payment, and the indents which had been received for the money deposited at the commencement of the war in the treasury of the State, amounting to about $11,000, which, though frequently urged, it had wisely declined to sell, were funded and rendered valuable. It was then ordered that this stock should be sold; that $6,400 should be subscribed to the Bank of the United States, and that the remainder, with whatever sum should be received from their bonds or notes, should be applied to the purchase of books. The resolutions for the establishment of an academy were at this time finally repealed. The books which were imported in consequence of these orders, and which, from many circumstances, were delayed until the close of the year 1792, may be considered as the foundation of our present collection. From this time the increase of the library has been regular though moderate, and the early misfortunes of the society will account for its deficiency in ancient literature, and even in the political writings which preceded our revolutionary contest. In 1808, the books in the library amounted to 4,500 volumes; by the catalogue of 1811, to 7,000; and the number now probably exceeds 12,000.

"If this library should be found small, it must be remembered that it has been formed within a few years, from the very moderate contribution of its members. It has no patron to boast of—no act of public munificence to record. If we except a few donations of single volumes or sets of books,* and one legacy from Benjamin Smith, in 1770, of about $600, (£1,000 currency,) we find no memorial of other assistance.

"Previous to 1765, the library was kept at the houses of the respective librarians.

"Gabriel Manigault, esq., who had been president or vice president of the society for many years, then presented the society with a lease for twenty-one years of a convenient building, in or near Kinloch court, and prepared it for the library at his own expense; and the library was removed there in the beginning of 1765, and continued until the fire of 1778. Mr. Carwithen died in the summer of 1770, and Will. Hort was appointed librarian; he resigned in a few months, and Thomas Powell was elected on the 4th February, 1771; after holding the office fourteen months he resigned, and Samuel Price succeeded in April, 1772; he continued in office until the end of 1778, and Fr. J. Fariau was elected in 1779, and again in 1780, and continued librarian until the summer of 1783. After the fire of 1778, temporary accommodations were procured for the library. In January, 1780, Will. H. Gibbes, esq., offered a part of his office; the remnants of the library, however, appear to have been cased up after this time, for, in April, 1783, a committee was appointed 'to inquire for a proper room, that the books may be opened.' Mr. Dan. Cannon loaned the society a room in Queen street for a short time; but when Mr. John M'Call was elected librarian on the 1st July, 1783, he removed the books to his office. In April, 1784, the intendant and wardens of the city offered the society a room in the Exchange, whither the books were removed. In October, 1787, the council required their room, and the library was placed at the corner of Broad street and the bay. In January, 1788, it was removed to the corner of Tradd street and the bay. In January, 1791, it was again removed to the corner of Broad and Church streets, and in November, 1792, finally placed in the room it now occupies in the upper story of the court-house.

"When the court-house was rebuilt by subscription, after having been burnt in 1788, the members of the Library Society subscribed very liberally, and promoted the subscription with their influence, with an understanding that their books would be permitted to occupy some portion

---

*"It deserves to be noticed that the individual to whom this society has been most frequently and perhaps most extensively indebted, is an inhabitant of Paris. Passing some time in Carolina with his father, many years ago, they received from some of its inhabitants those hospitable attentions which the citizens of this country take so much pleasure in paying to strangers, and the courtesy has never been forgotten. Scarcely a year for some time past has elapsed without our receiving from him some volume or work as a testimonial of his remembrance. I allude to Andre Michaux, the younger, the author of the splendid work on the Forest Trees of North America."

of the building—and in this arrangement there has been hitherto a liberal acquiescence."

Apprentices' Library—8,500 *vols.*—The society was incorporated 18th December, 1824, and rechartered in December, 1840. The library was first opened June 1, 1824. It now contains about 8,500 volumes; about 50 maps and charts, and six portraits of gentlemen distinguished in the Revolution; also a philosophical apparatus, worth about 500 dollars, and a pair of globes of three feet diameter, and new. The average annual increase is about 500 volumes. The average annual expenditure for books is about $150. A brick building with a tin roof was erected for the institution in 1840, at a cost of $14,500. It is 78 feet long, 34 feet wide, and two stories high. The upper story is occupied solely as a lecture-room. The lower story contains a library 37 feet by 29, and two reading-rooms, each 23 feet by 12. A catalogue (336 pages small 8vo.) was printed in 1840.

The library is open every day (except Sundays) from 4 o'clock p. m. till 9 in winter, and 10 in summer. Books are lent to members of the society, their families, and apprentices, and to other young persons recommended by members as beneficiaries. Each member pays one dollar for admission, and two dollars and fifty cents per annum in advance. About 800 or 900 books, and sets of books, are taken out annually; or, on a daily average, about 22 books to about 18 applicants. All strangers are welcomed to the use of the books at the library. Besides these, eight or ten residents resort to it daily as a reading-room. "The old books, and those not often consulted, unless bound with Russia leather, are apt to be injured by insects. They may be saved by taking them out every week or two and striking the backs together, also by clippings of Russia leather scattered about on the shelves." William Estell, secretary, treasurer, and librarian.

The Library of the College of Charleston—2,000 *vols.*—In the year 1785, three colleges—one at Charleston, another at Winnsborough, and a third at Cambridge—received a common charter from the legislature of South Carolina. In 1791 a separate charter was granted to the College of Charleston. This institution was reorganized on the 20th of December, 1837, at which time an act of the legislature was passed authorizing the transfer of all the college property to the city council of Charleston. The city council is bound to maintain the college.

The library was commenced about 40 years ago. In the year 1828, a considerable donation of valuable books was made by the citizens of Charleston. The library contains at present about 2,000 volumes. "A Catalogue of the books in the Library of the Charleston College," containing 36 pages 12mo., was printed at Charleston in 1849. William Peronneau Finley, president of Charleston College.

The Medical College of the State of South Carolina—2,450 *vols.*—The library of the Medical Society contains 2,450 volumes. About 120 dollars are yearly expended for books. The library occupies a room, say 22 by 18 feet, in the Medical College. A catalogue was printed in 1834, and another, containing 40 pages 8vo., in 1842. The library is open four times a week for two hours, and is freely accessible to members of the Medical Society, and all others to whom they may grant permits. About 350 volumes are annually lent out; and about 250 persons each year consult the library without taking away books. Dr. S. L. Lockwood, librarian.

COLUMBIA.

South Carolina College Libraries—18,400 *vols.*—In 1802, there was an act of the legislature to purchase books for the college library. The collection at present contains above 17,000 volumes, including an unusually large proportion of elegantly illustrated works. Its annual increase is about 500 volumes. There is an annual appropriation by the legislature of $2,000 for the library. A brick building was erected in 1838, for the use of the library, at a cost of $22,000. There are two rooms on the sides of the passage in the lower story. The library room is 100 feet by 40, and is modelled after the Congress Library. An architect was sent to Washington to copy the plan. A catalogue was printed in 1836, of 112 pp. 8vo., prepared by Edward W. Johnston. Another, 151 pp. 8vo., was published in 1849. It is intended merely for temporary use, whilst a more perfect one is in preparation.

The library is open every day in the week, except Sunday, from 9 o'clock till one.

Persons entitled to the use of the books are the trustees, faculty, and students; all who present $100 worth of books, and others who have a special permission from the trustees. Any gentleman can get a book by using the name of a trustee or professor. F. W. McMaster, librarian.

Students' societies—

Clasiosophic Society Library	- - -	700 volumes.
Euphradian Society Library	- - -	700 "

The college library is one of the best selected in the country. The learned aid of Professor Lieber has been bestowed upon it. The collection is far more valuable than many of twice its size. The legislature of South Carolina has abundant reason to be proud of its liberality, and satisfied with the manner in which it has been seconded by the officers of the college.

Theological Seminary of the Synod of South Carolina and Georgia—4,754 *vols.*—This institution was established by the Presbyterians in 1828, went into operation in 1831, was incorporated in 1832. The library was commenced in 1830, and contains 4,554 volumes. Most of the books have been presented by individuals; yet, for the whole time since the library was commenced, the average annual expenditure for books has been $243. The library is temporarily placed in a lofty room, 25 feet by 20, in one of the buildings of the seminary, and is open four or five times a week, one hour each time. There is no printed catalogue. The officers and students of the seminary, and, by courtesy, clergymen of the town, are allowed the use of the books. About 1,300 volumes a year are lent out. In answer to the question, "Have the books been injured at any time by insects?" the librarian writes: "Much injured by a small shiny moth, which eats off the pasted titles of cloth-bound books, and sometimes by a blackish worm of the caterpillar kind, the product of a brown miller or moth, which eats leather binding. It is also found that, in this climate, except in the driest situations, and occasionally even in these, leather-bound books suffer much from mould—English leather-bound books less than American, and French perhaps less than English. One gentleman amongst us has suffered so much from this cause, that he will only have books bound in cloth; and these, if the letters are stamped on the back, without being on a title which is pasted, are injured less by mould and insects than any other."

The "Society of Inquiry," composed of students of the seminary, possesses about 200 volumes. It maintains also a reading-room, in which the principal newspapers and reviews of this country are taken, as well as the reviews of Great Britain, and one or two German publications. This room is accessible at all hours. There is also under the control of this society a museum, containing articles illustrative of the natural history and superstitious usages of heathen nations. Rev. George Howe, D. D., librarian of the seminary.

FAIRFIELD DISTRICT.

Furman Theological Seminary Library—1,500 *vols.*—This is a Baptist institution, established in 1826.

GREENWOOD, ABBEVILLE DISTRICT.

Hodges Institute—500 *vols.*—The Sopronean Society of this institution possesses about 300 volumes. There is, besides, a reference library of 200 volumes. The institute was incorporated in 1848. It is the design of the trustees to make the institution one of the first order. Issachar Howard, librarian.

LEXINGTON COURT-HOUSE.

Theological Seminary of the Evangelical Lutheran Church—1,560 *vols.*—The library, founded in 1833, contains 1,560 volumes, besides many pamphlets. The library is kept at present in the house where the lectures are given, and occupies a room 25 feet long and 10 feet wide. It is hoped that better accommodations will soon be obtained. There is a written catalogue, somewhat in arrears. The library is open for taking out and returning books every Wednesday from 8 to 12 o'clock. The library is intended for the use of the students of the seminary and the ministers of the Lutheran church. Others may be admitted to its privileges on application to the professor of theology, who has the superintendence of the library—Professor Ernest W. Hazelius, D. D., Librarian.

GEORGIA.

ATHENS.

Franklin College Libraries—10,267 *vols.*—The present college library was commenced in 1831, the former one having been destroyed by fire in October, 1830. It contains 7,267 volumes, 59 maps and charts, a medal struck in commemoration of the victory at Saratoga, 3 gold, 94 silver, and 249 copper coins, ancient and modern. The yearly average increase for the last ten years has been about 132 volumes. The annual expenditure for books, during the same period, about $600. The income of the library is derived from appropriations by the trustees of the college. In 1835, a brick building was erected for the accommodation of the library and mineralogical cabinet, at a cost of $3,000. It is 50 feet long and 40 feet wide, measuring from the outside of the walls. It is two stories high, with two rooms on each floor. The books are arranged according to subjects. A catalogue was published about twelve years ago. Another was printed in 1847, entitled "Catalogue of Books in the Library of the University of Georgia, by Professor James Jackson, librarian; published by order of the board of trustees: Athens, 1847:" small 12mo., 69 pages. The titles are distributed under twenty-eight classes, corresponding with the arrangement of the books upon the shelves. The library is opened four times a week—Monday to Thursday, inclusive—and is kept open from half an hour to an hour each time. The trustees, faculty, resident and under-graduates are allowed the free use of the books. Under-graduates are required to return or renew them every two weeks. Literary gentlemen and ministers of the gospel in the place are, on the responsibility of the faculty, admitted to the privileges of the library. The trustees and faculty alone are allowed to take books out of the town. Professor James Jackson, librarian.

The Libraries of the Franklin Society and of the Phi Gamma Society contain 3,000 volumes.

AUGUSTA.

Library of the Medical College of Georgia—4,000 *vols.*—This library, founded in 1833, contains 4,000 volumes. The average yearly increase is about 150 volumes. The expenditure for books, $200. The library occupies a room in the college building 25 feet by 35, and is opened daily during the forenoon. The faculty are allowed the use of the books by having the work taken out charged to the borrower; the students, by depositing $10 as security for the return of each volume. L. A. Dugas, M. D., librarian.

The Young Men's Library—1,510 *vols.*—The Young Men's Library Association was founded 27th January, 1848. It expends about $200 a year in the purchase of books. The society rents two rooms, each 40 feet by 20, in a brick building—one for the library, and the other for a reading-room. The library is open daily (Sundays excepted) from 8 to 10 a. m., and from 3 to 10 p. m. Persons become life members by paying $50. Regular members pay $4 a year. Members are allowed to introduce strangers to the use of the library for two weeks. The library at present contains about 1,510 volumes. Thomas Courtney, librarian.

MACON.

Wesleyan Female College Library—350 *vols.*—The college was incorporated in November, 1837, and opened for students in January, 1839. The library was commenced with the college, and now (January, 1850) contains about 350 volumes, a few valuable ancient coins, a respectable cabinet of minerals, and a few antiquities, mostly the fruit of private donations. The library occupies a room in the college edifice, and is accessible at all hours of every day. The use of the books is free to the officers and pupils of the school.

MILLEDGEVILLE.

Oglethorpe University Libraries—4,000 *vols.*—The college library was founded with the college, in 1838. It contains about 2,000 volumes, mostly donations, and occupies a large and airy room in the college edifice. It is opened twice a week—one hour each time. The laws allow of the books being lent, within a mile of the college, at the discretion of the president. Persons connected with the college may use them without fee. The two literary societies (the Thalian and the Phi Delta) have well-selected libraries of 1,000 volumes each.

OXFORD.

Emory College—2,700 *vols.*—The college library, founded in 1839, contains 1,020 volumes, increasing by donations alone. It occupies a room 20 feet square in the college building. There is no printed catalogue. The library is opened four days each week, half an hour at a time. Professors and students are allowed to use the books without charge. About 250 volumes are taken out each year. There are two societies of students having libraries. The Few Society has 725 volumes; the Phi Gamma Society, 960 volumes. Rev. J. M. Bonnell, librarian.

PENNFIELD.

Mercer University—4,000 *vols.*—The library was commenced when the college was chartered in 1838, and now contains 3,000 volumes. The available funds of the college have hitherto been devoted mainly to the purchase of apparatus and the erection of buildings, whilst the library has remained nearly stationary. It is, however, expected soon to receive more attention. There are two other small but annually-increasing libraries connected with the college. S. P. Sanford, librarian. The Baptist Theological Seminary is connected with the university.

SAVANNAH.

Historical Society Library and Savannah Society Library—7,000 *vols.*—The Georgia Historical Society was founded in June, 1839, and incorporated the 19th of December of the same year. It has published several volumes of Collections. The legislature confided to the care of the society the invaluable documents obtained in England by the Rev. Charles W. Howard, at a large expense to the State. "These are comprised in 22 volumes folio. Fifteen are from the records of the Board of Trade, six from the State Paper office, and one from the King's Library; forming a body of historical information full of the most interesting statements, letters, and reports relating to the colonial period of Georgia."

The Savannah Society Library has been lately united with that of the Historical Society. They together contain about 7,000 volumes.—[See Account of the Georgia Historical Society, by W. B. Stevens, M. D. American Quarterly Register, May, 1840, p. 344.]

"This province [Georgia] was scarce thirty years settled before it had three fine libraries in the city of Savannah, the fourth at Ebenezer, and a fifth 96¾ miles from the sea, upon the stream of Savannah. In these libraries could be had books written in the Chaldaic, Hebrew, Arabic, Siriac, Coptic, Malabar, Greek, Latin, French, German, Dutch, and Spanish, besides the English, viz: in thirteen languages."—[De Brahm's Georgia, privately printed by G. W. Jones, of Georgia, in 1849, from an old MS. in Harvard University Library.]

ALABAMA.

LA GRANGE.

College Library—3,000 *vols.*

MARION.

Howard College.—The library, founded in 1842, contains 1,500 vols. It is opened once a week for half an hour. S. S. Sherman, president. This is a literary and theological institution, and the library is consequently designed to be literary and theological.

MOBILE.

The Franklin Society, founded 17th January, 1835. The library contains 1,454 volumes, with a few coins and maps. Of late years but few additions have been made to the library, the attention of the society having been mostly turned to maintaining a reading room. The Franklin Society and the societies of Free Masons have erected a brick building for their joint accommodation. The room of the Franklin Society is a parallelogram, 62 feet by 32. The library and reading-room are open daily for the use of members of the society and subscribers to the reading-room. The books are used in the room. P. Hamilton, president.

SPRING HILL.

College Library—4,000 *vols.*

TUSCUMBIA.

The Literary and Scientific Club, formed in 1849, meet weekly to discuss questions and submit essays, some of which have already been published. A fund is accumulating gradually for the purchase of books. The secretary is G. M. Wharton.

TUSCALOOSA.

The University of Alabama—7,123 *vols.*—The library was founded in 1831, and contains 4,500 volumes. The yearly average increase, for the last ten years, has been 159 volumes. There is a stated annual appropriation of $200 for the library. Within the last five years the trustees have made two extra appropriations of $500 each. The library is in the "Rotundo," which is occupied, besides, as a chapel, and for public exhibitions. The library room is a large circular apartment, 85 feet in diameter. The whole building cost $75,000. The foundation, to about four feet above the surface, is of sandstone; the residue of brick. The first printed catalogue—a pamphlet—was published in 1838. The last—a volume of 257 pages 8vo.—was printed in 1848.

The library is opened twice a week, and kept open about an hour each time. The trustees, faculty, resident graduates, students, and donors to the amount of $100 to the library, are entitled to the use of it, and may take out books. About 800 volumes are lent annually. Robert S. Gould, librarian. The two students' libraries contain 2,623 volumes.

The first catalogue of the library was prepared by Mr. Richard Furman. It was classified. The second was prepared by Mr. Wilson G. Richardson, M. A., now professor in the university. It is on the plan of the catalogue of Brown University Library. This elegant catalogue is highly reditable to the institution, and honorable to the industry, taste, and earning of the gentleman who prepared it. A few such publications will establish a high standard of excellence for the catalogues of even small libraries, and will demonstrate their value. "A catalogue," says Mr. Van der Weyer, "is like the eye of a library." Let the eye, therefore, be perfect, that the whole body may be full of light.

FLORIDA.

PENSACOLA.

The Naval Hospital.—The library of the Naval Hospital was founded January 16, 1847, and contains at present 1,337 volumes, besides pamphlets. The library has been raised by voluntary subscriptions of the inmates of the hospital, and of benevolent individuals, officers of the navy, &c. Mr. Secretary Mason directed $150 to be given from the Naval Hospital fund. A considerable number of donations have been received. The library room is in the hospital, and measures 27 feet by 24, and 17 feet high. It is open from morning to evening every day. Any inmate of the hospital may take out one book at a time. The library is the property of the hospital, and is under the direction of the surgeon in charge. The present incumbent is Isaac Hulse, M. D., U. S. Navy. The steward of the hospital, Mr. G. L. Brown, is acting librarian.

ST. AUGUSTINE.

Judicial Library—2,000 *vols.*

TALLAHASSEE.

State Library.—The State Library was founded in 1845, and contains 2,000 volumes. The use of the library in the room is free to all persons. The library is under the care of the Secretary of State, Charles W. Downing.

MISSISSIPPI.

JACKSON.

State Library—5,000 *vols.*—Founded by act of legislature, passed February 15, 1838, appropriating $3,000 for the purchase of suitable books. Previous to 1842 there was an annual appropriation of $1,000 for the purchase of books; since then the appropriation has been $500—one fifth of which is for law books. The library is on the third floor of the State capitol. "A Catalogue of the Library of the State of Mississippi, arranged alphabetically, under different heads, with the number, size, and cost of the volumes of each work specified, to which are prefixed the rules and regulations provided for its government," 27 pages 8vo., was printed at Jackson in 1839; the same, with additions, 34 pages 8vo., 1841; same, 1845, 43 pages 8vo.; same, 61 pages 8vo., 1847; same, 51 pages 8vo., 1849. The price of each book is given in every catalogue, and forms a novel but interesting feature. The library is opened every day during the session of the legislature, Sundays excepted, from 9 a. m. to 3 p. m. All persons are allowed to use the library when open, but no one is allowed to take out books but the trustees, State treasurer, adjutant general, judges of the United States circuit court, and members of the legislature while in session. Persons who have filled the office of governor of the State, chancellor, judge of the high court of errors and appeals, United States senator from the State, whilst they may be in the city of Jackson, are allowed to borrow books. For every book issued, a receipt or note of twice its value, or twice the value of the set to which it may belong, must be given, conditioned on its safe return, and the payment of all forfeitures and penalties for detention beyond the time limited by the laws. John W. Patton, librarian.

CLAIBORNE COUNTY.

Oakland College—6,000 *vols.*—The college library, founded in 1831, contains 3,589 volumes, 200 maps and charts, 800 engravings, and 200 medals and coins. In 1841, $3,000 were appropriated for books, but the library has been increased principally by donations. An apartment in the college chapel, (a brick building,) 26 feet by 22, and 14 feet high, is used for the library. The books are arranged according to donors. The library is opened once a week for an hour, and frequently at other times. Books are lent to all who apply for them: few, however, are taken out except by the officers and students of the college. Professor John Chamberlain, librarian.

The students' libraries contain 2,411 volumes.

OXFORD, LAFAYETTE COUNTY.

The University of Mississippi, near Oxford, went into operation in November, 1848. Its library contains about 1,600 volumes. The State has made an appropriation of $3,000 a year for books and apparatus. The college has an income of $16,000 per year: seven professors and eighty students.

WASHINGTON.

College Library—1,000 *vols.*

LOUISIANA.

BATON ROUGE.

State Library—7,000 *vols.*—The State Library was founded the 12th of March, 1838, and contains about 7,000 volumes, some MSS., maps, engravings, &c. The library has lately been removed to Baton Rogue and placed in a room in the capitol. A correct description and inventory of it will soon be prepared. As yet, there is no printed catalogue. The average annual increase is about 300 volumes. An annual appropriation of $1,000 is made by the State legislature for the increase of the collection. The library is open daily from 10 a. m. to 3 p. m. Admittance is free to all persons, but no book is to be taken away except by members of the legislature during their sessions. Paul Caire, librarian.

College Libraries—1,000 *volumes.*

BRINGIERS.

Jefferson College Libraries—6,000 *vols.*

JACKSON.

Louisiana College Libraries—2,000 *vols.*

NEW ORLEANS.

Public School Library—10,000 *vols.*—"The Public School Library and Lyceum Society of Municipality No. 2" was founded December 3, 1844. The library contains [1850] 10,000 well-selected volumes. It has also two books of paintings, and five books of sketches. It is supported by subscriptions, donations, and voluntary contributions of the pupils of the public schools, and is fast increasing. An elegant room, 75 feet by 35, and 20 feet high, has been recently provided for the permanent accommodation of the library, in the new 2d Municipal Hall. The exact cost of this room is not perhaps known; the cost of the entire building is estimated at $300,000. There have been two printed catalogues: the first, numbering 29 pages, was published in 1846; the second, 155 pages, in 1848. The library is open daily (Sundays excepted) from 2 to 8 o'clock p. m. Subscribers pay $5 per annum. Pupils of the public schools may become life members by paying $9. The teachers of the public schools are entitled to the privileges of the library without charge. The librarian is Samuel H. McConnell.

TEXAS.

AUSTIN.

The State Library.—The collection of books usually styled the State Library was commenced in 1837, and has been derived from donations. It numbers at present 1,001 volumes. The average annual increase is about 80 volumes. The books are kept in the building of the State department, and are accessible to the public, without charge, during business hours, every day. About 300 are annually taken out, and perhaps 300 or 400 persons annually consult the collection without borrowing books. The library is in charge of the secretary of state, who is considered *ex officio* librarian.

HUNTSVILLE.

Austin College, incorporated in 1850, is in vigorous progress, and collecting a library.

INDEPENDENCE.

Baylor University Library—300 *vols.*

ARKANSAS.

LITTLE ROCK.

Lyceum Library—1,000 *vols.*

TENNESSEE.

COLUMBIA.

Jackson College Libraries—2,500 *vols.*—The college library was begun in 1834, and contains about 2,000 volumes. About 400 volumes have been added during the last ten years. There is a manuscript catalogue. The library is opened once a week for an hour. Students pay 50 cents per session for the use of the books. Rev. Joseph Sherman, LL. D., librarian.

Students' libraries, 500 vols.

The Female Institute Library—3,500 *vols.*—Established February, 1839—contains 3,500 volumes, and the richest collection of engravings in the State. About 350 volumes per year are added to the library. About $150 are annually expended for the purchase of books. There is a manuscript catalogue. The library is opened one hour each day. Members of the institute pay $1 per annum for the use of the books. Books are not taken from the institute except by day pupils. F. G. Smith, rector.

GREENVILLE.

College Libraries—3,000 *vols.*

JACKSON.

West Tennessee College was incorporated in 1843, and reorganized in 1849. It has four teachers and ninety-two students. It has begun to collect a library.

KNOXVILLE.

East Tennessee University—4,500 *vols.*—The college library, founded in 1819, contains 2,300 volumes. It is supported by fees for the use of the books, with occasional appropriations from the funds of the university. It occupies a room 20 feet square and 14 feet high, in the main building of the university, which is of brick. The library is open regularly once a week, and, on application, at other times. Officers of the university are allowed to use the books without charge; students pay $1 a year for the privilege. About 150 books are lent out in a year; and about 240 persons consult the library without taking away books. There are two literary societies connected with the college, (the Chi-Delta and the Philomathesian,) which have each about 1,100 volumes, in rooms belonging to the university, connected with the society halls. These libraries have been founded but a few years, are rapidly increasing and much used. Albert Miller Lea, librarian E. T. University.

LEBANON.

Cumberland University Library—4,000 *vols.*—The library, commenced in 1844, the date of the charter of the university, contains some 4,000 volumes. William Mariner, librarian.

MARYVILLE.

College Libraries—3,700 *vols.*—This institution was founded in 1821, and was called the "Southern and Western Theological Seminary." A charter was obtained from the legislature in 1842, and the name of the institution changed to "Maryville College." The library, commenced in 1821, contains 3,200 bound volumes, and about 500 pamphlets. The increase has been very slow, not more than 25 volumes per year. The library is in a room 20 feet by 12, in the second story of a brick building belonging to the college. It is opened whenever application is made for books. Students of the college, and persons in and near the town, pay $1 a year for the use of the books. Clergymen educated at the college, and residing within one hundred miles, are allowed the use of the books without charge. The "Beth-Hacma Society" of students has 125 vols. The "Beth-Hacma-ve Berith" Society has 375 vols. John S. Craig, librarian of the college.

MURFREESBOROUGH.

Union University Library.—500 *vols.*

NASHVILLE.

State Library—8,000 *vols.*—The State Library has no legal existence or distinct name, but is merely the depository, under the care of the secretary of state, of books and charts which have been accumulating ever since the foundation of the State. It contains now about 8,000 volumes, mostly reports, public documents, and books presented. There is no appropriation for its increase. A large and elegant room, 36 feet square and about the same in height, in the new capitol, will be assigned to the library. The library is now opened daily from morning to evening, (Sundays excepted.) It is accessible to all persons, and books are freely lent to all who apply for them. W. B. A. Ramsey, secretary of state.

Nashville University Libraries—9,456 *vols.*—"Davidson Academy" was incorporated by the General Assembly of North Carolina 29th December, 1785. Its name, property, and rights were merged in "Cumberland College," incorporated by the legislature of Tennessee, 11th September, 1806. The legal style and title of this college was changed to "*The University of Nashville*" by an act of the legislature, 27th November, 1826. The library was founded in 1824, and contains (1849) 3,144 volumes, and a few MSS. During the last four years the sum of $1,216 75 has been paid for books. There is a catalogue in manuscript, but none printed. Professor N. Cross is librarian.

There are two society libraries, namely: the Agatheridan, with 3,576 volumes, and the Erosophian, with 2,736 volumes; making with the college library a total of 9,456 volumes deposited in the college building, and which may be consulted or borrowed by any member of the university; also by others on certain easy conditions. The president, Philip Lindsley, D.D., and Professor Troost, have private libraries, containing 7,000 or 8,000 volumes. The three public libraries are said to contain "many rare books in various languages, and very few that are not useful."

Franklin College, (near Nashville,)—2,100 *vols.*—The college library, commenced in 1844, contains 1,200 volumes, and increases about 100 a year. The expenditure for books and collections in natural history is about $200 per annum. The library is opened twice a week for one hour. The members of the faculty have free use of the library, and the students pay $2 per annum. Perhaps 1,000 persons visit the library in a year. There are two societies of students, the Euphronian and the Apollonian, with libraries containing together about 900 volumes.

WASHINGTON COUNTY.

Washington College Library—1,000 *vols.*

KENTUCKY.

AUGUSTA.

College Libraries—2,500 *vols.*

BARDSTOWN.

St. Joseph's College—3,000 *vols.* The college library was founded in 1824, when the college was incorporated by the legislature of Kentucky. Before August, 1848, the library contained about 6,000 volumes. At that time the board of trustees divided the library between this and several other institutions which they directed, leaving to St. Joseph's College about 500 volumes of theological, historical, and literary works, with a set of congressional documents. A new board of trustees, at present, controls the affairs of the institution, and they are determined to form a permanent and valuable library. It already numbers about 2,000 volumes. It has also about 400 medals of the 15th, 16th, 17th, and 18th centuries, and about 200 modern coins. The expenditure for books from the general funds of the college is about $250 a year. The principal reliance for the increase of the collection is upon donations. The library occupies a room 24 feet by 15, and 13 feet high, in the college building. The books are arranged according to subjects—each subject having one or more panels. There is no printed catalogue. The library is opened every day twice, to allow the professors opportunity for consultation—three-quarters of an hour in the morning and one hour in the afternoon. Books are freely lent to persons connected with the college, and, by permission of the superintendent, to others residing in the immediate vicinity.

There are two societies of students possessing useful libraries; the

Eurodelphian (or English) Society has a collection of works in English literature, and the Eucerophradic (French) Society possesses a library of French books. Rev. John Roes, S. J., librarian.

COVINGTON.

Library of the Western Baptist Theological Institute—2,000 *vols.*—The library was founded in 1845, and contains about 2,000 volumes. One thousand dollars a year is hereafter to be appropriated from the general funds of the institution for the increase of the collection. The library is opened on Tuesday and Friday of each week from 8 to 9 o'clock a. m. All members of the institute and ministers of the gospel in the city are entitled to the use of the library. Rev. Prof. A. Drury, librarian.

DANVILLE.

Centre College—5,050 *vols.*—The college library, begun in 1824, contains 1,850 volumes. The endowment of the college is nearly completed to $100,000. After it reaches that point, systematic efforts will be made for raising a large library fund. There are two libraries belonging to societies of students—the Deinologian (1,600 volumes) and the Chamberlain (1,600 volumes.) John C. Young, president Centre College.

FRANKFORT.

State Library—9,000 *vols.*—Founded in 1834, and contains about 8,000 or 9,000 volumes, mostly law books and public documents. There are not more than 200 volumes of miscellaneous works. In 1840, the legislature appropriated $3,000 for law books for the courts and the legislature. The library is kept in a room, 50 feet by 20, in the State-house. A catalogue is in preparation and will soon be published. The library is opened daily during the sessions of the courts and legislature. Officers of the State government, members of the legislature, and lawyers attending the courts in Frankfort, are allowed the use of the books. The books are not lent out to others. R. D. Harlan, librarian.

GEORGETOWN.

Georgetown College Libraries—7,280 *vols.*—The library was founded in 1837, and contains 6,500 volumes, comprising many costly works in philology and theology, but chiefly scientific and historical books, a few manuscript journals of early settlers of Kentucky, and many maps and charts. It has also 64 medals and 676 coins, comprising those of Burmah, Siam, Hindostan, the East India Company, South America, Dutch East Indies, &c. The average annual increase is about 500 volumes. The late additions of 800 volumes have been obtained by the president as donations, as have also all the coins, medals, and other articles, as idols, statues, &c. There is a charge of $1 per annum on each student for keeping the books in repair. The library is in a room of the main building of the college, 45 feet by 32, with lofty ceiling. The coins, medals, pictures, &c., are kept in a room devoted to the purpose, on the same floor as the library. The books are arranged on the shelves according to subjects, under twenty divisions. A catalogue *raisonné* was printed in ——, containing 76 pages 12mo. The library is open twice a week, half an hour each time. All persons connected with the college are allowed the use of the books; undergraduates are taxed $1 each per annum for the privilege. By permission of the president, books may be taken out by citizens. No application has ever been refused. Prof. Danford Thomas, librarian.

Two voluntary societies of students are attached to the college—each having a convenient hall and a library. The two libraries contain 780 volumes.

The Female Collegiate Institute—organized 1838—"has a select library of 500 volumes."

HARRODSBURG.

Bacon College.—The college possesses about 1,800 volumes, accessible to all persons, but no regularly organized library.

LEXINGTON.

Transylvania University—14,000 *vols.* The college library, founded in 1798, contains about 12,000 volumes, in three library rooms in the three departments of the university, under the control of the faculties of arts, law, and medicine. Several catalogues have been published, but none of recent date. H. B. Bascom, president T. U.

The students' libraries contain 2,000 volumes.

LOUISVILLE.

The Louisville Library—3,500 *vols.*—was chartered as the "Mercantile Library Association." Two years ago it was reorganized and received the name of the Louisville Library. The library contains 3,500 volumes. The stockholders of the library are about to erect, on the court-house square, a handsome building of stone and brick, 60 feet by 30, to cost $5,000, for the joint accommodation of this library, that of the Kentucky Historical Society, and that of the Louisville Law School; which, united, will form about 6,000 volumes. The room for the Louisville Library will be 60 feet by 30, and 25 feet high, fitted up with alcoves and galleries. A catalogue was printed about 10 years ago, and reprinted in 1848. The library will be open every day and evening till 10 o'clock. Stockholders and subscribers alone are entitled to take out books. William Johnston, librarian.

Kentucky Historical Society—1,000 *vols.*—This society was organized March, 1838, and has a library of 1,500 volumes. [See, Louisville Library.]

Louisville Law School has a library of about 1,000 volumes. [See Louisville Library.]

Medical Department of the University of Louisville—1,000 *vols.*—"The library is enlarged from year to year by the purchase, not only of new medical works, but of costly books pertaining to the allied sciences. Handsome additions have lately been made to it, and other purchases will be made in the course of the coming vacation."—[Annual catalogue, 1849–'50.]

MARION COUNTY.

St. Mary's College Library—5,000 *vols.*

PRINCETON, CALDWELL COUNTY.

Cumberland College (near Princeton)—1,210 *vols.*—The college library was founded in 1825–'6. It contains about 1,000 volumes. Exertions are now making for its enlargement. A new room, 30 feet by 18, has lately been fitted up for its accommodation. There are in connexion with the college two literary societies: the "Erodelphian," organized in 1842, reorganized in 1847. It has a large hall, 30 feet by 18, well carpeted and furnished, and a library of 160 volumes. Number of members 22. The other is the "Amicitiæ Societas," constituted April 28, 1849, with 8 members. It has a large hall well fitted up, and about 150 volumes. Richard Beard, president of Cumberland College.

SHELBYVILLE.

Shelby College Libraries—4,000 *vols.*—"An extensive theological and classical library is attached to the college, which will be accessible to such students as may choose to enjoy its advantages. The number of volumes amounts to about 4,000. A reading-room is connected with the library, which is furnished with the leading American and English reviews and other periodical publications." "Two literary societies exist among the students: one—chartered in 1848, under the name of Phi-Mu—has some 25 members, a small but well-selected library, and receives regularly the pricipal reviews, English and American, as soon as published. The other, auxiliary to this, is for the benefit of the younger portion of the students. Both are making strenuous exertions to increase their libraries and other means of intellectual improvement. Any aid the public may see fit to afford will be thankfully acknowledged. Convenient rooms will be provided, and handsomely fitted up, during the coming session of 1849–'50, in the new building." [College catalogue, 1849.]

OHIO.

ATHENS.

The University of Ohio—2,750 *vols.*—The college library was founded in 1804, and contains 1,250 volumes. A catalogue was printed in 1828, containing 12 pages. The library is opened once a week for an hour. All connected with the university may use it without charge. The institution has lately been reorganized, after a suspension of three years on account of debt. Professor William J. Hoge, librarian.

Students' libraries, 1,500 volumes.

BLENDON, FRANKLIN COUNTY.

Central College Library—550 *vols.*—The library was commenced in 1843, and contains 550 volumes. It is open one afternoon in two weeks. The faculty and trustees are entitled to use the books without charge. The students pay a small fee. J. S. Henderson, librarian.

CINCINNATI.

The Young Men's Mercantile Library Association—10,000 *vols.*—The association was formed in 1835, and incorporated January 5, 1836. It possesses a library of 9,767 volumes, a few maps, globes, portraits, engravings, &c., &c. In July, 1846, at which time the library was removed to its present location, it numbered 4,000 volumes. The rate of increase, for several years, had been about 700 volumes per year. For the last two years 2,000 volumes a year have been added. The annual appropriation for books, for the last two years, has been 2,500 dollars a year. Previous to that, it had been about $800 per annum. The funds for the increase of the library are derived from the annual subscriptions, which amount to say $5,000, from which current expenses are to be deducted and a reading-room sustained. In 1846 a building was erected at the joint expense of the Cincinnati College and the Library Association. It cost $35,000, of which the Association owns $10,000. The style of the edifice is Grecian. Dimensions—front, 140 feet; depth, 100 feet; height, (four stories) 58 feet. The construction is of the most permanent character, of Dayton limestone, the roof covered with iron. The rooms of the Library Association form the entire front of the second story. Library 29 feet by 45; reading-room, 29 by 45; directors' room, 16 by 14, with a room for stowing away newspapers, &c.; and a room now occupied as the Merchants' Exchange, 59 feet by 45, intended hereafter for the library. The "Catalogue of the Young Men's Library Association in Cincinnati," printed at Cincinnati in 1846, contains 145 pages 8vo. The "Supplementary Catalogue," &c., was printed in 1848, and paged continuously with the catalogue, the two forming 260 pages 8vo. The catalogue is alphabetical, with a classified index; is very well prepared, and handsomely printed. An earlier catalogue was printed in 1844, 62 pages 8vo. The library is open daily (Sundays and holidays excepted) from 9 a. m. till 10 p. m. The library is for the use of the members of the association and others, at the discretion of the board of directors. Members pay $1 initiation fee, and the further sum of $3 as an annual subscription. About 15,000 books are lent out each year; and about 2,000 books are consulted, by about 100 different persons, in a year, without taking them away from the library. The present librarian is Thomas Gales Foster. Besides the library, this institution maintains an annual course of lectures. The printed annual reports of the board of directors show that the establishment is conducted with great energy and intelligence, and that it is eminently and increasingly useful.

Lane Seminary, at Walnut Hills, near Cincinnati.—This institution was incorporated in 1829, and commenced full operations in 1832. It is under the direction of the Presbyterians. The library, founded in 1837, contains 10,000 volumes, 4 ancient manuscripts, and 33 volumes of engravings. It is intended to appropriate $500 a year, from the funds of the seminary, for the increase of the library. There is a manuscript catalogue. The library is open twice a week, regularly. It is for the free use of the faculty and students. Other persons wishing to consult the library are always accommodated by the librarian. Professor C. E. Stowe, librarian.

St. Xavier College Libraries—5,600 *vols.*—The library was founded in November, 1841, and contains something over 5,000 volumes. It increases at the rate of about 400 volumes a year. The college having no endowment, nor any established fund, there is no permanent appropriation for the library, but only such as occasion justifies. The library is in a hall of the college building, 40 feet by 25. There is a manuscript catalogue. The library is open daily from 7 to 8 a. m., and from 4½ to 5 p. m.; on Thursdays from 9 to 12. The use of the books is confined to those belonging to the college; but by courtesy any literary, or other respectable person, may have access upon application. There are two societies of students possessing libraries: the Philopedian has 300 well-selected books; and the Philhermenian, nearly the same number. Rev. J. De Bleeck, president.

The Ohio Mechanics' Institute—3,265 *vols.*—The library was founded and incorporated in 1829, and contains 3,265 volumes. The institute possesses also a philosophical apparatus, said to be the best in the State. For the last ten years the annual average increase has been about 200 volumes, and the expenditure for books about $100. The library is supplied principally by donations and occasional special subscriptions. The institute is erecting, by subscription, a building on the corner of Vine and 6th streets. It is of brick and iron. Estimated expense, $32,000. It will be finished in 1850. The outside dimensions are 90 feet on Vine street, 75 feet on 6th street. It has four stories, attic and basement. It is intended to lease about three-fourths of the building to others.

A catalogue, 48 pages 12mo., was printed in 1841. The library is open six days in the week from sunrise till 10 o'clock p. m.; Sundays, from sunrise to sunset. Members pay $3 per annum, ladies and minors 50 cents per annum, for the use of the books. The total number of volumes lent out from September 1, 1848, to September 1, 1849, was 5,069. Samuel Warner, acting librarian.

The Historical and Philosophical Society of Ohio.—Founded February 11, 1831. The library contains about 1,000 volumes, and about 2,500 pages of historical manuscripts, in English and French. All the books have been procured by donation. The library is opened daily for four hours, and accessible to all who wish to consult it. Perhaps one hundred and fifty different persons a year avail themselves of its privileges. G. Williams Kendall, librarian.

Apprentices' Library—2,200 *vols.*

The Medical College of Ohio.—The library, founded in 1826, contains 2,129 volumes, 50 volumes of engravings, and the manuscript theses on medical subjects by the graduates. It occupies two rooms in the college edifice. The books are arranged in 9 chapters, viz: 1, anatomy; 2, chemistry; 3, surgery; 4, materia medica; 5, obstetrics; 6, theory and practice of medicine; 7, periodicals; 8, miscellaneous works; 9, engravings. A catalogue was printed in 1832, but the library has been considerably enlarged since that time. The library is open Mondays, Wednesdays, and Fridays, from 1½ to 5 o'clock p. m. It is for the use of the trustees, professors and students of the college. Alexander Denniston, librarian.

Orphan Asylum.—Founded 1840: has 400 volumes. Miss Wood, librarian.

Woodward College Libraries—1,400 *vols.*

CLEVELAND.

The Western Reserve Medical College—1,000 *vols.*

Cleveland University.—A tract of 275 acres of land has been purchased for $34,000. It is expected that, after some 50 or 75 acres shall have been reserved for the college, the remainder will yield a handsome fund for the purposes of the college. It is proposed to erect one large edifice for public rooms. The students will lodge in private houses. Active measures are in operation to open the institution for students by 1st March, 1850. [Letter of A. Mahan, president, in New York Tribune, November 28, 1850.]

COLUMBUS.

State Library—12,500 *vols.*—The State Library of Ohio was founded in 1817, and contains (1850) 12,500 volumes. It increases at the rate of about 500 volumes a year. The State publishes its own reports, the profits of which, amounting to about $800 per annum, are appropriated to the purchase of books for the library. The library is under the control of commissioners, consisting of the governor, secretary of state, and State librarian. The room occupied by the library is 118 feet by 22. A catalogue is published every three years. The last, printed in 1848, contains 92 pages 8vo. The library is open daily, (Sundays excepted,) from 7 o'clock a. m. to 6 p. m. in summer, and from 7 a. m. till 9 p. m. in winter. The library is free to members of the legislature and officers of State, and it may be used by others by consent of the library commissioners. The number of volumes lent annually is about 1,800. About 3,000 persons annually consult the library. John Greiner, State librarian.

DELAWARE.

Ohio Wesleyan University—2,780 *vols.*—The college library was founded in 1845, and contains 2,000 volumes. It is open once a week for an hour. The students pay 50 cents a term for the use of the books. The faculty use them without fee. Professor McCabe, librarian. The Letagothian Society of Students, instituted 1845, has a library of 335 volumes, increasing about 100 vols. each year. It has also about 250 mineralogical specimens and curious coins. The Chrestomathian Society, instituted 1846, has 450 volumes; annual increase, 60 volumes.

GAMBIER.

Kenyon College Libraries—7,550 *vols.*—The library of this college is called the Library of the Theological Seminary of the Diocese of Ohio. It was founded in 1824, and contains about 4,550 volumes. The library is kept in the building of the Theological Seminary, and occupies a room 40 feet long, 18 feet wide, and 12 feet high. A catalogue was printed in 1837, containing 76 pages 8vo. The library is open one hour each week, and is free to the members of the college and seminary. Rev. M. T. C. Wing, librarian.

The students' libraries contain 3,000 volumes.

GRANVILLE.

College Libraries—3,000 *vols.*—The library, founded in 1836, contains 1,000 volumes. Open every Saturday for the use of the officers and students. Rev. Silas Bailey, president.

Students' libraries, 2,000 volumes.

HILLSBOROUGH.

The Library and Museum Association of Oakland Female Seminary.—The association is composed of the pupils of the seminary and ladies in Hillsborough. It was formed in 1840. The library contains about 400 volumes, besides a collection of shells and minerals. About 40 volumes a year are added to the library. A catalogue (8 pages) was printed in January, 1848. Another will be published soon. The library is open every school-day, whenever the pupils or others wish to exchange books. Pupils pay $1 for membership; other ladies, $2. About 3,000 volumes were taken out the last year, which is a greater number than ever before. Nancy F. Parker, librarian.

HUDSON.

Western Reserve College—7,634 *vols.*—The college library was founded in 1826, and contains 4,568 volumes, exclusive of periodicals and pamphlets, unbound, which amount to about 200 volumes. The average annual increase for the last ten years has been 133 volumes, mostly donations. About $50 a year have been appropriated for books. A brick building 62 feet by 42 was erected for chapel and library. The library-room is 40 feet square. A catalogue (18 pp. 12mo.) was printed in ——. The library is open each Saturday afternoon. The faculty use the books without charge. The students pay $1 50 per annum. About 1,000 books are lent out each year. There are two societies of students connected with the college possessing libraries, containing together 3,066 volumes. Professor Henry N. Day, librarian.

MARIETTA.

Marietta College Libraries—6,400 *vols.*—The college library was founded in 1835, when the present college charter was obtained. It now (1850) contains 4,300 volumes. Its average rate of increase has been of late about 120 volumes annually. The library is open for one and a half hours every Saturday. The use of the books is free of charge to the trustees and faculty: the students pay $1 per year. A subscription has lately been opened for $10,000, and is nearly filled up, for the benefit of the library. It is proposed to expend about half of this sum immediately in the purchase of books, and to fund the other half. A brick building, 65 feet by 53, and three stories high, has just been completed. On the first floor are the laboratory, room for philosophical apparatus, and recitation-room for the senior class. On the second floor, the library, the cabinet, the Hildreth cabinet, and a rhetorical-room, used at present as a chapel. In the third story are two large rooms for the societies, with recesses for the libraries. The whole cost of the building was between $7,000 and

$8,000. The library-room is, say 53 by 25 feet, and 14 feet high. A catalogue of the library (42 pp. 8vo.) was printed in 1840.

"The college library embraces, in addition to works of general literature, a valuable collection of philological works, procured in Europe.

"It also contains a large collection of text-books, which furnishes, at a trifling percentage, nearly all the text-books used in the preparatory and college courses; and a considerable portion of these are the best German editions of entire works.

"In addition to these, there are three libraries belonging to the college societies, carefully selected, and placing within the reach of students a considerable amount of useful reading.

"The present number of volumes in the several libraries is as follows:

College Library, general literature	2,650
" " philology	1,000
" " text-books	650
Psi Gamma Society Library	850
Alpha Kappa " "	750
Society of Inquiry "	500
Total	6,400"

Dr. S. P. Hildreth has lately presented his valuable cabinet to the college. This cabinet contains "more than 4,000 specimens in the various departments of natural history, arranged in cases and drawers, labelled, numbered, and entered in a catalogue under their respective heads."

The Marietta Library Association—1,000 *vols.*—This association has been in existence many years. A brick building, two stories high, was erected by it some twenty years ago for a library and lecture room. A thousand dollars have lately been raised for the purchase of books. The librarian is Thomas Vinton.

There is also at Marietta a library collected from the proceeds of a part of the township reservation for religious purposes. It is now under the care of the Universalist Church.

NEW ATHENS.

Franklin College Libraries—2,000 *vols.*

OBERLIN.

Institute Libraries—4,000 *vols.*—This institution was chartered with university privileges in 1833-'4. It embraces a theological, college, teachers', ladies', and preparatory department. There are about 4,000 volumes in the libraries, as stated in the American Almanac for 1850.

OXFORD.

Miami University Libraries—6,786 *vols.*—Miami University was founded in 1809. A grammar school was established in 1818. The university began its operations in 1824. The library of the university was founded in 1812, and contains 3,486 volumes. It increases at the rate of about 200 volumes a year. Some appropriation is generally made for each year to purchase books: for five years previous to August, 1847, it was about

$250 a year. Now, it is $150. The university library and the two society libraries occupy three separate rooms, each 32 feet in length, 18 feet in breadth, and 18 feet high. The university library is open every Saturday morning for half an hour, and generally for two or three hours every afternoon. Persons entitled to the use of the books are—the faculty, free; students, who pay fifty cents a session; also the inhabitants of Oxford, on the same terms as the students. The number of volumes lent out of the library during the year ending October 1, 1848, is 489. This is perhaps about the average.

There are, in connexion with the institution, two students' libraries: the Erodelphian, containing 1,500 volumes, and the Miami Union, containing 1,800 volumes. James C. Moffat, librarian.

SPRINGFIELD.

Wittenburg College Libraries—5,265 *vols.*—The library was founded May 4, 1846, and contains 1,406 volumes. About 100 dollars per year are expended for books. The library is opened once a week, and kept open one hour each time. H. K. Geiger, librarian.

The Excelsior and Philosophian Societies, composed of students of the college, possess valuable libraries. The Excelsior library contains 2,054 volumes and increases about 600 volumes per annum. About 150 dollars are each year expended for books. The Philosophian library contains 1,805 volumes and increases about 522 volumes per annum. About 135 dollars are annually expended for books.

Lyceum Library.—The Springfield Lyceum was formed November 19, 1832, but till 1849 it had but few members. Its library numbered but about 300 volumes. Lately a new impulse has been given to the institution: a reading-room has been opened and supplied with 33 of the best reviews and newspapers, and public lectures have been commenced. The number of members has increased to 150, paying annually three dollars each. The room is open daily. Edward M. Doty, librarian.

STEUBENVILLE.

City Library.—The Steubenville City Library was founded in 1847, and contains 550 volumes. A catalogue is in press. The library is open every Saturday evening from 6 to 8 o'clock. Members pay 10 cents a month for the use of the books—others 20 cents. David F. Cobb, librarian.

ZANESVILLE.

Athenæum Library—3,580 *vols.*—The Zanesville Athenæum was incorporated in 1828. The library contains 3,580 volumes, and increases at the rate of about 100 volumes a year. Two catalogues have been printed: one, 20 pp. 12mo., 1831; the other, 72 pp. 8vo., 1843. The library is open daily. The librarian is in attendance Wednesday and Saturday evenings. Stockholders pay five dollars per annum: subscribers three dollars.

INDIANA.

BLOOMINGTON.

Indiana State University Libraries—5,000 *vols.*—This institution was founded in 1816. In the catalogue for 1848 are the following notices of the libraries connected with the university: "The college library is open to all of the students on paying a subscription of 50 cents per session. Each subscriber is permitted to take out a volume every Saturday.

"This library has recently been augmented by a purchase of about 2,000 dollars worth of books, some of them rare and valuable. It embraces a choice collection of Greek, Latin, French, and English classics, the best standard works on history, biography, and the sciences, together with a selected variety of miscellaneous literature."

"There are two literary societies connected with the university—the Philomathean and Athenian Societies. Each has a well selected library of several hundred volumes."

In the Law School, a good law library is provided for the use of the students.

The aggregate number of volumes in the libraries may be stated at 5,000. A catalogue was printed in 1840, containing 50 pages 8vo., prepared on the plan proposed by Professor Park in his "Pantology."

Monroe County Library—4,000 *vols.*

CRAWFORDSVILLE.

Wabash College Libraries—6,100 *vols.*—Wabash College was established in 1833. The library was commenced in 1835, and burnt in 1838. It was a choice collection of about 2,000 volumes, exclusive of the text-book library. A new collection was begun in 1839. It contains 4,300 volumes. There is a small fund slowly accumulating for the purchase of books. It is proposed soon to erect a new building for the library and other purposes. The library is open once a week, and is accessible to all persons connected with the institution. Students pay 25 cents a term for the use of the books. There are two societies of students—the Lyceum and the Calliopean. Each has 900 volumes. Professor Caleb Mills, librarian.

EVANSVILLE.

Vanderburg County Library—2,000 *vols.*—The sum of $1,000 has been placed in the hands of the treasurer, and about an equal sum is due from the county, for the purpose of founding a county library. An agent will purchase the books in the spring. The library will be open to all inhabitants of the county on the payment of $— per year. John Ingle, jr., treasurer; J. A. Corbet, secretary.

FRANKLIN.

College Libraries—600 *vols.*

GREENCASTLE.

Indiana Asbury University Library—2,700 *vols.*

SOUTH HANOVER.

Hanover College Libraries—4,700 *vols.*—This institution was founded in 1829. In the triennial catalogue for 1849, it is stated: "By the liberality of friends in the East and elsewhere, a very valuable library, and an extensive and excellent cabinet of minerals, have been recently obtained." The number of volumes at present (January, 1850) is 1,700. There are two societies of students possessing libraries—the Union Literary Society, 1,500 volumes; Philalethian Society, 1,500 volumes.

INDIANAPOLIS.

The State Library—7,000 *vols.*—Founded by act of legislature, February 11, 1825, and contains about 7,000 volumes, exclusive of duplicates and surplus legislative acts and journals. It has also many valuable maps and charts; some curious Mexican armor and arms; a portrait of "Beato Simon de Cassia," painted in 1751; a painting of the "Tippecanoe battle-ground," 150 square feet; and a small collection of minerals and fossils. The average increase is about 250 volumes per annum, including congressional documents. The average expenditure is about $200 a year. The legislature makes, annually, a specific appropriation for the increase of the State library. It is usually $300—part of which goes to pay for newspapers, periodicals, and binding. The library occupies four rooms on the first floor of the State-house—together, 80 feet long, 24 feet wide. The last printed catalogue was published in 1841, and contains 36 pages 8vo. The library is open daily (Sundays excepted) from 9 a.m. to 6 p. m., during the sittings of the legislature, the supreme court of Indiana, and the district court of the United States—at other times, every Saturday from 8 a. m. to 4 p. m. Persons entitled to the use of the library are: members of the legislature, ministers of the gospel, editors of newspapers, physicians, engineers on the public works, judges of the United States and State courts, attorneys of the supreme court, officers of State benevolent institutions, secretaries and clerks of the legislature, and all persons elected to office by the legislature. To such persons, the books may be lent out for a period not exceeding 30 days—the books not to be taken from the seat of government. About 1,600 are taken out annually. John B. Dillon, librarian.

LAPORTE.

Indiana Medical College—the medical department of Laporte university. The catalogue for 1845–'6 states: "During the past winter, a medical and scientific library association, connected with the institution, was formed. Students can have access to the library by complying with necessary regulations."

LOGANSPORT.

The Sigourney Library—3,000 *vols.*

NORTH BEND.

St. Mary's Library—2,000 *vols.*—The University of Notre Dame du Lac, at North Bend, established 1842, possesses a library of the above name, containing 2,000 volumes. It is kept in a fine room, 21 feet by 14, in the college, and is open daily from 1 to 5 o'clock for the use of the professors, students, and neighbors. About 1,000 books are lent out annually. E. A. Dussaulx, librarian.

VINCENNES.

Public Library—1,700 *vols.*—The Vincennes library was established July 20, 1806, and contains (1850) 1,700 volumes. It is kept in a room, 15 feet square, in the City Hall. The first catalogue was printed in 1813; the next and last in 1838, of 17 pages 8vo. The library is opened once a week for three hours. Any individual may have the use of the books by paying $2 annually. Willis M. Hitt, librarian.

COUNTY LIBRARIES.

The State of Indiana provided, in the law laying out the State into counties, for the appropriation of a piece of land in each county to the establishment of a public library. The income of the money arising from the sale of certain reserved lots was to be appropriated to the purchase of books. Monroe county has already procured a valuable library of 4,000 volumes: it is located at Bloomington. Vandenburgh county, as already stated, is about to establish one. Other counties, it is believed, have already commenced their collections, but we have not as yet been able to procure exact statistics concerning them. In some cases, the attempt to establish these libraries has failed, and the books collected have been sold at auction. The difficulty arose from the want of a librarian. No salary having been provided for such an officer, the books were neglected, and the library finally abandoned.

Historical Society of the County of Vigo.—From the anniversary lecture delivered before this society in March, 1844, by Rev. Robert B. Croes, we learn that one principal object of the society is to collect a library.

ILLINOIS.

CHICAGO.

Mechanics' Library—1,000 *vols.*—The Chicago Mechanics' Institute was founded in 1842, and possesses 1,000 volumes, 40 maps and charts, and 500 minerals. It expends for books about $150 a year. The institute has a bequest of real estate, situated in the city, valued at $5,000, as a permanent fund, but at present unavailable. The library is at present kept in a brick building adjoining the Mechanics' Hall. Two catalogues have been published—one printed in 1843; the second, (30 pages 12mo.,) in 1847. The library is open for consultation every evening, and for the delivery of books once a week. The library is free to all persons for special reference. Members of the institute, their families and apprentices, may use it without charge. Other citizens pay $3 per annum; apprentices, $1. About 2,000 volumes a year are lent out. A. D. Taylor, librarian.

GALESBURG.

Knox Manual Labor College Library—1,400 *vols.*—The library was founded in 1844, and contains 1,400 volumes, besides 400 text-books and 500 volumes belonging to the preparatory department. About $40 a year are expended for books. The library is open once every two weeks for an hour. College students pay $1 a year for the use of the library. About 300 volumes a year are lent to the faculty and students. The Adelphi Society of Students has a small library, purchased a few months ago for $100. The "Gnothautic Society" has $75 subscribed for the purchase of books. J. S. Kuhn, librarian.

GODFREY.

Monticello Female Seminary, 4 miles from Alton, Illinois, founded 1838.—"The library consists of more than 1,000 vols. It is accessible to all pupils." [See 11th annual catalogue.]

JACKSONVILLE.

Illinois College Library—4,000 *vols.*—The library was founded in 1830, and contains 4,000 volumes. It is open twice a week, one hour each time. William Coffin, librarian.

LEBANON.

McKendree College Libraries—1,825 *vols.*—The college library was founded in 1820, and contains 1,200 volumes. The average increase is about 100 volumes a year, mostly donations. A catalogue will soon be printed. The library is free to all persons connected with the college. About 400 volumes are taken out annually. The library is open once a week for one hour. The Philosophian Society of Students, founded in 1846, has a library of 465 volumes. The Platonian Society, formed 1849, has 160 volumes. Professor A. W. Cummings, librarian, McKendree College.

SPRINGFIELD.

State Library of Illinois—4,000 *vols.*—This library contains 4,000 volumes or more, exclusive of duplicates. From the last annual report of the librarian, presented to the legislature 9th January, 1849, it appears that the sum of $191 29 was expended the preceding year for miscellaneous books. This sum was the proceeds of the sale of the State laws, which are by law appropriated to the library. The secretary of state is *ex officio* librarian; but, in the report referred to, he suggests "whether this department, consisting of this peculiar description of property, belonging to the State, of thousands of dollars in value, does not merit the personal sole attention of a competent person, selected for the exclusive purpose," &c. "A catalogue of the books belonging to the Illinois State Library, prepared by H. S. Cooley, secretary of state and *ex officio* librarian, January, 1848," was printed at Springfield in 1848, containing 47 pages 8vo. The catalogue is divided into seven parts: 1, jurisprudence; 2, miscellaneous works; 3, laws and judicial reports of the State; 4, legislative journals and reports of the State; 5, laws of the several States; 6, laws, documents, &c., of the United States; 7, pamphlets, maps, &c

The library is required to be open every day, (Sundays excepted,) during the session of the legislature, from 8 a. m. till 6 p. m. Books may be taken out by members and officers of the General Assembly during its session, and at any time by the governor, officers of the executive departments, justices of the supreme court, and attorney general. The librarian says, at the close of his last report: "The undersigned would respectfully call the attention of the legislature to the fact that our library probably embraces a less number and a less valuable and useful collection of miscellaneous books than is found in any of the libraries of our sister States, which suggests the importance of providing, by law, for a small sum to be appropriated yearly, from the public treasury, for the purchase of scientific and other works for this department of the library."

ST. CLAIR COUNTY.

The German Library of St. Clair county—1,821 *vols.*—We are indebted to Mr. Anthony Schott for the following interesting account of the library founded and sustained by the intelligent and educated German settlers in St. Clair county:

"About the year 1830 the wave of immigration from Germany reached the Mississippi river, and but shortly afterwards it was swelled to an unprecedented height by political causes on the old continent. The consequences and reactions of the French revolution of that year, in and on Germany, caused a great number of persons to despond of any meliorations in the State affairs of Germany, and to seek for an asylum from the renewed and increased oppressions in their fatherland. Those who wended their way to America were in great numbers from the professional classes, and mostly men in the prime of their lives, who, with youthful ardor, had entered into the political arena, and many of whom had been more or less implicated in the efforts fruitlessly made to obtain the liberty of the press and more liberal constitutions. Upon them the following book exerted an immense influence: 'Duden's Account of a Residence in the Western States of North America;' (first edition: Ebberfield, 1829.) It was written in an earnest and philosophical manner, in a style, as it were, expressly adapted to the well educated classes. To that book, it may safely be ascribed, that between 1830 and 1840 so large a number of German emigrants settled in the counties of St. Louis, St. Charles, Washington, Franklin, in Missouri; and of St. Clair, in Illinois. Thus, in 1836 we found some 5,000 to 6,000 volumes of books in the possession of new settlers in St. Clair county, Ill., who lived not very far apart and mostly in social intercourse. It was, therefore, practicable to provide for a common centre, in which these books, if not immediately, yet in the future, might be collected, instead of being scattered and lost. The impulse was given by Sparks's Writings of Washington, offered by a trading agent and desired by many, but too expensive for any one alone. This book was fitly made the corner-stone of a common library, to be built up by a very small annual contribution, ($2) by donations, (and of course they were very often books discarded from the shelves of the donors for their worthlessness to them; though I have had the satisfaction of seeing many of them used to good purpose, which I never had expected to take down again,) and eventually by legacies. Our small means have been since 1840 still more limited, by a deduction of 20 per cent. of the yearly income for a reserved fund, designed to purchase at the county seat a building for the library, when our books shall have become too numerous to be contained in a room of the librarian's farm-house, (not in a log-house built for that purpose, as Dr. Ludewig says in his article on the libraries of the United States, in Naumann's Serapeum, No. 9, Leipzig, 1846, where he also errs in giving another library to the Germans at Belleville,) and to buy, by free lodgings therein, the services of a young professional man as a librarian, when they would no more be rendered gratuitously.

"Under these circumstances, we feel some satisfaction that the German Library Society of St. Clair county, Illinois, incorporated by act of our legislature in 1839, now contains 885 works, in 1,821 volumes; that there are among them some collections of comparative value, (the works of the great men of our Revolution;) Congressional documents, due to the favor of our senators and representatives; continued files of several German and American newspapers and periodicals; publications in reference to the liberal movements in Germany since 1830; on emigration; on ancient German literature; on agriculture; on mathematics, &c.; and that we have reason to hope that our library, whenever it will be proper to transfer it to Belleville, will be firmly enough established to pass through the increase of expenses coincident with the expected increase of means and usefulness, which has frequently prostrated similar institutions—e. g., the St. Louis Library, in 1839.

"In the catalogue, as far as it has been printed, the books are numbered according to the time they came into the possession of the society; but we have an alphabetical catalogue, containing the full titles on detached leaves; and thirdly, (not a so-called scientific catalogue, for which our library is too small, but) a *catalogus materiarum*, where, under proper heads, all our books treating on the same subject are named."

UPPER ALTON.

Shurtleff College Library—1,520 *vols.*—The library contains 1,520 books, and 700 pamphlets and magazines. About 60 or 70 books are added each year. The library is open one hour each week. Trustees, the faculty and students of the institution, and such literary gentlemen in the vicinity as the committee may designate, are entitled to the use of the library. The Alpha Zeta Society of Students, recently established, possesses a small library. Washington Leverett, librarian.

MISSOURI.

CAPE GIRARDEAU.

St. Mary's College Library—2,400 *vols.*

COLUMBIA.

Missouri University Libraries—1,200 *vols.*—The college library was founded in 1842, and contains 675 volumes. One appropriation, which was of $1,200, has been made for books. It is not wholly expended. The endowment of the university is $100,000, invested in bank stock. The library-room in the university building is 36 feet by 24. It is open one hour every two weeks. The use of the books is without charge to officers and students. The Athenian Society of Students has 200 volumes; the Union Literary Society, 325 volumes. R. S. Holmes, college librarian.

FAYETTE.

Howard High School Library—500 *vols.*—This flourishing institution occupies the buildings designed for Fayette College, which, though chartered, never went into operation. It has a library of 500 volumes, commenced in 1849. There is a fund yielding $100 annual income to be continued for the increase of the library till it reaches 2,000 volumes. It will probably be continued longer. W. T. Lucky, principal.

JEFFERSON CITY.

State Library of Missouri—4,637 *vols.*—The library was established by law in 1829. In 1831 the sum of $150 a year was appropriated for the purchase of books. In 1833 the annual appropriation was raised to $450. On the 15th November, 1837, the library was destroyed by fire, and everything valuable lost. The library at present contains 4,637 volumes, and 32 maps and charts. It derives a small income from the sale of the State reports, laws, &c. The library-room is in the State House. It is one half of a circle, 56 feet in diameter, 16 feet high. During the session of the General Assembly it is kept open from 9 a. m. to 5 p. m. daily. During the recess it is opened occasionally, as the librarian may direct. State officers and members of the legislature may take out books, by giving receipts to the librarian. All other persons who desire it may consult the books in the room. The clerk of the supreme court is made, by law, *ex officio* librarian. Present officer, William E. Dunscomb.

The Historical and Philosophical Society of Missouri, 300 *vols.*—From the first number of the "Annals" of the society, (29 pp. 8vo., 1848,) we take the following account of the society and its collections:

"In the year 1844 a few individuals made an effort to establish a Historical and Philosophical Society for the State of Missouri, similar to institutions successfully established in other States. On the 18th of December, in that year, a meeting was held in the Senate chamber, in the city of Jefferson, at which measures were taken to organize the society, addresses were delivered explaining its object and utility, a constitution adopted for its government, fourteen gentlemen enrolled their names as members, and a committee was appointed to apply to the General Assembly for an act of incorporation. The Rev. Dr. Goodrich presented to the society a volume of ancient travels in America, and a fac-simile engraving of hieroglyphics, found in an Indian mound in Illinois, and these constituted the beginning of a library and cabinet which will probably become extensive and valuable. The constitution declared the objects of the society to be to collect and preserve all papers, memorials and documents connected with the early history of Missouri, and all statistics in any way pertaining to the population, mineral, navigable and agricultural resources of the State, and to make publication thereof from time to time. In conformity to the request of the society, an act of incorporation was passed and approved by the governor on the 27th day of February, 1845. Since that time an act has been passed granting to the society the use of a room in the capitol, well adapted to its purposes. The society is located at the city of Jefferson, but branches or auxiliary societies may be established in any other part of the State.

"The first annual meeting of the society was held on the 20th of January, 1845, at which officers were chosen for the ensuing year, new members admitted, several distinguished citizens of other States were elected as honorary members; the presentation of some books, mineral specimens, and other articles, was announced, and resolutions were passed requesting the co-operation of the citizens of the State.

"The second annual meeting of the society was held on the 19th of January, 1846, at which addresses were delivered, the presentation of additions to the library, cabinet, and museum, announced, resolutions passed, and officers chosen for the succeeding year.

"The third annual meeting occurred on the 19th of January, 1847, at which reports of officers were heard, resolutions adopted, officers for the year selected, and addresses delivered.

"On the 17th of January, 1848, the fourth annual meeting of the society was held, at which the reports of the officers were made and approved, some appropriate speeches were delivered, and officers for the present year selected.

"A room has been fitted up for the reception of books, pamphlets, papers, manuscripts, curiosities, and other articles, and the foundation for a library, cabinet and museum has been laid; and hopes are entertained that the liberality and public spirit of the citizens of Missouri will cause the same to be rapidly increased by many valuable additions.

"All editors and publishers of weekly newspapers and periodicals are solicited to present to the society regular files thereof, in order that they may be bound in volumes and carefully preserved. The authors of all books, pamphlets, and publications of every kind, are requested to donate a copy of the same for the use of the library. The society invites the contribution of all old letters and manuscripts, illustrating the history of the discovery and early settlement of Missouri and of the western country. Files of all newspapers and periodicals that have been heretofore published in the State, will be very acceptable. Ancient and curious books and pamphlets are desired as additions to the library, particularly all such as relate to the western country. A copy of every book and pamphlet that was ever published in the State is desired; no publication should be considered too unimportant to enter into such a collection. One object of the society is to collect and preserve the fleeting and ephemeral publications that otherwise would be buried in oblivion. Citizens throughout the State may make many contributions to the society without much trouble or inconvenience."

PALMYRA.

Masonic College Library—2,500 *vols.*
Saint Charles College Library—390 *vols.*

ST. LOUIS.

University Libraries—13,580 *vols.*—The college library, founded in 1829, contains 12,500 volumes, increasing at the rate of 200 volumes a year. It occupies a room 40 feet by 20 in the college building; opened once a day. All persons connected with the university are entitled to the use of the books. Others are permitted to consult the library at any time. There are three libraries belonging to societies of students: The Philalethian, with 630 volumes; the Orthological, 200 volumes; and the Phileuphradic, 250 volumes. Caspar Girsch, librarian.

Mercantile Library Association—4,299 *vols.*—This association was founded in 1846. From the fourth report of the directors (January, 1850) we gather the following facts: The present number of members is 589. During the year 1849 $1,888 40 were expended for 1,060 volumes; and 470 volumes were presented. From the origin of the library $4,901 40 have been expended for books. Those presented during the same time were valued at $1,766. Whole number of volumes in the library, 4,299. An alphabetical catalogue, with a classified index, forming about 300 pages 8vo., is now in press. Use of the books during the year, 4,743 volumes. 38 periodicals are taken. Of 20 of these the sets are complete. The librarian is William P. Curtis. Great pains seem to have been taken in the selection of books; and all the affairs of the institution appear to be conducted with much energy and good judgment.

Law Library—1,500 *vols.*—The Law Library was established in 1840, by members of the bar, and is kept in a room of the court-house.

MICHIGAN.

ALBION.

Wesleyan College Library—700 *vols.*—The Wesleyan College, founded in 1848, is making arrangements for the gathering of a library. The preparatory department, which has been longer in operation, has a library of about 700 volumes. C. T. Hinman, president.

ANN ARBOR.

Michigan University—5,000 *vols.*—Founded in 1837. "The library of this institution was purchased a few years since in Europe, and consists of between 4,000 and 5,000 volumes of well-selected standard works, in the various departments of literature and science. There are two literary societies connected with the college, which hold weekly meetings during term time, and possess valuable libraries of select and miscellaneous books." [Catalogue, 1848–'9.] Professor Abram Seager, librarian.

DETROIT.

St. Philips College Library—3,000 *vols.*

Young Men's Society Library—1,815 *vols.*—The Detroit Young Men's Society was formed in 1833. Its library at present contains 1,815 volumes. The annual increase has been about 100 volumes; but of late a new and vigorous impulse has been given to the society. The number of paying members is 103, including many of the first citizens of the place. A new brick building has been erected by the society, and will be ready for occupation in October, 1850. The building is 95 feet by 24. The lower story will be rented for stores. The second story contains, besides two offices, a large hall for lectures, 70 feet by 40. The third story is divided into two rooms: one for a library, and the other for a committee-room, &c. This edifice, when completed, will have cost about $8,000. The lot on which it is built (valued at $5,000) was given to the society by the land board of the then district. It is eligibly situated on Jefferson avenue—the principal commercial street of the city. It is expected that the rent of those parts of the building not occupied by the society will, in the course of a few years, pay for the building, and yield a considerable revenue for the support and enlargement of the institution. The library, when removed, will be placed in permanent glass cases, and arranged according to subjects. The rooms will be open at all times of the day, for members of the society, and their friends not citizens. Members are elected by the board of managers. They pay $2 each as initiation fee, and an annual assessment of $2. The society is not solely a library association, but it embraces also another department—that of lectures and debates. A catalogue of the library (43 pages 8vo.) was printed in 1842. John S. Van Alstyne, librarian.

LANSING.

State Library—4,400 *vols*.—The library was founded A. D. 1836, and contains 4,400 volumes. From 1839 to 1848 there were no additions by purchase. In 1848, 395 volumes were purchased for $620, and 226 volumes were presented. In 1849, about 400 volumes were added to the collection. The library is kept in a room of the capitol. A catalogue was printed April 1, 1846. The library is open every day from 9 a. m. to 12 m., and from 2 to 4 p. m. State officers and members of the legislature are entitled to take out the books. The secretary of state is *ex officio* State librarian. A clerk in his office has charge of the library, under his direction.

MONROE.

Public Library—1,500 *vols*.

SPRING ARBOR.

Central College Library—1,600 *vols*.

300 TOWNSHIP LIBRARIES,—43,926 VOLS.

"The law has for several years made it the duty of the supervisor to assess a half-mill tax upon each dollar of the taxable property of his township for the purchase of a township library, a portion of which tax may, when certain conditions are complied with, be applied to the support of schools.

"The constitution of the State provides that 'the clear proceeds of all fines assessed in the several counties for any breach of the penal laws, shall be exclusively applied to the support of said libraries.'

"Although, according to the returns, there are but 300 township libraries in the 425 townships of the State from which reports have been received, still, there is a very gratifying increase in the number of these libraries, the number of volumes they contain, and the extent of their circulation. There are thirty more township libraries reported this year than last, containing in all 43,926 volumes, which is 6,938 more than they contained, according to the reports received, for the year 1846. These libraries circulate through 1,349 districts, which shows an increase of 268 over any former year. Communications received from several counties afford very gratifying evidence of their increased usefulness." [Mr. Mayhew's report, 1847.]

The amount of mill tax for township libraries in 1847 was $7,368 75. The amount of fines, &c., collected, $807 15.

74 SCHOOL DISTRICT LIBRARIES—3,294 VOLS.

The statutes formerly provided for these libraries. Now, however, the money formerly applied to them is devoted to township libraries. There are, however, still left seventy-four of these district libraries, with an aggregate of 3,294 volumes.

IOWA.

BURLINGTON.

"The '*Iowa Historical and Geological Institute*' was organized December 18, 1843, but ten years after the departure of the 'red men,' by four citizens of this city, and now [December, 1849] numbers over thirty members. The object of the association cannot be better communicated than by transcribing a portion of the preamble of the constitution: 'We, the undersigned, agree to organize an institution, to be located permanently at Burlington, Iowa, the object of which shall be the establishment of a cabinet of curiosities, of a library, and of a depository of records and papers relating to the primitive settlement, early history, and geological features of Iowa.'

"The objects of the association have been steadily kept in view, and constant additions are being made to the geological and historical departments, as well as to the library. The geological and mineralogical specimens amount to about two thousand, and some of them are exceedingly rare and valuable. The collection of historical papers, records, and facts relative to the early settlement and history of this State has demanded the special attention of some of the members; and thus has many an important historical fact, that otherwise, by the death or removal of the actors, would have been lost, been collected and preserved among the archives of the institute." [Letter from David Rorer, corresponding secretary.]

DAVENPORT.

The college at Davenport, Iowa, is in active operation. It has commenced the formation of a library.

IOWA CITY.

State Library of Iowa—1,600 *vols.*—The State Library was founded in 1839, and contains about 1,600 volumes. The yearly additions have been very small, derived from an exchange of law books and public documents between the States, and donations by Congress, probably not exceeding ten volumes a year. The library-room is in the capitol, and measures 42 feet by 21, and 14 feet high. A catalogue was printed in 1839, and another in 1845, containing 18 pp. 8vo. The library is open every day during the sessions of the legislature and the supreme court, from 9 o'clock a. m. to 9 p. m.; at other times it is open on Wednesday and Saturday afternoons. State officers, members of the legislature, and members of the supreme court bar, are entitled to the use of the books. Lemuel B. Patterson, State librarian.

This infant State has already made legislative provision for a State university, with several branches; a system of district schools, with normal schools, and district libraries. A superintendent has been elected—Mr. Thomas H. Benton, jr. He has lately published, in a handsome pamphlet of 140 pages, "Statutes of the State of Iowa relating to Common Schools, including forms, regulations, and instructions, respecting proceedings under those Statutes," 8vo: Iowa City, 1849. This contains plans of school houses, selections of books for district libraries, &c.

There is a Presbyterian College at West Point, Lee county.

WISCONSIN.

BELOIT.

Beloit College Libraries—1,000 *vols.*—The catalogue of Beloit College and Seminary for 1849–'50 states that "the libraries connected with the college now amount to over 1,000 volumes, and arrangements are made which will insure their progressive increase."

MADISON.

State Library—4,000 *vols.*—Founded in 1836; contains about 4,000 volumes, including pamphlets and magazines. The sum of $5,000 was appropriated by Congress in 1836 for the purchase of books. Since then no additions of importance have been made, except the laws and reports received from the different States. The library is placed in a room of the capitol, measuring 18 feet by 42. There has been no printed catalogue, but one will be published by January 1, 1850. Books are lent out to the members of the legislature, judges of the supreme court, and the State officers, to be returned in six days. About 5,000 persons consult the library yearly. It is opened during the sessions of the legislature and supreme court, from 9 a. m. to 8 p. m. Privileged persons can always have access to the books. George P. Delaplaine, State librarian.

University of the State of Wisconsin, at College Hill, near Madison.—This institution was incorporated in 1849.

A State Historical Society has been formed, and has commenced the gathering of a library. The first annual meeting of the Society was held at Madison, January 15, 1850.

MILWAUKIE.

The Young Men's Association of the City of Milwaukie has a library of more than 1,000 well-selected volumes. In the reading-room are to be found many of the valuable periodicals of the day. The library is open for the delivery of books every Wednesday from 2 to 5 o'clock, and Saturday evenings. The reading-room is open every evening. A catalogue of the library (18 pp. 12mo.) was printed in 1848.

MINNESOTA.

ST. PAUL.

Minnesota Historical Society.—This society was incorporated by the legislative assembly of the Territory on the 10th of October, 1849. It has already issued "Annals of the Minnesota Historical Society," 8vo., 28 pages: St. Paul. The officers of the society invite exchanges and contributions towards the formation of a library. Alexander Ramsey, president.

Territorial Library—3,000 *vols.*—The act of Congress establishing the Territory of Minnesota, approved March 3, 1849, contains an appropriation of $5,000 for a library, to be kept at the seat of government, for the use of the officers of the Territory, and other persons, under suitable regulations. The library (December, 1850) has been organized: 3,000 volumes of good books (law and miscellaneous) have been purchased, and a catalogue (30 pages 8vo.) published. Charles Cavileer, librarian.

ST. ANTHONY FALL.

The St. Anthony Library Association was incorporated November 1, 1849. During the winter of 1849, a series of lectures was delivered before the association. Just after the incorporation of the society, a purchase of books was made, as a nucleus of the proposed library. There are now, perhaps, 200 volumes upon the shelves.

CALIFORNIA.

MONTEREY.

"A good beginning for a public library has been made by the formation of the Monterey Library Association, and a subscription of $1,400. The plan meets with decided public favor, and an order has been forwarded to New York for books."—*New York Observer, May* 18, 1850.

TERRITORIES OF OREGON, NEW MEXICO, UTAH.

The acts of Congress establishing these Territories contain appropriations of $5,000 to each for the purchase of Territorial libraries. The library of Oregon has already (January, 1851) been purchased. Dr. Bernhisel, an energetic and intelligent agent, has been appointed to collect the library for Utah, and has made good progress in the work.

MILITARY LIBRARIES.

We are indebted to a distinguished officer for the following account of the military libraries connected with the United States army:

"Under authority of the 'General Regulations for the Army,' libraries, consisting of newspapers, pamphlets, and bound books, are formed at most, if not all, the military posts occupied by our army. The fund for the purchase of these is accumulated by savings in the bake-houses on soldiers' bread, and taxes on the sutlers of the posts.

"The number of volumes is generally but a few hundred, and not more than a thousand, probably, at any one of the largest posts; and the number is constantly varying, by the wear and tear of the books in the hands of soldiers, and by the interruptions occasioned very frequently of late by the removal of the troops or division of the companies comprising the garrison, as, in all such cases, the detached troops are entitled to take with them their proportionate shares of the library.

"The formation of these libraries, and the instituting of schools for instruction of soldiers and children at the military posts, have had a very beneficial effect, in the education of those who, without these advantages, would never be able to read, and inducing an application of time to books which otherwise would be spent in idleness and indulgence in evil habits."

CLASSIFICATION.

In the following Table are exhibited, in seven classes, the number of libraries in each State, with the number of volumes which they contain—gathered from the foregoing notices. These several classes of libraries may be characterized, in general terms, as follows :

1. *State libraries*, including those of the general government and of the executive departments, and those of the State courts. Almost all the States in the Union have organized State libraries. Those which have not, possess collections of books which will ere long serve as the foundations of such Libraries. These libraries are composed, to a great extent, of public documents of the general and State governments, with works on statistics, political economy, history, &c. Some of them, as the Library of Congress, the New York State library,&c., take a much wider range, and are extremely valuable collections for general reference.

2. *Social libraries*, including athenæums, lyceums, young men's associations, mechanics' institutions, mercantile libraries, &c.—These libraries are generally composed of popular works for reading rather than for reference. But among them are many of the best collections in the country. We think, that any one, looking over the catalogues of these libraries, would be surprised and gratified to find them generally so well selected.

In some States, almost every town has, under some name, a social library. Most of these collections, it is true, are very small, containing less than a thousand volumes ; but there doubtless are a great many, far more considerable in size, which have been unintentionally overlooked.

3. *College libraries*, (exclusive of students' libraries.)—Our colleges are mostly eleemosynary institutions. Their libraries are frequently the chance aggregations of the gifts of charity ; too many of them discarded, as well nigh worthless, from the shelves of the donors. This is not true of all our college libraries ; for among them are some very important collections, chosen with care and competent learning, purchased with economy, and guarded with prudence,—though ever available to those who wish to use them aright.

4. *Students' libraries*, in colleges, professional schools, academies, &c.—The societies formed by students in our seminaries of learning, for mutual improvement in debate and composition, for the most part possess libraries. These are generally useful collections of books of a popular character. Sometimes (in Yale College particularly) they are large, well selected, and admirably arranged and kept. Dust seldom gathers on the books in such collections.

5. *Libraries of professional schools and incorporated academies.*
This class includes theological seminaries, law schools, medical colleges, and military academies as well as high schools, generally termed in this country "academies." The professional schools, several of them, possess the best special libraries in the country. These institutions (particularly the theological) are so frequently connected with academies, that it was found most convenient to group them together. The notices in the body of this work will generally enable the reader to subdivide this class, as well as the other classes, if desired.

6. *Libraries of Learned Societies*,—scientific, literary and historical. These libraries are mostly composed of the Transactions of similar societies and of periodicals which contain the current records of science and letters. They have been mostly procured by donation and exchange. Some of these collections are extensive and important. The historical societies are doing great service in gathering and guarding the precious memorials of our early annals.

7. *Public School Libraries.* Several of the states, have taken great interest in supplying every township and school district with a library. Other states have commenced such collections, and it is to be hoped that they may be greatly multiplied. They are not intended for pupils alone, but for all the population of the district or township to which they belong. They are composed of valuable books, designed and adapted to communicate useful knowledge in a popular way, and to cultivate all the higher elements of character. They are in continual use, and it is impossible to overestimate their beneficial influence.

Another class of libraries of which it has not been in my power to collect the statistics comprises *Sunday School Libraries.* The aggregate number of books which they contain is very great. These books, though mostly for juvenile readers, are always of a moral or religious tendency, and they have vast influence in forming the intellectual as well as the moral character of the people.

Tabular view of public libraries in the United States.

States.	State libraries.		Social libraries.		College libraries.		Students' libraries.		Libraries of academies and professional schools.		Libraries of scientific and historical societies.		Public school libraries.		Totals for States.	
	No.	Volumes.	No.	Volumes.	No.	Volumes.	No.	Volumes.	No.	Volumes.	No.	Volumes.	No.	Volumes.	No.	Volumes.
Maine	1	9,000	2	6,370	2	16,800	6	13,134	2	10,800	1	300	17	452	31	56,856
New Hampshire	1	4,700	9	13,878	1	6,400	5	16,200	7	10,700	2	2,800	25	2,500	50	57,178
Vermont	1	3,500	....	....	3	13,032	6	8,667	....	....	....	....	13	*9,100	23	34,299
Massachusetts	1	7,400	23	126,269	4	71,693	15	28,735	9	45,450	10	44,572	700	91,539	762	415,658
Rhode Island	....	....	5	25,104	1	24,000	2	7,600	....	....	2	3,000	35	19,637	45	79,341
Connecticut	1	3,000	3	14,234	3	29,138	7	38,666	3	6,300	1	7,000	1	*300	19	98,638
New York	3	34,099	21	151,894	8	43,376	7	19,319	171	143,465	4	25,253	8,070	1,338,848	8,284	1,756,254
New Jersey	1	5,000	3	4,300	3	18,000	2	7,000	1	9,000	1	825	6	*2,180	17	46,305
Pennsylvania	1	10,000	16	125,385	10	37,875	12	29,350	7	38,300	5	38,478	29	*8,131	80	287,519
Delaware	1	4,000	1	4,000	1	2,500	2	6,200	....	....	....	....	....	....	5	16,700
Maryland	1	15,000	9	32,156	6	25,592	4	1,700	3	3,150	1	1,500	22	*5,467	46	84,565
Dist. of Columbia	10	100,200	2	7,000	2	29,500	4	2,800	....	....	2	9,173	....	....	20	148,673
Virginia	1	14,000	4	3,313	9	45,790	8	10,466	5	12,951	1	1,200	2	*1,460	30	89,180
North Carolina	1	3,000	....	....	3	9,401	2	8,846	2	3,000	....	....	....	....	8	24,247
South Carolina	....	....	2	28 500	2	19,000	4	1,900	5	10,264	....	....	1	*250	14	59,914
Georgia	....	....	1	6,510	5	15,637	4	4,685	2	5,000	1	2,000	11	*1,800	24	35,632
Florida	2	4,000	1	1,337	....	....	....	....	....	....	....	....	1	*200	4	5,537
Alabama	....	....	1	1,454	4	13,000	2	2,623	....	....	....	....	30	*1,000	37	18,077
Mississippi	1	5,000	....	....	3	5,189	2	2,411	....	....	....	....	102	*3,050	108	15,650
Louisiana	1	7,000	1	10,000	4	13,000	....	....	....	....	....	....	....	....	6	30,000
Texas	1	1,001	....	....	1	300	....	....	....	....	....	....	2	*330	4	1,631
Arkansas	....	....	1	1,000	....	....	....	....	....	....	....	....	....	....	1	1,000
Tennessee	1	8,000	....	....	9	20,844	8	9,912	1	3,500	....	....	2	*5,100	21	47,356
Kentucky	1	9,000	1	3,500	10	37,150	10	7,190	3	4,000	1	1,500	1	*1,100	27	63,440

Ohio	1	12,500	8	21,295	13	35,510	19	20,205	3	12,529	1	1,000	3	*1,595	48	104,634
Michigan	1	4,400	2	3,315	4	10,300							374	47,220	381	65,235
Indiana	1	7,000	4	10,700	6	17,300	4	4,800					1	*200	16	40,000
Illinois	1	4,000	2	2,821	4	8,120	2	625	2	2,000			16	*2,350	27	19,916
Missouri	1	4,637	2	5,799	5	18,465	5	1,605	1	500	1	300	4	*6,200	19	37,506
Iowa	1	2,500											4	*160	5	2,660
Wisconsin	1	4,000	1	1,000									33	*2,163	35	7,163
Minnesota	1	3,000	1	200											2	3,200
Total	39	288,937	126	611,334	126	586,912	142	254,639	227	320,909	34	138,901	9,505	1,552,332	10,199	3,753,964

* For the sums marked with an asterisk, I am indebted to the courtesy of Mr. Kennedy, superintendent of the 7th census. Much valuable information respecting public and private libraries will be furnished by the Census, when the returns are all received and digested.

GENERAL SUMMARY.

Whole number of Libraries, exclusive of those of the public schools	694
Aggregate number of volumes - - - - -	2,201,632

Whole number of Libraries containing, each, 1,000 volumes, and upwards - - - - - - - -	423
Aggregate number of volumes in these Libraries - - -	2,105,652
Average size - - - - - - - -	4,977

Number of Libraries reported, containing less than 1,000 volumes, each - - - - - - - - -	271
Aggregate number of volumes in these Libraries - - -	95,980

*Number of Libraries containing 1,000 volumes and upwards, and less than 5,000 - - - - - - -		198
Number of Libraries containing 5,000 volumes and upwards, and less than 10,000 - - - - - - -		175
Number of Libraries containing 10,000 volumes and upwards, and less than 20,000 - - - - - - -		43
Number of Libraries containing 20,000 volumes and upwards, and less than 50,000 - - - - - - -		11
There are but five Libraries containing, each, 50,000 volumes and upwards, Namely: - - - - - - -		5
Harvard University—		
Public Library - - -	56,000	
Law Library - - -	14,000	
Theological Library - -	3,000	
Medical Library - - -	1,200	
Students' Libraries - -	10,000	
		84,200
The Philadelphia Library, (including the Loganian Library) -		60,000
Yale College—		
College Library - -	20,515	
Medical Library - -	900	
Law Library - -	1,900	
Students' Libraries -	27,166	
		50,481
The Library of Congress - - - - - -		50,000
The Boston Athenaeum - - - - - -		50,000

*In this statement, and in those which follow, the Libraries of societies of students and those of professional departments are counted with the Libraries of the Colleges or Seminaries with which they are connected.

INDEX TO THE APPENDIX.

Page.

Erratum.—Page 35, line 28 from the top, for "Williams College" read *William and Mary College.*

www.ingramcontent.com/pod-product-compliance
Lightning Source LLC
LaVergne TN
LVHW011209110826
845150LV00006B/1381
9781425517632